Inner Logic—Engineering Your Life

By Christopher Gorog

Published in the United States of America by Logic Central Online.

ISBN-13: 978-1508461944

ISBN-10: 1508461945

For more information, media content, and interactive support visit

www.logiccentralonline.com

Prelude

When someone sets out to describe what drives them, what motivates them, what direction they're heading, and what makes them tick inside, words are not what first come to mind. For me, it's a set of feelings—chemical releases that I can feel even now. How do you sum up a person, a life, a set of urges to move forward, a driving force that propels us? Answering these questions may be the only real thing I have accomplished in life. This self-knowledge is what I will begin to share with you now. I am aware that I will probably not do any justice to solving the complex issues that we as humans have with defining ourselves, but if I help one person grasp the details that I have learned in my life, then all the effort will have been worth it.

To describe myself briefly, I am someone who has experienced life, someone who has taken in more input, experiences, and situations than many people could ever desire. The highs and lows that life presents come with experiencing life, and I have had my fair share of those.

- I have been an underachiever with low self-esteem
- I have been the life of the party and the center of attention
- I have been broken to the point that I did not care whether I lived or died
- I have savored life and the pursuit of happiness
- I have exceeded expectations in organizations consisting of the top percentile of the most elite people
- I have questioned my own sanity
- I have confidently traveled the world
- I have shut myself off and hidden from the world
- I have spent my life in pursuit of knowledge and education

- I have been mentally confused to the point that I could not hold a thought

- I have built my body to its top performance capability

- I have lost my health to the point of near death

- I have been a top expert

- I have been a fool

I have had a great, successful life. If you had asked me as a child to consider what would have been possible for me to achieve in my lifetime, I would never have imagined that I could accomplish 1 percent of what I have accomplished. With my success have come many challenges. Overall, I consider myself a contradictory person at best—but one who has experienced highs and lows and who has identified what makes success and what does not. By looking at my own life and identifying which traits, influences, and surroundings I have had during the contrasting times of my life, I hope I can help others to navigate through potential pitfalls and to build upon the strategies that I have found create success.

My most significant talent, which is an extremely logical and sequentially oriented mind, has simultaneously been both my greatest gift and greatest curse. My extremely logical bent has made me successful at everything with a logical nature that I have attempted, but not everything in this world follows logical patterns. Though I hope you find insight in my logical explanations of how people approach and rationalize situations, I arrived at these explanations through countless failures and wrongly assessed situations. The question of whether I am gifted or whether I am unique in the sense that I cannot relate to any other human has plagued me and has driven my highs and lows, detailed above in my self-descriptive list. I believe that I am living proof that a human can achieve any mindset that another human visibly possesses.

After much deliberation on whether I am unusual or whether everyone experiences similar things, I feel that I am not alone and that each person has the same prison of uniqueness: our own minds. I believe that every human can adopt any mindset observable in another person and that the position in which we find ourselves is an important part of our influences, our knowledge, our self-motivation, and to an extent, our biological limitations. These factors can make a person achieve the status either of the president of the United States or of a homeless person on the street. Those who think, as I did earlier in my life, that they could never find themselves in some of the lowlier mindsets with which they see other people struggling will find that their arrogance enables them to enter into such situations more easily than most. As chance has some part in life, a person may never experience the right set of influences to get them to a proper mindset. Whether good or bad, I challenge you not to think that you are more or less of a person, but one unchallenged by the situations that may have driven a lowlier mindset in others.

How Can I Help People?

My latest quest in life is to help others by sharing my own life experiences. Though I feel this falls under the category of self-help, I admit that, like my gift in logic, my approach to this topic is different from any other I have read from modern authors. My sampling of those around me at first suggested that my work was probably not valid. A few people, whom I consider self-help junkies, have directly referred to my work as "something that no one would read." After the initial hit to my self-esteem, I looked at why such people would say this regarding my work. In order to move forward in our lives, we all need to justify ourselves, and my process of self-justification (whether valid or not) uncovered something regarding the personalities of people who typically consume self-help topics. The best way to describe this is with the following joke I heard once, which goes like this:

There are ten types of people in this world:

1. Those who don't finish lists

2.

3.

Like this joke, people who write or consume self-help material often identify themselves according to their demographics. The humor in the joke is the absence of any mindset other than the one that does not finish the list. Likewise, the nature of self-help consumers is in the existence of the material itself. People who don't talk don't write their stories. I believe that the reason that self-help material has not been of interest to me is the same reason that people with personalities similar to mine do not often consume self-help material. I have described myself above as an extremely logical, strategic person. The strategic life of a systematic person does not often contain the large, miraculous changes that frequently seem to be the basis of self-help material. What I personally consider self-help is just smart living, the desire to improve small things, and the self-reward from touching lives. I believe it is more accurate to say that self-help material for systematic, logical people may not exist.

People who make drastic changes write about their changes because that is the nature of such a personality. Systematic people like me often view these types of personalities as living life as if it were a slot machine. Live for the next miraculous opportunity. The bigger the miracle—i.e., opportunity—the more desirable it is to chase. Status for those with this mindset accrues to the people who have performed the biggest miracle—made the largest change—one that defines them. This lifestyle involves constantly changing as many things as necessary until those who live it achieve great success, always believing that the right change will trigger that success. People I have known with this personality type usually rely on a person or a group with systematic stability to support the miracle-seeking lifestyle, while always believing that the same systematic personalities on whom they depend are lackluster and in need of change.

In watching people who live a lifestyle in which everything needs to change, I have seen the focus seem to turn to what things to fear and to whom to blame for the lack of each previous miracle. A logical, systematic lifestyle does not need to include blame and fear, because the only blame falls on you and the only thing to fear is not moving forward. The value of a logical mindset is in systematically addressing the next achievable objective that advances you on your path and adds to your life, rather than simply setting a goal to change.

The problem with miracle-seeking lifestyles is that so few people hit the big one. I have not met one person with this type of personality who did not believe that they were the next one who would hit it big. Unfortunately, the odds suggest that few people do. They may be the most exceptional, the luckiest, the most popular, or some combination thereof, but what ultimately must transpire is stratification involving a ratio of one of these exceptional people to countless numbers of supporters or followers. However, the nature of this support system requires individuals to believe that they are the next miracle. In truth, the odds of making it big indicate that the ratios are probably similar to hitting a jackpot at a casino.

I represent what I refer to as the silent majority of systematic people who believe that slow and steady wins the race. We cannot be classified as conservative or liberal, religious or agnostic, urban or rural. We are just logical, progressive thinkers who see the value in understanding the progression of life and in not changing everything to escape each previous phase. Engineering your future is about augmenting your life with needed influences and following proven processes that generate success. I look at life from the perspective of an engineer who evaluates the current situation, identifies what is possible, and proposes a possible solution that makes the future more effective.

I was shown success and stability by nature and example; however, throughout the course of my life, the influence of others has convinced me to give up certain aspects of my personality in order to conform to the standards of others. To my surprise, giving up or changing some traits made me lose my competitive edge. I found that I became like those surrounding me, reduced to levels that I had previously considered tantamount to incompetence. In conforming and striving for the next big thing, I also became ineffective, as did my influences. I had lost what made me successful, what made me healthy, my motivation, and my desire to savor life. After determining which parts of myself I had changed thereby reducing my effectiveness, I restored those traits and, to my delight, was able to reestablish my effectiveness. What I discovered about myself amounts to an understanding of human nature—revealing things I had ignored or did not believe would or could happen to me—but I found that certain things, whether you believe they will or not, will catch up with you anyway.

After having a heart attack at an early age, my approach to life and to what is important changed dramatically. I shifted my focus from acquiring material things toward distributing what I can offer to people who could use it earlier in their lives than I had the opportunity to do so. My driving force is to document myself for my thirteen-year-old son, with whom I do not have the opportunity to spend my reduced number of remaining years. Max, remember that I love you even if I may not be around to physically show it, and know that everything I have done here is for you. I also hope that others reading this will benefit from it. Every old man says, "If I only knew when I was younger what I know now, how much more I could have accomplished!" Let me help you avoid the mistakes I have made and improve from the lessons I have learned.

Chapter I

The Best Year of My Life Is "Next Year"

This wonderful concept came to me this morning. As I was looking back and thinking about each year of my life up to now, some stood out as amazing, some as so-so, and others were disasters. I tried to figure out what was different about me at those times in my life. Was it my mental focus, my environment, some unforeseen outside force, or fate? I very quickly ruled out both fate and an unforeseen, supernatural intervention and focused on the things over which I did have control, such as the situations I was in, the people I was with, and the mindsets that I had at the various times. I realized that all three were related and that all three set up a cycle. The people I was around drove the situations, which drove my mindset, and my mindset drove my selection of the people who surrounded me.

What a revelation! Any time I changed any part of this circle in a positive or negative direction, my life veered in the same direction. The overall feeling, mindset, and measurable results of each year matched the direction of the change made in these areas for the majority of the year. Any year that I looked back on that was so-so was defined by this circle, which builds in a negative direction. Any year that was bad was when this circle went through a zero-acceleration period (no change) and then shifted from "building, or good" to "declining, or bad." Any year that was good showed continuous, positive growth at a constant rate. Now, every year that was exceptional was one that went from a decelerating, negative period to a positive period.

Therefore, it was the change in my life cycle that, in retrospect, shaped my memory of each year.

How did I get to any of these improving or declining stages? How did I change the cycle to affect my life's direction? Was it something I did on purpose, or something that just happened? As I thought about these areas, I started to categorize each input into the three areas. These areas comprised the people I was around, the situations I faced, and the mindset I had. As someone who has recently realized a certain nature of humanity within himself that I cannot just ignore, I am using this enlightenment to compile how to manage it. By manage, I mean to understand myself, to recognize my needs as a human, to see the direction I am heading, and then to make a small change in order to actually attempt to control that direction.

Bad Years

The first thing that comes to mind is how I got myself into the bad years. In each of these years, I found myself surrounded by very negative people. These people had peaked at some point in the past, had low self-esteem, were concerned about maintaining their status, were afraid in general, and were lashing out at someone or something. A negative mindset surrounded these people, and they needed continuous positive input to keep themselves from a full-blown meltdown.

Mindset

My personality determines my mindset when I am exposed to people and situations. I am naturally a helper, and like many men, I have a strong human need to support and help the people around me and to improve the situations in which I find myself. I love to rush in, take some action, scurry around rapidly, and make it better immediately. After the initial phase of making it better, the strongest part of my personality really kicks in: the need to set up maintenance to keep the initial, rapid changes intact, to the point of being OCD. After setting up a maintenance routine, I then follow up on the feeling of fulfilment by slowly advancing the initial progress further in a positive direction. Once again, I have defined three steps that can now be analyzed: the initial scurry, the maintenance, and the march forward.

People

I have found that my mindset is highly affected by the progression of these three areas. If I enter a situation and cannot scurry around and help, I feel helpless. If I can't maintain the initial work, I feel frustrated, and if I can't march forward, I feel ineffective and unneeded. In the bad years, I was often unable to help in certain situations. One reason was that the people I was around believed they had peaked in the past and did not accept that situations could be better. Another reason was that I was with people who were afraid of change and who thus resisted the initial scurry and forward march. A third reason was that, in some cases, people around me with negative mindsets accepted that their circumstances were becoming continuously worse, which prevented me from meeting my need for maintenance. Lastly, at other times, I was around people who were so worried about status that they languished in the stage of scurrying around. For them, one episode of scurrying negated the previous one and caused a need for the next. However, because of this they were never able to reach the maintenance or forward-march states. When I get into a situation in which others hinder progress entirely in one or more of the three areas, I feel stressed out, which leads to emotional outbreaks because I feel overwhelmed.

Situations

The situations I found myself in were a product of my mindset, and I was always feeling stressed out and having emotional outbreaks from the overwhelming feelings. I was not in control of my direction and not progressing, and in the bad years, I was even regressing when it came to maintenance. The situation I was in influenced the situation toward which I migrated. In bad years, I was trying to regain control, maintain, and move forward. The only way to do this in any given circumstance was to reduce the complexity of the situation. Reducing the number of things to manage was the primary objective during those times. The interaction with others was a product of the people surrounding me and of my mindset, which was focused on attempting to pull these people out of negative states. This exhausted my energy to affect their well-being. My mindset added to the situation as I became frustrated and handled the situational interfaces poorly. In bad years in general, I did not handle situations well, which lowered my self-esteem. I

10

then selected new people to associate with who also had low self-esteem, which caused the situation to spiral further.

Great Years

I jump straight from the bad years to the great years because of another personality trait of mine, which is that I feed on and grow positive from negative situations. From my exposure to people during my lifetime, my assessment was always that this particular trait is very rare, but as I researched and thought about the process of engineering one's life, I found that this is something that can be reproduced and taught to anyone. I have read a lot of classical material about such a personality type, which was always portrayed as an innate human quality in writings from exceptionally dark parts of human history. I have pondered the question of whether it is necessary to have exceptionally bad times to push from bad years to better years. Do people have to go through exceptionally low points to turn their lives around? I will explore these questions later in the book. However, the one thing I can say with certainty is that, when I look back at the great years of my life, they have always emerged from something exceptionally negative.

People

The people I find myself around in great years are at the tops of their games. I have lost track of many people from my past, as I have become so busy with people at the tops of their games that the people from the bad years fall off the chart. My question to myself is whether this happened because I removed the influence of these people, because these people disconnected from me since they didn't fit in with those at the tops of their games, or because they felt inadequate when associating with the improved version of me. It was probably a bit of each, but in the best years, I definitely willfully severed relationships with some very negative persons. In each of these cases, I have felt miserable about the lost relationship, but in retrospect, this has caused my personal growth, both in mindset and situation, to skyrocket. The people who surrounded me in the great years had pushed themselves beyond what they previously thought was possible and had cleared a well-defined path for their futures.

Mindset

My mindset in the great years was defined by the fact that I did not concern myself with status or negative thoughts about what I had done in the past. I reached the point where I decided I had messed up so badly that I did not care anymore. In these times, I did not care if I lived at all, just that I was going to make the best out of what I was, who I was, and what I had. At these times, I felt that I had so much more than the people around me did, though I have to admit that this may have been a foregone conclusion, based on the perception of measuring myself against my previous mindset. However, I can say that in each great year, I snapped, and I became more focused on what I could do, instead of on what I should have done. In every occasion, this meant disconnecting from the people who were worried about appearances and status. The social pressure of others around me, especially those closest to me, during these times was to fall back into what I had been doing that had led up to the so-so years and that had bottomed me out in the bad years. My mindset in great years was to break away from that social pressure and to do what is best for and what works for me.

Situations

The situations in which I found myself during the great years were improving in the three areas that my personality needed. I was surrounded with people who provided me with the opportunity to enter into situations, scurry around, and improve matters. I was also in environments where the work I had done was not continuously degrading, which gave me the opportunity to have the time to work on a march forward. These situations were free of people who were convinced that they or I had done the best in years past, and they were full of those who looked forward to being better next year. My current situation at any given time always included defining the next step beyond what I was currently working on. In addition, the path was clearly defined, giving me the ability to maintain and march forward without continuously pausing to redefine goals.

Good Years

The years I describe as good were almost a break from the great years, and they were when I slowed down a bit. Several, mostly social, reasons were behind this. The social reasons I refer to are the same reasons that the stock market goes up and down—the same reasons that economic trends fluctuate—which is something I have referred to as "the rule of one hundreds" because it affects the stock market. Simply put, it is that no stock can go up forever, no matter how good it is. This is why people have a problem perceiving that others are passing them up. If one of your peers had received a promotion this year, then no matter how well he might do in his management role, there is almost no chance he will receive a promotion to the next level the year after. It has nothing to do with his capabilities at all, but rather the social acceptance of others in that situation and the fact that, socially, you have to prove yourself over time at one level before you can move on to the next.

People

The people who surrounded me in these years were positive and comfortable with themselves, but often modest and content that they had peaked in the past, or they were just happy not to push the envelope too much. They were very orderly, maintained themselves, and even slowly marched forward. There was mutual acceptance and social respect, but they often conformed out of concern for maintaining their status with those around them. There was also a common level of acceptable competition and social conformance.

Mindset

My mindset was definable by meeting my needs for maintenance and marching forward, but it was often missing the scurry around and improvement phases. In truth, my assessment of these years may have only been less than lustrous because in my mind they followed a great year with an exceptional benchmark. Many would call these building years. The years that fit this description were 1) my second and third years of undergraduate study in college, 2) my second year of graduate studies, and 3) my second year at a new job after graduation. These years provide a few case studies, and they fit the mold of goals set incrementally to conform to socially accepted rates of improvement. For example, when you start a new four-year degree, you are classified as a freshman and are not accepted for, or even expected to achieve, exceptional results. You may have the same accomplishments as upperclassmen, but not the same level of acceptance. People in these phases often sit back and embrace these expectations as a rite of passage, as a trade-off for future expectations.

Situations

The situations and environment in these years were mostly unchanged or in a state of maintenance, but they were often, in retrospect, absent any positive or negative feeling. My most significant memories from these years involve situations that were relatively constant and that did not have any notable changes. Thus, a good year in this respect was not great because of the sense of decreased acceleration.

So-so Years

The balance in the so-so years tipped away from the good years and toward the life circle moving in a negative direction. When I've tried to determine which of these tipping effects were actually in effect, causing the negative direction, I have found that it is different each time. On different occasions, I have seen that any of the three—people, mindset, situation—have been the cause, but usually a combination of two changed the overall outlook to negative and pushed the circle in a downward direction. When just one area changes to trigger a downward shift, it is easier to pinpoint and even stop the shift, but when two are in effect at the same time, the spiral can start to turn downward out of control. So-so years have often spanned several straight years in my life, and when this happens, my personality trait to help, support, and grow something positive from negative situations is so strong that I will circle the wagons and try repeatedly to improve each of the areas of the circle.

People

Persons in my life during these years are usually the same as in good years with one or two exceptions, which usually end up making the difference in the year. In my experience, several of these downward circle trends have involved people in my life who had made a change in one of the following areas:

1) They resolved that they could no longer improve some aspect of their own lives.

2) They determined that either they or I had peaked in the past.

3) They started to draw more emotional energy from me than I felt returned by them.

4) They initiated a pattern of being overwhelmingly afraid or helpless.

5) In general, they introduced an overpowering disruption of my basic human needs to scurry, improve, maintain, and march forward.

Many times, these people had been in my life prior to these years, and my mindset may have affected the balance in one of the above five ways.

Mindset

My mindset is usually one of the factors in the so-so years, whether my mindset causes the change or some outside influence changes my mindset. At different times, I have found that, when I changed my mindset, it caused the traits of another person, with whom I was already in contact, to affect me. Other times, some individuals near me changed, which caused my mindset to change. The ultimate effect, though, is that personality clashes with someone resulted in my mindset becoming less tolerant of certain characteristics, which at times went as far as total frustration with the other person's trait. My mindset shifts to a state of avoidance. I repeatedly focus on whatever I am at odds with and push back, only slightly at first, with comments registering my dissatisfaction, until I eventually avoid situations altogether that accentuate the differences, and then I start to get upset at the events or traits that those situations accentuate. When I get to the point of being upset, my mindset slides even further toward the point at which the events that highlight the differences upset me. This causes my mindset to spiral, and I often struggle to restrain myself from tipping over the edge. If I do tip over the edge, the trigger is usually a stressful situation, and the outcome is that I behave badly and my behavior appears unwarranted.

Situations

The situations in which I find myself are sometimes the factor that produces my mindset, and other times, my mindset brings about the situations. Often, others have spoken at length about economic events that cause situations beyond their control, leading to their circle spiraling downward. On one occasion, a negative economic situation I experienced added to the negative balance late in the cycle of a downward spiral and led to a bad year. Other times, the situation I was in directly resulted from appealing to others and allowing something, which I thought would be not be an issue for me, to define my entire environment. Sometimes allowing others to define aspects of my situation did not affect me, as long as the situations allowed me to meet my human needs of scurrying, improving, maintaining, and marching forward. However, when someone was allowed to make a decision that affected my situation greatly and when there was a perceived disruption to any of my three areas of basic human needs, a pessimistic mindset began to grow within me.

The Making of a Good Year

So I ask myself, how do I take positive control of these areas and make a good year? Do I need to have positive control in every way, or just some knowledge of how to affect matters when the balance is tipping? At the point in my life when I first wrote this chapter, I had not yet attempted to understand these aspects of myself. I had at times been what I considered successful, but I was unsuccessful at other times. I could see that, with a bit of time and analysis of these various periods of my life, a pattern emerged that could help determine how to positively affect the amount of effective, productive time in my life. Since nothing can be great all the time, much like nothing can go up forever, I cannot expect that each year will be a great year, but it should be possible to have enough of an effect on the overall course to at least determine when a negative effect is under way, note the inflection points, and attempt to make a change before I get too far into a so-so situation.

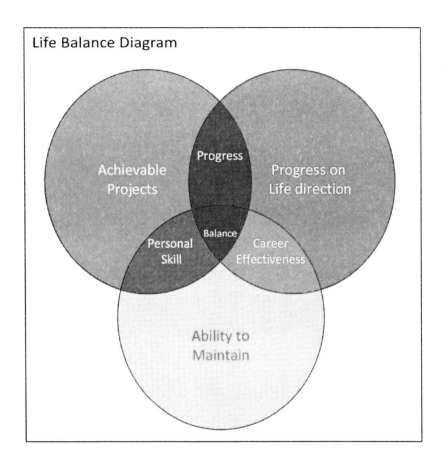

I determined that the bad years had always come from ignoring a so-so situation for an extended

period of time, which led to a meltdown caused by simultaneous changes in all three of the

factors—people, mindset, and situation. It appears to me that each of these areas changes slowly

over time along with everyone else's around me. The life cycles of individuals and those of the

people surrounding them, regardless of the components that comprise each, end up migrating in

and out of a state of affecting each other. Thus, each person's life cycle will continuously change.

My objective is to minimize the downward cycles in myself by addressing my identified basic

needs, which I cannot control, and by making an effort to align my mindset, the situations I am

in, and the people I choose to surround me.

When my mindset slips, it is usually because of the loss of control in one of the three areas I need to have in my life in order to feel validated. I need to set up projects that I can start from scratch and that have exceptional need, and thus I can show some rapid improvement. At the same time, I need to live in an environment that can be easily maintained with my current level of effort and amount of available time. Lastly, I need to have large projects that I can continuously work on while marching forward in a positive direction. The situation I am in needs to provide enough time and an environment that supports what I select to fill these needs. The people I am with need to support these goals and need not be exceptionally disruptive to the situation, meaning that they should add as much to the overall situation as they take from it. They also need to have their own path and direction, which should show an equal level of motivation and compatible areas that are not mutually exclusive with my own. My mindset needs to allow me to be human and to have variety in my life, but it should keep me moving in the overall direction that I am heading.

Identifying and Affecting

When identifying the times in my life that I was not effective, I also found that they related to the times when I was unfulfilled. I wanted to determine what had changed from the effective times and whether any of these could be changed back. What I found was that there were definable traits that I had changed and that set the path in the new ineffective direction. A difficult realization was that I had often in my life voluntarily given up certain traits for a situation I had encountered or for a person who needed appeasing.

How could someone or something external to me make me change enough to render my entire life cycle ineffective? Digging into this had me exploring some weaknesses in my own personality that had enabled this dynamic to occur. Was this also something over which I could gain control,

20

or even mastery? I did not want to be the person who swayed in the wind, whose entire life's direction could be determined by external environments. I knew I had been extremely successful before and that I could do it again in the future, but this time I would understand the process of how this occurred as it unfolded. I decided to quit trying to be something that I thought I had to be and instead to be the thing that I knew worked for me. Identifying which areas of my life cycle had been affected was more difficult than it may seem. I realized that I had exceptional problems with this area because of my upbringing, specifically the deep-rooted training I received from my family that it was wrong for me to think about myself and that it was selfish of me to desire for myself things that only benefited me.

Once again, turning the corner required me to understand my upbringing and to determine what made me capable of being affected so completely by something that was not my choice. My first self-exploration into why I had entered into several controlling relationships led me to understand the fact that obvious weakness existed in my personality. These weaknesses pointed to some areas of interpersonal interaction that I needed to explore further. Identifying how people interact and what portions of the transfer between people could be handled more effectively to gain control over my own weaknesses was a key point of my exploration. What I have found has changed my life, because not only can I be more effective and more productive again, but also I now understand how to accomplish this and how to help others do the same in their lives.

Chapter II

An Eternity Followed by Twelve Lifetimes

When I consider the stages of my life, I notice they have defining points that stand out. I can go through each year of my life and tell you, "At this point in my life, I changed," and from that time on, I had a different perspective. These perspectives each defined a stage in my life. My mindset, along with the thought process I had before each defining point, was not fathomable in the phase after that point. Why was this? Why do we all turn a corner and can never go back to the person we were before? In my life, I've found that I could link these stages to how my perspective corresponded to the length of time I had already been alive. When I compared these stages closely with many other people's experiences, they appeared to be relatable to many other people.

To understand this, let's start at the end of someone's life and add perspective. Follow me for a minute and think about the day when you will get the message (which is coming in everyone's life) that you have reached the end and that you are going to die soon. You've heard story after story about the things that everyone wants to do as a last wish, the clarity in their understanding of it all. This is what I am calling the last perspective lifetime. This I define as the time between when a person gets the knowledge that the end is here and when they actually pass on from this Earth.

Now that I have placed that thought into your mind, let's look at the beginning. Humans base their understanding of memory, knowledge, and wisdom on occurrences in their lives—things and events that affect, include, surround, or happen to them. These events need to be related to time to have some perspective of how many events occur in a given period or of how much time passes between events. When a human is developing in the womb of a mother, the events and stimuli are limited, the sounds muffled, and for the most part, they do not include the infant. Up until the day when the mother's contractions begin, the perspective of events related to time is not large enough for them to trigger memory building of any large amounts. Then something changes.

For a visual, think of someone living on a tropical island that readily provides for everything the person needs to survive. If you have known this your entire life and if all you have ever had to do is gather natural resources and drink coconut milk while playing on the beach, then your life has been uneventful. Imagine that you have had this environment throughout adulthood without ever going through a hard time. What does the first hurricane look like to you? Now imagine that you are the only survivor of this hurricane and that you find out the entire island has changed. All of the landscape has changed, and all of the plants and animals have completely vanished. The events of that hurricane would seem like an eternity. The hurricane would not be just one negative event, but a string of events that included hours of torment. Your life from that point on would relate to what you currently know, and it would have nothing in common with your life from before.

When a child is born, they have never experienced pain. Many of their organs have never had to function before. They have limited experience with their eyes, ears, sense of touch, and so on. This experience is a lifetime from their perspective, each second experienced as a gasp for survival from one moment to the next. We look at them, see a cute face, and smile with awe. If you look closely, you can also see they are struggling through each moment of consciousness waiting for the sense of discomfort they are experiencing to be resolved or waiting until they fall asleep with these senses unresolved. The time from when the first discomfort of the birth process starts until the time when infants become comfortable in the aftermath of adapting to all of their new senses and to all of their needs seems an eternity, much like the hurricane, compared to their previous uneventful life. Everything they experience after that will be measured against the birth process from the new human's perspective.

The experience of the birth process (though the human does not have vivid memories of it) establishes all of their perspective for their future life. It is likely different for each person, but I am guessing that this average experience for most people lasts less than two weeks. At this point, the infant knows a week of hell, which is their first reference to events. Their first lifetime includes the time interval beyond the length of this eternity of events in their memory that they continue to live. To advance past the first lifetime is to arrive at the realization that the extreme discomfort of the birth experience will not return and that the future is what they see around them, not the struggle they associated with the hurricane-like eternity before. Since humans are more instinctual than they are capable of cognitive thought and memory at this stage, the time that it takes them to get past this is ostensibly short. Though no one knows for sure, my sense is that each time you double your existing knowledge and experience in life, it feels like another lifetime in your perception.

The Master Key system says that the laws of periodicity fall into increments of seven—that everything that lives has periods of birth, growth, fruitage, and decline—and the assessment of the authors of that system is that, every seven years, a human enters a new phase of growth (Haanel, 1916). The interesting thing I found when looking at perspective lifetimes, other than the first seven years from birth until the seventh perspective doubling, was that this pattern roughly held its form. Since logic seems to have a universal nature, even when Haanel first realized this correlation to seven-year phases, he was able to approximate what we feel in relation to sequences with which he was familiar at the time.

24

As I watched my son grow through these early years, I saw major milestones, both for him and for me, in each doubling of perspective. Thus, the relation to perspective appeared to be a better gauge than using seven-year intervals. From birth until about two-weeks, he was mostly struggling to learn how to control his bodily functions, without much reflection outside of himself. In the second two weeks, there appeared to be a realization of the external world. At two-months old, another phase of consciousness showed subtle changes.

Neuroscience tells us that human brains develop more rapidly during the earlier stages of life. In fact, synaptogenesis in the human striate cortex was found to be most rapid between the ages of 2-4 months (Huttenlocher, Courten, 1987). The maximum synaptic density, the absolute number of synapses, and the number of synapses per neuron are reached by one year of age. Subsequently, progressive synapse elimination is most rapid during the preschool years (Huttenlocher, 1984). The higher levels of brain growth during these earlier years explain the more powerful gains in logic and in responses to the environment during these earlier times in our lives.

This growth, compared to our ability to perceive only the future in relation to what we already know, makes these earlier lifetimes appear in our memory to have the same effective relational scale and the same magnitude of later perspective lifetimes, which are exponentially longer in length. To relate this in terms of computers, the program to run a game of checkers on an early computer system may have used up 50 percent of the capability of the machine. A modern computer may be able to run a program that can analyze the Gross National Production of goods from several countries, containing millions of points of data, and still only use 50 percent of its capabilities, but the perception of usable resources to the scale of capability has changed by many multiples as the computer industry has grown by a multiple of two in each cycle over the years.

25

If I think relatively in multiples of two, then between 2-4 months, my son was able to reach some big milestones, such as holding the bottle himself and using his hands to do things he wanted. At eight months or so, I saw my son starting to imitate what he saw in adults, and the desire to walk and be mobile was beginning to surface, and so on. Now, I am not interested in proving a point on childhood development or in trying to predict the behavior of children. My objective here is to give you some perspective on what happens in adult conscious life. My experience tells me that people throughout their lifetimes have approximately twelve of these changes in consciousness at which point they turn a corner in their lives, and from that point on, they are never the exact person they were previously. My point is that these segments of people's lives are in relation to their knowledge and to what they have already experienced, and when they reach a point at which they have doubled what they already know or at which their perspective changes to reassess their remaining time to a more conservative expectation, they will go through a defining point.

These defining points are not set in stone or determined exactly by age, but rather by the individual's growth and absorption of events, which they have digested into memory due to the emotional influences that were occurring in conjunction with those events. While exploring these defining points in my life, I found out that, though these correspond to my perspective in relation to the rest of my life, they also require a triggering condition or a set of circumstances that precede turning such a corner. These turning points are always uncharted territory and can cause some people to collapse, but they can cause others to excel to unimaginable levels. These corners and triggering points have been the most wonderful and exciting portions of my life.

The lifetime that someone is in at the current stage of their life will display a few main characteristics that relate to their current perspective and awareness. Some of the things I have noticed the most include the following:

26

1) The things that will be most important

2) The values that they base their decisions on

3) The scope of their cognitive recognition

4) Emotional maturity

5) Social awareness

6) The efforts that they desire to pursue

The things that are most important to you in each stage of your life are the things that you focus on in that lifetime. This is a large area, which changes from one point to another when life-defining points occur.

The first turning point I remember from my conscious life was when I was at one of these perspective-doubling points and a stimulus event gave me the insight to make a decision for myself that totally turned my world upside down. I was in the third grade, around eight years old, and I was at one of the transition points between awareness that I relate to the sixth doubling of perspective since my consciousness. I will talk about this decision and transition point later in this book.

Perspective Lifetime Mapping

When I originally wrote this chapter, I did not include this section because, as I mentioned before, I am not trying to make a point about childhood development. However, since I will reference this topic several times later in the book, I need to establish a baseline for the events and enlightenments of the basic items that could characterize people in each of their perspective lifetimes. The items and developmental characteristics that I relate to each perspective lifetime are just some of the things that I either remember personally or experienced while watching my son develop. They are in no way all-inclusive or authoritative, just my thoughts on the subject to lay a foundation for later discussions.

- Birth to Two Weeks Old: Eternity
    - Blank looks, struggling with internal feelings
    - Reacting to discomfort
    - Involuntary and biological triggers seem to be in focus
    - Instinctual actions

- Two Weeks to One Month Old: First Lifetime
    - External focus starts building
    - Focusing on faces and responding to others
    - Combining multiple instinctive actions
    - Birth to two months—crying, touching, feeding, hearing, seeing (ZERO TO THREE, 2006)

- One to Two Months Old: Second Lifetime
    - Discovery of motion and motor capabilities
    - Uncontrollable or confusing mechanics of self
    - Imitating and copying facial features
    - Emotional connection to external cues

- Birth to two months—crying, touching, feeding, hearing, seeing (ZERO TO THREE, 2006)

- Two to Four Months Old: Third Lifetime

    - Usefulness of motor skills and own body

    - Combining multiple instinctive actions to influence desired results

    - Emotion stemming from interactive and external stimuli

    - Social connection to emotional influences

    - Two to six months—movement, touching, language, hearing, seeing (ZERO TO THREE, 2006)

- Four to Eight Months Old: Fourth Lifetime

    - Desire to self-initiate

    - Exploring mechanics and physics of surroundings

    - Movement of objects and spatial relationship

    - Emotion developing to internal desire (independence)

    - Reacting appropriately to surrounding social situations

    - Six months to eighteen months—cognition, learning, movement, language, social, emotional (ZERO TO THREE, 2006)

- Eight to Eighteen Months Old: Fifth Lifetime

    - Desire to explore

    - Practice of imitation other people (walking etc.)

    - Physical/mechanical reaction to emotional cues

- Six months to eighteen months—cognition, learning, movement, language, social, emotional (ZERO TO THREE, 2006)

- Eighteen Months to Three Years Old: Sixth Lifetime

  - Verbal participation

  - Non-physical social Interaction

  - Understanding social expectations

  - Outward emotion from internal desire (often characterized as uncontrollable)

  - Cognition, learning, movement, language, social, emotional (ZERO TO THREE, 2006)

- Three to Six Years Old: Seventh Lifetime

  - Determining expectations of social environment

  - Building self-guided patterns of social compliance

  - Determination of logical thought processes from multiple influences

  - Stimuli exploration, understanding of consequences to actions

  - Like and dislike, opinion building, and pursuit

- Seven to Fourteen Years Old: Eighth Lifetime

  - Developing supporting trends for personal likes and dislikes

  - - Self-guided decisions prompting desire

  - Building the ability to conceptualize consequences

  - Developing conceptualization capability for lifelong impact of decisions

- Fifteen to Thirty Years Old: Ninth Lifetime

- o   Reproductive expansion and exploration

- o   Control and exploration of biological influences

- o   Exponential growth in physical capability

- o   Health becoming less of a concern, perception of invincibility

- Thirty to Sixty Years Old: Tenth Lifetime

  - o   Growth through development of higher thought-length skills

  - o   Largest period of building wealth, social status, and productivity in life

  - o   Comfort with self and self-direction

  - o   Status and differentiation between peers

- Sixty Years Old to The Imminent End: Eleventh Lifetime

  - o   Continuing all of the previous

  - o   Gaining perspective of less time left than already lived

  - o   Health not taken for granted

  - o   Avoiding suffering becoming larger driver than biological (hormonal) needs

- The Imminent End Until Death: Twelfth Lifetime

  - o   Perspective that today is a gift

  - o   Worldly or physical possessions are meaningless

  - o   Revisiting of unexplored self or experiences

Perspective Lifetime Correlation

The determination of ages that I have associated with each perspective lifetime is just to provide an understanding of the concept of the mental, or perceptual, relationship to time. These perspective lifetimes will span different lengths of time for each individual, and each individual will experience or develop some of the items under each at different points in life. Anyone who has raised a child can attest to the development of people in general, following a progression of the capability to utilize cognitive thought. In addition to that, each child is different and follows a different progressive path. As you can see, even some of the references I cite related to development have employed different categorizations of ages in relation to development than the direct multiple of twos that I use.

Since my background is in technology, I have watched the development of the computing age with the same progression steps that I saw my son and stepchildren surmount as they developed their own cognitive abilities. The abilities required for the developmental levels that I relate to these perspective lifetimes build like each new generation of computing products. People who have been around since the inception of the computing age can relate to computers and technical products with the childlike capabilities and characteristics that resemble each of these levels.

If you did not fully catch the details of perspective lifetimes, do not worry, as it will become more apparent as I provide more examples and more details over the course of the book. This will especially be apparent in the next chapter where I offer a detailed description of my son's and my own development in relation to these perspective lifetimes. The connections I will make throughout this book flow from this thought process, which will be outside the box of most human cognitive and behavioral theories. Though I am only making points for the development

32

and control of one's internal self by using these theories, I also hypothesize that some of this approach could resonate in human behavioral models, as well as reveal a possible correlation to future artificial intelligence designs in computing.

References

Chugani, H. et al, (2001) "Local brain functional activity following early deprivation: a study of post-institutionalized Romanian orphans." Neuroimage 14 :1290-1301.

Haanel, C. F., (1916), The Master Key System, Psychology Publishing, St. Louis and The Master Key Institute, New York

Huttenlocher, P. R.,(1984) Synapse Elimination and plasticity in the developing human cerebral cortex, American Journal of Mental Deficiencies, March;88(5);

Huttenlocher, P. R., Courten, C., (1987) The development of synapses in striate cortex of man, Human Neurobiology; 6(1):1-9

ZERO TO THREE, (2006) BrainWonders, a collaborative project (1998-2001) between Boston University School of Medicine, Erikson Institute and ZERO TO THREE

Chapter III

Building Blocks of a Person's Core

In the Beginning

I was the fifth child born to a family of six children. My parents were born and raised during the Great Depression. Looking back at my parents now, I realize that their upbringing made them extremely cautious. They also had a note of distrust for the government and brought strong religious undertone to everything in their lives. Along with this, my father in particular had a strong desire to keep social control, especially in the family environment, which I attributed to the fact that when he was a child during the Depression his family became separated. I saw that this gave him a failed sense of family in his emotional wiring as a child, and it later drove much of the story of my young life.

Adding to the social conflict at the time of my entry into the world, the country was near the height of civil unrest that erupted in response to the Vietnam conflict, and the local area where my family lived was in terrible economic times. We lived outside of Pittsburgh, PA, and since the current rotation of the U.S. economy had shifted away from raw material smelting, which had been the largest source of employers for generations of workers, unemployment rates were at all-time highs. Overall hopelessness seemed to plague much of the adult community, all of whom could remember living in better times.

In order of birth, my five siblings and I are Brian, Peter, Betsy, Jonathan, I, and later Benjamin. We all lived together in a three-bedroom home. My parents had one bedroom, my sister had the smallest bedroom, and we four older boys shared a bedroom with two sets of bunk beds. I don't remember much of where my younger brother was until my parents added a larger bedroom onto the house. This larger bedroom then housed the four older boys, and our old bedroom went to my much younger brother.

My mother was a full-time homemaker for my entire childhood, and my father worked a very taxing blue-collar, service-industry job that provided pipe-cleaning services to the declining steel industry. My memories of childhood were of a controlled chaos in close quarters with extended family present nearly all the time. My parents' house, though small, was always clean and tidy, at least as much as it could be with at least six children present nearly all the time. Unsurprisingly, we only spent enough time to eat and sleep inside the house.

As you probably have already determined if you did a quick math problem, my parents were relatively older than the average parents were when I was born, especially for the 1970s. This age difference was another defining aspect of my existence, as my parents had three children, took a break for several years, and then had another set of three children. This made for a rather interesting dynamic, as my oldest brother and sister were old enough to be parental figures in the younger children's lives. By this point in his life, my father already seemed to lack the energy and stamina that he once had, which was apparent from photographs of when the older children were younger. On top of that, he was now working an excessive amount of hours at his job. From my earliest memory, it appeared that due to the nature of his emotional state most evenings after work, my father rather disliked his job.

My childhood was full of outdoor activities nearly all of the time, with large numbers of people around. Our family was always involved with something related to a large church, of which both my immediate and extended families were parishioners. My grandfather, of whom I have little memory, was a greatly admired church leader, and though my parents tried to distance themselves from this fact in an effort to create their own importance in these circles, much of their identities were based on this relationship. I have also recounted that the hard times from the late 1960s through the 70s and the social trend for communal activities seemed to influence them to embrace this church-heavy social environment. This style of living had them involved in church activities and groups for more than half of each week.

As my life has progressed, I have come to a few realizations related to some genetic predispositions that my family and I share that truly define the next aspect of my life that I will describe. My family, especially my father and I, are plagued with anxiety. It shows up in us in different ways than in most people, as we are very good at reacting to stressful situations; we maintain our grace under pressure, which makes us excel in work environments. However, my father's and my ability to handle long-term stress is not actually good, as it leads to a buildup of anxiety over time and to excessive mood swings. In hindsight, this is probably the reason that I thought my father was often upset and did not appear to enjoy his job.

In any case, due to my father's excessive mood swings, I learned not to bother my father, to the extent of never being around him at all. In such a large family, this was possible because one child could slip through the cracks and go unnoticed almost indefinitely. I had my oldest brother as a father figure, and I went to him in every instance when I needed a father. I really felt like I was living with a father and a grandfather. My brother Jonathan, who was one year older than I, had really taken to attaching himself to my father, and anytime there was a trip or something planned, Jonathan was with my father while I did the same activity or work with my brother Brian. This just seemed to be the natural order of things in our family, and I can't remember one occasion when it was reversed. Looking back at the situation, I see that my father's stress and anxiety didn't give him much chance to look past himself or give him any ability to plan or react to this dynamic.

The dynamic of being raised by my older brother and learning to avoid my father at an early age is probably the most defining aspect of my life. As my father figure—Brian—went through high school and struggled for his independence, he became more and more at odds with our father. The two of them had very long, very loud quarrels. I was too young to remember what they were about, but I knew one thing: I hated the guy who I perceived to be after my father figure, by which I mean that I hated my real father because of the discord between him and my surrogate father, my older brother. I remember these struggles ending with Brian rendered very meek and with my father overpowering Brian verbally until he had collapsed into subservient submission. Through this time, my brother Brian became more and more distant from the family. Given that he was a teenager himself at the time, I am sure that even to this day he does not understand what dynamic emerged for the young child who looked to him as a father.

My earliest memories of this avoidance pattern with my father were of knowing where he was and what he was doing at any given time so that I would not be anywhere near him. Every evening, he sat in the living room, resting from the mental anguish of work, dozing from dinnertime until our bedtime, and it would not go well for anyone who woke him up. About the time we would go to bed, he would awaken and suddenly have all kinds of energy to work on something in the garage for hours into the night.

My relationship with my father is something that has caused me much unresolved conflict, but I will address this topic later. Interacting with the rest of my family members—a few of them more than others—contributed a great deal to my development, but unfortunately, the way I learned to interact and react with all of them was exactly the same as with my father.

My brother, who was a year older than I was, seemed to spend his existence trying to please my father, which I did not understand. Interactions with Jonathan were defined by his admiration for my father. He would do whatever it took to elicit approval from that man, who I saw as angry, miserable, or unhappy most of the time. This required positioning himself as the good kid in my father's eyes, and he needed to have someone with whom to contrast. Out of this dynamic, I developed as the bad kid. At first, it was to make Jonathan happy because, for some reason, I was under the impression that it was one of my responsibilities to make people happy. At a young age, I found out that if I let him portray me as the bad kid so he could be the good kid, he would share his stuff and be my best friend whenever we played together. For young, cute kids in a large family, this is an acceptable trade-off since they are with siblings 95 percent of the time, so their approval during that 95 percent of the time avoids most of the conflict in their lives. In addition, most trouble a little kid causes is merely funny when the kid is young enough not to know any better, so the conflict for parental figures is minimal as well.

However, this shifted during my seventh perspective lifetime (ages 3-6), which is the development level during which children are expected to know for themselves the socially accepted actions in a given situation. The outcome of this shift was that I lost the ability to appease these two parties at the same time. I had been the contrast to Jonathan's good kid persona for so long that he had come to expect it, and if I disrupted that dynamic, my life during playtime became much less enjoyable. At the same time, the parental end of the equation had gained the perspective that, if something mischievous or disallowed occurred, yours truly was the first person assigned blame.

This magnified to epic proportions through my eighth perspective lifetime, to the point that my brother learned that he could blame me for anything and that I would be punished without verification. At some point he realized that he could inflict physical punishment on me (usually a

38

beating with a belt) based on his word alone. Though this is probably common in large families, it was the second strike on my young psyche. Even my playtime had someone who could inflict physical punishment (not directly, but by enlisting my father), and several times my brother proved that point by flexing this power and creating a ruse in order to prompt my father to beat me, just because I did not follow his lead at playtime.

Thus, my brother Jonathan became a second person whom I began to avoid as much as possible. The problem was that either my brother or my father was always around, so unfortunately this meant that I essentially needed to avoid my family entirely. As my eighth perspective lifetime progressed, I became extremely detached from my immediate family. Accentuating this, my oldest brother, who had been my father figure and protector, was around less and less and finally not at all.

My mother defended my father at all costs, so any child who got in the way of that would meet her wrath as well. This relationship also defined me, as when my father was not around, my mother was always there to console me and to be understanding of the dynamic that existed between my brother, my father, and me. But the minute he came in the door, a bubble of fear climbed up my throat because I knew I once again had no one. The change in my mother's demeanor toward me was apparent on her face: it was like a soft stuffed animal that had turned to stone. The comfort that I associated with any compassionate feelings dried up. My world became full of hazards in every direction, and it was like watching frost grow from the corners of a window on a frigid winter day. All aspects of the environment around me became dangerous, with sharp emotional needles in every corner in which I tried to hide. The only safe places were where no one wanted to be, and that was where you would find me: hiding, avoiding, and reducing conflict.

My sister, younger brother, and middle older brother are the three I have not addressed here, and that is because they were relatively neutral parties in my young perspective lifetimes, which may be the reason that I am closest to my younger brother and sister to this day. If I had to correlate the strength of my relationships with my family members to something, it would correspond to the largest part of my personality, as I relate to the people with whom I have the least conflict. This feature mostly defines my personality, as I am a conflict avoider at the core of my personality.

Personality-Defining Traits

The personality traits of people are what make them identifiable and unique. Some famous people are known for a deformity that makes them extremely identifiable, while others are known for their voices or facial gestures. Almost all of us have traits that we feel distinguish us from others. Many of us, including me, see themselves as having a very narrow set of traits or even a single, core, defining trait that has created nearly our entire personality. In any case, these traits are the building blocks that make up our core.

The defining trait of my personality is conflict avoidance. From my earliest few perspective lifetimes, this trait became ingrained in me. Though I can explain situations that emphasized this trait in my conscious memory, I cannot fully account for how I first began to develop it. My earliest memories of self-awareness are confusion based on having unresolved feelings of conflict that affected me in an exceptional way. In the section in which I described my family interactions, I described the first instance of this and explained how my inability to make my brother and my parents satisfied with my behavior became the first of my irresolvable conflicts. Ever since then, my logical mind has struggled with any similar irresolvable conflicts.

It is my belief that each of us has a similar personality-defining trait, one that guides the formation of all of our beliefs—a trait to which we can attribute the majority of our personality. What is yours? Years of therapy have helped me to understand myself well enough to identify my defining traits, but understanding is only the beginning of effectively changing one's wiring to resolve the negative effects that have been left unchecked for many years.

As part of the process of engineering your path and life positively, start to identify these personality traits within yourself. That is the first step to confronting them and starting to unravel the onion of your personality that you have developed for so many years. The main reason why each perspective lifetime seems to possess the same relevance, or length, in your mind is the fact that these defining traits have so much more effect on you during the earlier lifetimes when you react to stimuli without understanding or being able to process the reasons why you react.

The most poisonous mindsets, situations, or people in your life (which we will talk about in the chapter, "Thriving at the Low Points of Our Lives") will be the things that reinforce the weaknesses in your personality. They can affect you in negative ways like nothing else you will ever experience. Overcoming and recovering from their effects starts now as we begin to explore what these traits are in your life. Let's look at some examples from my life that may help give you a clearer idea of your traits.

When the Package Does Not Fit the Contents

Watching my son grow up and seeing some of the difficulties he endured helped to illuminate how I felt when I was younger. Watching him gave me the opportunity to see how I must have looked from the outside to the people trying to help me. My son was a very mild-mannered child with many curiosities. He seemed to learn very well in real-life settings and reacted well to stimuli that directly influenced his life. However, when he went to school, sat in a room, and listened to the teachers all day long, he had difficulty absorbing verbal content into his thought patterns. What was obvious was that he wasn't learning in the same manner that was successful for other children in his classes. His IQ testing showed that he had higher than normal intelligence, but he was unable to display this in a normal classroom environment.

Officials at his school requested an evaluation of him for learning difficulties, and the doctor explored several things, including autism spectrum disorders. They decided that he didn't really fit any of the standard categories for autism spectrum disorders. Instead, they just addressed the two areas in which they determined he had the most difficulty, which were focusing and executive functioning. Most people can understand not being able to focus, but the second thing is what has interested me the most. Executive functioning is the ability to change from one thought inside your mind to another. I understood this well, as I believe I have experienced the same issues my entire life. In both of our cases, we could sit through a class at school and fully grasp the entire content when it related well to something we already understood, but then when the teacher switched to the next subject, my mind could not switch to the new topic, especially when it did not relate in any way to the previous one.

The evaluation of my son's learning disabilities made me take a deeper look into what it actually means to have autism or an autism spectrum disorder. In so doing, I began to sense that the medical community essentially applied the label of autism spectrum disorder to children who did

not learn or adapt to conventional education patterns in the same way as others. Also, the more

I watched my son and the more I learned about these behaviors, the more I saw that I probably

exhibited the same behaviors when I was younger, but I had not been diagnosed because schools

did not explore these learning challenges nearly as much at the time.

A large aspect of my personality is a product of the fact that I make decisions differently than

most of those around me. While most people seem to react instinctively to stimuli, I describe my

process as more akin to observing the stimulus and then making a logical decision about how I

should react. In many cases, this looks like a delayed reaction to everyone around me, much like

when a digital TV feed pixelates or freezes because something slows or disrupts the feed's

bandwidth for a moment. When I was in an intellectual cognitive thinking mindset, I would go

through scenarios that I had seen based on the same or a similar stimulus, and my reaction

would spring from the logical determination of what was acceptable for the situation or stimulus.

I also noticed both when watching my son and in my own behavior that this feature within our

personalities of delayed reactions as well as executive functioning challenges did not occur all the

time. There was another side that enabled rapid access to instinctual functioning. However, the

two were very separate, and one could not be accessed while in the other mindset and vice

versa. It was as if the other mindset were not even understandable while firmly within the

opposite mindset. This brings me back to the topic of the section. What this looks like from the

outside is not what one might expect from the inside.

Consider the example of the digital television freezing for a moment for no apparent external

reason. This change in thinking pattern, which seemed to fit the medical condition that they

labeled as executive functioning disorders, often made outward reactions and actions not fit the expectations of others. The knowledge that something was different—not always, just some of the time—became a large portion of my personality. The fact that I had briefly frozen or paused was not always noticeable to me. In fact, often I only realized it had happened after the odd glares or confused looks of people around me. I became very easily convinced that my behavior was odd, and so I would enter an apologetic mode in which I assumed that I was the variable that had inaccurately approached a given situation.

The effect of this on my personality has been significant. Only in recent years have I come to understand it enough to begin addressing and influencing this dynamic. When looking at my or my son's visual appearance, the first impressions of outsiders often do not fit the opinion that they later adopt. In many cases, I have been lumped into the category of a business or marketing personality because of my appearance, but then later my detail-oriented mind will usually change the opinion of the same people. Many times, people have also commented on my voice being much softer and less aggressive than their expectations. In any case, the change viewed from my perspective has appeared as a disappointment to the person because of what they found after interacting with me.

Though what I perceived as disappointment was most likely a reassessment of the person's perception followed by a reevaluation of the value to them of our relationship, it affected me negatively. This aspect within me, along with the knowledge that I also had the appearance of a skipping TV, led me to question myself more than those around me did. Thus, building on my primary weakness, this made me assume that I was wrong more often than others were.

Building My Character Through Hardship

Being easily convinced that I was the incorrect variable in situations was not the only key aspect of my personality, however, because one personality trait often enables another. I attribute my robust work ethic to individual belief patterns that were established because of my constant assumption that I was the incorrect variable in situations. I repeatedly allowed people to convince me that I had inappropriately addressed a given situation, to the point that they always expected me to submit to their correctness. Admitting that you are always wrong makes those around you feel empowered to believe that they are always correct, even when they are not.

I permitted the pattern of my acceptance of the incorrect action or opinion and the pattern of others' assumptions of correctness to continue for extremely long periods. Those patterns persisted until they stepped too far over the line by proclaiming correctness when they were obviously logically incorrect. At this point, I realized that not only had I relegated my own opinion to just another opinion, but that the other person had gained an understanding of how on a whim they could completely manipulate me into illogical patterns. In other words, I had been played as a fool. The realization of how this had happened compelled me to construct belief lines in my logic that I would never again allow myself to cross. One of these early belief lines established an insatiable work ethic that has followed me for my entire life.

Life in my family was an oddity that did not fit the rest of the world around me. Whether it was the influence of '70s communal living or the fact that both of my parents had grown up on farms, they seemed to strive for fiscal independence by growing all of the food we needed on their single acre lot. Often I describe my family to others as one generation out of an Amish lifestyle. The summers were spent tilling gardens, planting, pulling weeds (my absolute most hated activity in the world), then canning or freezing everything that we grew. My mother took the opportunity whenever possible to make homemade clothing for the children, but when she did buy clothing, our economic situation required such extreme financial conservation that discount stores such as Kmart were the most common places for her to shop.

You might have detected a bit of sarcasm in the paragraph above, and that's because I remember feeling as though I was dressed like a clown for many public events. Since I was already aware of unsavory looks and attention thanks to my mental delays and resets, any additional attention bothered me in the extreme. Attending grade school through the 1980s, a time when television broadcasts and media awareness were growing, made my family's financial position and retention of older trends draw negative attention from my peers, which I resented at the deepest level of my core. When it came to my first instance of human individualization and differentiation, the point at which one becomes self-aware, clothing definitely served as that first area for me. At eleven years of age and in sixth grade, having already experienced ridicule at increasingly greater levels for the previous two years, I determined that I was no longer going to wear clothing that made me the target of ridicule. I would do whatever it took.

Since I understood that it was not an option to change the economic condition of my family, I knew it was entirely in my hands to change this aspect of my fate. I set out to work and get money to change my life. I was resolute that, if I had to work every waking hour, I would. In hindsight, I regard this as the determining factor that led to persistence becoming my primary strength.

Absorption of Surroundings

Considering the influences that each of my perspective lifetimes has had on my interactions with the world also led me to see how different these influences are for different people, just based on their time of birth. I have often examined how other people (starting with my siblings) view the world and how they have established personalities that are extremely different from mine. My brother, who was a bit more than a year older than I, was born in early November. His birthday was just after the colder weather started, when everyone was indoors more often, but before the winter holidays got into full swing. In my large family, visits through this period averaged about 3-6 a week, sometimes with multiple visits in a single evening or weekend day. The celebration of my brother's birthday became a large event each year because it was the season's first event, and everyone was excited about gearing up for family visits and indoor gatherings.

From watching this, I realized that his birthday kicked off the holiday season each year, and this festive mindset continued in everyone for essentially a two-month period. Now, the festive events were not all due to his birth, but with twenty aunts and uncles, countless cousins, and much more extended family in the local area, the holiday season was hectic and nonstop with visits, pseudo-parties, and community or church events. When looking at the early development of a child who entered the world at this time, the first two perspective lifetimes were filled with exceptionally many happy faces, exciting visits, festive disregard for health, and patterns of splurging resource spending.

When children are in the first two perspective lifetimes, they are beginning to focus on the external, responding to the facial features of others and putting together the first combinations of multiple actions. At the same time, the brain development and synaptic growth is exponentially larger than at any other time in their lives. In my brother's case, through the most festive time of the year, he was learning to imitate and copy facial features and to connect his own emotions to external cues. People attending parties have time for youngsters, while at other times of the year they may not pay nearly as much attention. A child gaining perspective in this environment would have a heightened value of self—others give them attention and thus validate their self-worth.

Over the years, the same patterns will recur as this person's birthday falls at the same time. I remember large parties each year and my brother having a sense of entitlement in his expectations for this recurrence. I remember looking forward to my brother's birthday each year as the event that mattered. In large families, children around the same age tend to be viewed in pairs. I remember feeling as if I was the less capable twin who was born a few minutes later with physical and mental disabilities that rendered me less capable.

In contrast, my birthday was just after the New Year, right when everyone was feeling partied out and resigned to return to the grind, when everyone starts to feel remorse and guilt from the holiday season, and when everyone buckles down to pay the piper after two months of extravagant spending and careless eating. My first two perspective lifetimes, during which I was developing external focus, responding to the facial features of others, and putting together the first combinations of multiple actions, were much different from my brothers' experiences. It was the most serious and focused time of the year. I learned to imitate busy faces and saw detached, worried, emotional cues. Focused and preoccupied, people had worried looks and less time to pay attention to youngsters.

I gained my perspective on my own individual importance at a time when people were tired of social interaction. Then I followed up with my third lifetime, developing motor skills, during the

48

busy spring planting season, which for my family involved exceptionally hard work and long hours. Like a papoose on the back of an Indian woman, I am sure I was just included in all the activities with the expectation that I would cause minimal disruption. In these times, children are expected to set their emotional reactions to the social expectations of their environment. For my situation, the expectation was that I should be silent and content because everyone was busy.

As the years passed, like my brother's birthday, mine also formed patterns. I remember the bothered, exhausted looks on everyone's faces when birthday parties were held for me, followed by the early, tired exits. Often I received fewer Christmas presents than everyone else did because my financially strapped parents just saved some for my birthday. Other years, everyone—including me—forgot about my birthday entirely. The feeling that everything was over after New Year's seemed to resonate with everyone. On two occasions, I remember being the only one who remembered my birthday. It was entirely skipped. My self-worth was such that, even when I knew it was my birthday, I did not feel it was my place to desire or command any attention to celebrate myself. It was not remembered until someone else recalled the omission several days (or weeks) later, and then remorse fueled a late, half-hearted celebration.

The perception I gained at an early age was that I was much less important than those around me were. Often, I have categorized life as though some people are born to be the center of resources while others are utility persons relegated to providing for those people who are entitled to resources. As it pertains to the development of and links between perspectives in the early perspective lifetimes, time of birth has a great impact. This is why I believe the signs of the zodiac have maintained relevance. They can categorize people based on how they react to stimuli at different times of the year based on which months their first few perspective lifetimes spanned.

In my case, I did not see the holiday season that my brother experienced in his first two perspective lifetimes until my fifth perspective lifetime. Given my theory that each perspective lifetime is as long as all the others with respect to a person's psyche, I nearly went half my life before experiencing this exceptionally festive portion of the year (for my family). In addition, I did not fully grasp that it was a recurring event and not just a one-time experience until well into my sixth perspective lifetime, and not until my seventh perspective lifetime did I see enough holiday seasons to understand the pattern and learn to expect that they would occur on an annual basis.

Programming a Person

On this journey into my own origins and my own psyche over the last few years of my life, I have gained a new perspective for the importance of a parent's role in child development. Parents have the first opportunity to program their children. For 75 percent of children's perception of time on this planet, parents are the majority control of their shaping. Children will acquire beliefs from their parents that they will carry throughout their lives, beliefs that are entirely situational or their own creation.

I have started having discussions with my son that attempt to determine some of the beliefs he has gained that may have been just because of my inabilities as a parent. Some of the most dangerous beliefs you can give a child are the ones that will position them in opposition to the things that will make them successful in life. Let's explore some of these in relation to the processes we will discuss later in this book.

My father appeared to be a bitter man when it came to work. I described him as appearing to have a deep hatred for his job. At the same time, in our large family, we were treated as if we

50

were on an assembly line. As the older ones rolled off, the younger ones were expected to pick up any dropped tasks. No consideration was given to whether or not the younger children enjoyed the tasks that the older generation used to do and may have even done happily. There was no exploration of self, and the belief was solidified daily with the negative reinforcement that my father hated his work. The relationship to work revolved around this hatred and avoidance of discomfort. Later we will talk about enjoying the processes in life, but involuntary programming in my upbringing aligned me in opposition to this aspect of success.

My family's extreme, hardline religious views, which in retrospect had been adopted primarily by my father, established a set of beliefs in all of us that was in opposition to the next process area needed for success. My father and his traveling religious team frequently expressed a doomsday mindset towards the future. On several occasions, my father stridently stated that God had told him that the end of the world would occur in his lifetime. This end-of-days mindset required no plans for the future. In essence, the dark ages were resurrected in the minds of my family. Thinking about the future was not essential. Thus, working past where you are in life had no value, nor did a productive path in life receive positive consideration.

Parents often assume that such views do not affect children over the long term because they do not exist as anything more than an opinion in the parents' minds, but the end of the world with fire and brimstone is not something that is celebrated in a child's mind. The associated negative emotions instill beliefs that are in opposition to all three of the process areas required for success. Parents assume that their children will gain their valuable principles, but then they focus their outspokenness on their children with fear and opinions. This negative interface sets up the emotional process to create a logical thought-stopper in their offspring's minds. My early determination to look for any alternative to each thing that came out of my father's mouth was the only redeeming quality that prevented me from establishing the same beliefs so strongly.

Driving Self-Reliance

Another area in which parents have a large influence on their children's development is with their internal self-talk. It is much easier to help yourself to be productive in life if you are not redefining self-talk instilled in you during childhood. Often self-talk is what drives our self-confidence. Some people may hear from birth that they are a higher class of human than those from some other demographic. When these people interface with a member of the perceived lower class, they make value assumptions in comparison to that person and can manifest a lifelong elitist view. Conversely, children may repeatedly listen to the self-talk that says they should not trust their own opinions, which can produce the lifelong perception that others possess more value.

The way we address either overpowering or including children happens on many levels and for many reasons, but the resulting effect drives the self-talk, self-image, and self-reliance of the person as an adult. When continuously instructed to go along with others and scolded for questioning why, you learn to follow without understanding. If you constantly give this response to stimuli, a logical thought-stopper can be inserted to halt thought when the notion of questioning external influences arises. The effect of this is to program people not to think for themselves and thus not to be self-reliant.

In my own life, though, I was not prepared to be a parent until after my child-rearing years. In many cases, the solid guidance of grandparents probably more often influences the raising of children. We are typically in the child-rearing phase of our lives before we become aware of the influence we wield over our children's self-image. Driving self-reliance is a primary factor in programming children with the sets of beliefs that enable the process areas that create successful traits. The most important thing you can do as a parent, however, is to avoid instilling counterproductive beliefs in your children. Knowing the process areas required for success when you begin your family planning will make all the difference. I hope that expectant parents or new parents take note of these portions, which I will define throughout this book. I wish I would have known these things sooner, and I believe they will drastically improve the lives and capabilities of our future generations.

Stages of Life and Migration of Self

We all go through various stages of life in which we look back to the things that created our personalities. Some of these things changed us entirely, and some may have broken us, while others just became milestones or added memories. I will offer some examples of these from my own life later in the book, including some that are rather embarrassing and others that were just awakening. When I look at these through the lens of my perspective at the time, I can relate not only to what was happening to me, but also to how I felt in relation to what I then knew about life.

Three to Six Years Old: Seventh Perspective Lifetime

I actually have many vivid memories from the ages of three to six—my seventh perspective lifetime. Before this time of my life, I have a few reference points to events, mostly as feelings that relate to later life events. My physical need for sleep was similar even at this stage in my life. One of my earliest regular memories involves not having nap times and then waiting in the throes of boredom for my older brother to awaken from each day's nap. This special treatment that focused on my older brother—while I was often punished for something as insignificant as not being quiet—was confusing to me at the time, but a pattern of self-guided expectations formed my first understanding of the consequences to me individually, consequences that were not spread among my siblings. My likes and dislikes of patterns and the results of such patterns are what I remember the most in my perception of self.

Seven to Fourteen Years Old: Eighth Perspective Lifetime

The first self-directed decision I made in life, which I will discuss further, was early in my eighth perspective lifetime. To analogize to the development of the personal computer, something I will do often in this book, throughout this lifetime I recall grouping multiple patterns, which I started to see in the seventh lifetime. Being able at the eighth lifetime to process multiple, shorter thought processes from my last lifetime granted me the ability to see these patterns coming together and to see that, at their intersections, I could exert influence. This was my earliest instance of self-guided decision-making. I recall being excited when I constructed a conceptualization of self-determined consequences that aligned with the pattern of interaction points. The excitement of coming to a conclusion then watching it happen has stayed with me and has had a lifelong impact on how I enjoy the process of conceptualization as it affects self-anticipated occurrences.

This process of conceptualizing and anticipating events was what I remember the most through my teenage years. However, at the same time that I felt skilled at anticipating the future consequences that may unfold from situations, I also felt that my opinions were less valuable than those of people around me, so I would not stand up to take actions based on my self-perditions. The considerable struggle of disbelieving my own talent is the most defining part of my personality in this eighth perspective lifetime. Gaining the self-confidence to believe my own insight and then act on it is what I consider the turning point toward my ninth perspective lifetime.

54

Fifteen to Thirty Years Old: Ninth Perspective Lifetime

When you once again double your computing capability—or in this case, cognitive ability—as you do when upgrading to the next generation of personal computer, you develop the ability to perform multiple instances of operations, of which you could only do one with the previous generation of system. Our human cognitive capabilities grow in the same manner. We can now take the things that we did at a younger age, such as looking at the interaction point between two processes, and evaluate hundreds of such convergence points with the same effort as we used to require for one single conceptual point of convergence. Our new capabilities in this perspective lifetime allow us to begin to feel a mastery of what we have known for all of our lives up to that point.

The expansion and exploration into entirely new, previously unknown areas that others had completely mastered, as I felt I had mine, characterized this lifetime. The more I explored, the less I began to perceive that I knew. I relate the reduction in my sense of knowing to the fact that, if you learn about an entirely new area of study each day and realize you have knowledge of less than 1 percent of it, then you know exponentially less each day compared to what you learn that you do not know. I associate much of this lifetime of exploring and expanding with a reduction in desire to learn and master, mostly due to the impact of biological influences on the human mind. Along with peer comparison and differentiation, biologically triggered reproductive influences clouded my pursuit of skills and knowledge I felt I had mastered, even some from earlier perspective lifetimes.

I often ask teenagers who are early in this perspective lifetime, "What is the oldest age of a person of the opposite sex whom you would consider dating?" The response is usually in the late-twenties range. Why is this? It is because that age represents roughly the doubling of their perspective, of what they have known. At the same time, many of them will consider anyone over thirty too old, because those individuals fall outside their perception of time. I recall a time when my close cousin, Ken, and I were conversing about how long we thought we would live. Both of us saw thirty as the end of our lives while we were in this ninth perspective lifetime. The turning point in my life that I associate with progressing to my next perspective lifetime was the birth of my son. Not only did this have a mental impact, but also, shortly thereafter, the physical realization of a change followed when Ken died shortly before his thirtieth birthday, while I also had my first nearly life-ending event at about the same time. This ended the perception of invincibility that, in retrospect, drove much of the mindset for this ninth perspective lifetime.

Thirty to Sixty Years Old: Tenth Perspective Lifetime

The previous perspective lifetime had centered on a feeling of immortality and on reproduction-driven lower brain functions that kept me focused on how to individualize and differentiate myself from others. Turning the corner to this tenth perspective lifetime changed my focus with regard to each of the things I was doing, which shifted from a primal focus to an individual focus. That is to say, I did not change what I was doing but changed why I was doing it. This happened almost immediately, as if turning a corner, and after that, I could not see back around the corner behind me. For example, I maintained a very vigorous workout routine, even reaching the peak performance of my life. However, I no longer did it to get attention from the opposite sex, but rather to prove how much I could build myself. I began to compare my performance against the performance of others around the same age as me.

I started to achieve cognitive growth through the development of higher thought-length capability. Though I was not aware of this at the time, I was self-exploring both the enjoyment of the process that led to success and the stretching of my own cognitive ability. There is no question as to why this perspective lifetime includes the largest wealth-, social-, and productivity-building years of most people's lives. Each portion of my life built toward the next, and it seems to me that the building process became the mark of my skyrocketing success.

Sixty Years Old to the Imminent End: Eleventh Perspective Lifetime

You may feel as if I ended the description of the last perspective lifetime abruptly. That is because in my life I have had a great gift that many people do not have: the gift of a shortened tenth-perspective lifetime and of the forced entry into the twelfth, followed by the good fortune to return to the eleventh. While most only experience the eleventh lifetime after they have passed beyond the level of physical and mental ability necessary to take the best advantage of it, I am using it to give back my success, combined with what I can only describe as the clarity to understand the meaning of life and to communicate it to the next generation. I may have a few decades or only a few years, but the eleventh lifetime mostly signifies the ability to become at ease with this fact. I realize that our value in life is what we pass on to the next generation. Health cannot be taken for granted, and I am convinced that I can help each person achieve success and avoid the interference we all face from our own biological limitations.

The Imminent End Until Death: Twelfth Perspective Lifetime

All of the days since August 22, 2010 have been a gift to me, and I look forward to as many more of them as I may be given.

Chapter IV

Human Logic and Thought Patterns

The contents of this chapter were not originally a part of the plan for this book, but as I wrote

and followed my own logical thought patterns to pull together the story of my life, I learned a

few things about myself that I thought I would share with you. First, however, I will share a few

stories regarding the content of this chapter that greatly influence the manner in which I will

present the topic.

The first story is about one of the earliest times that I shared the content of this chapter with

another person. I had not yet realized the extremely sensitive nature of what I felt was just

another great concept I had discovered. So, excited to share this topic, I prefaced my experience

of how I came up with the concept by telling my own story, which is the second story I will share

after this one. I did this using my excited, teaching tone, until I got to one particular statement

that I will reveal in a moment; however, I will tell you that this statement caused such a violent

reaction from my interlocutor that I was entirely caught off guard. Her response to the

lighthearted content I was happily expounding was, "OMG, if you print that you will be

destroyed. No one will believe a word you write, and you will totally discredit yourself as an

author."

My first response to her reaction was a joking rebuttal. Since she was the closest thing I had at

the time to a significant other, I assumed that we were merely sharing lighthearted banter. Boy,

was I wrong! My next statement in response to her reaction unleashed the fury of hell upon me!

I did not know what to do other than to melt into a speechless stupor of emotional lockup. Her explosive response to my rebuttal was, "You will be a fool if you publish that! If you ever want to have any value, don't ever go there. If you say that, Tony Robbins will destroy you!" which sent me into a deep sense of worthlessness and shame.

Since I am only vaguely familiar with Tony Robbins' work, mostly through reputation and via my significant other, I did not know what his opinion was on the topic, but her authoritative reference to his work felt like an unexpected slap in the face from the person to whom I turned most for encouragement. After we had a few moments to loosen the emotional lockup and back away from the topic, I questioned the Tony Robbins reference. She reworded what she had said explaining that what she meant to say was that, "Tony Robbins fans would destroy me." Although this seemed to downplay her emotional reaction, it definitely showed me what I might expect when treading near this topic. I will return to what I actually said that triggered this reaction after the second story and a discussion of some research I have done on the subject.

The second story involves how I initially came up with the concept and content of this chapter. It may seem out of place to tell this story after the last one, since this one happened first chronologically, but both stories are just as powerful for the unveiling of this topic. Without the first one, however, I would not be able to impart the gravity of the fear I had regarding my inclusion of this topic. The nature of the destructiveness surrounding both stories made me completely stop writing each time I reached this point. Both made me lockup emotionally for some time, prompting me to re-evaluate my entire approach, and more or less how I felt about the meaning of life.

My second story begins months before the first story, while I was solidly immersed in writing the chapter about my background. The problem I will describe also resurfaced later when I was writing the chapter about the time I questioned my own sanity because of the influence of others. What I experienced was a mental block, which initially presented as writers' block. While writing several of the topics from my life, I realized that I was repeatedly experiencing mental blocks that caused me to lose track entirely of what I was writing. I often sat in front of my computer and just stared as the text blurred into organized lines of symbols that registered no meaning in my mind.

After some time passed, I became motivated to address a different topic and resume writing with purpose. Often I had stretches of productivity, even for weeks at a time, working on some other portion of the book that interested me. Anyone who writes often will relate to the fact that you don't write all sections or content straight through from beginning to end. However, when I completed the alternate topic that motivated me, I went back to the earlier chapters that had prompted the mental block. When I began work again, I found that I ran into the same mental block I had before when trying to overcome the same section that had previously produced the mental block.

After several attempts to work through the same material before reaching a mental block, I decided to take some time to understand why this mental block kept emerging at the same place. I pondered it repeatedly until I collided with a mental block from thinking about the mental block. Several times the only resolution I could come up with was to drop everything and just do something else. Then it hit me that each time I reached a mental block, I was following a logical thought process that crossed a point in my mind, and something that seemed to be a biological response made me stop thinking about the topic. Why had I done this? I am a logical person. I should be able to think through any logical pattern just by thinking about the next logical step. My brain had stopped at the same point in the logical progression each time. What was it that made my brain stop at that particular logical pattern?

What Does Neuroscience Tell Us?

Now let's shift gears and look at some research by professionals on how the human brain works from a neuroscientific and psychological perspective.

Allan N. Schore, PhD, an expert recognized for linking the fields of psychoanalysis and neuroscience focuses a chapter of his book, *The Science of the Art of Psychotherapy* (2012), on relational trauma and the developing right brain. The book in general focuses on joining psychotherapy and neuroscience, which seems to be a relatively new approach, as several comments throughout the book identify the correlation between the two as cutting edge.

Neuroscience and psychology have now converged in many aspects of the study of brain development. Researchers are able to ascertain which portions of the brain are active when certain functions of human behavior are exhibited, which thus reveals the portions of the brain responsible for specific thoughts or behaviors. Keenan, Gallup, And Falk (2003) note, "By casting the right hemisphere in the terms of self, we have a revolutionary way of thinking about the brain. A new model of the brain, therefore, must take into account the primary importance of the right hemisphere in establishing and maintaining our sense of awareness of ourselves and others" (p. 252). Since the right brain is where the self is developed, let's analogize a human infant to a new computer with an enormous, but entirely empty, hard drive. As the infant grows and experiences new things, it begins to fill its lifetime capacity for retention with logical patterns about what to do and how to act. These are self-items.

In Dr. Schore's book, the relation between trauma and the developing right brain of a child explains some of the processes behind how the human brain biochemically reacts to traumatic situations. He describes two separate response patterns—hyperarousal and dissociation (Schore, 2001, 2002c)—and elaborates:

> In the initial hyperarousal stage, the maternal haven of safety suddenly becomes a source of threat, triggering a startle reaction in the infants' right hemisphere, the locus of both the attachment and the fear motivational systems. The maternal stressor activates the hypothalamic-pituitary-adrenal (HPA) stress axis, eliciting a sudden increase of the energy expending sympathetic components of the infant's autonomic nervous system (ANS). This results in significantly elevated heart rate, blood pressure, and respiration, the somatic expressions of a dysregulated psychobiological state of fear-terror. This active state of sympathetic hyperarousal is expressed in increased secretion of corticotropin releasing factor (CRF)—the brain's major stress hormone. CRF regulates the sympathetic catecholamine activity, creating a hypermetabolic state in the developing brain.

> But a second, later-forming reaction to relational trauma is dissociation, in which the child disengages from stimuli in the external world—traumatized infants are observed to be "staring off into space with a glazed look." This parasympathetic dominant state of conservation-withdrawal occurs in the helpless and hopeless stressful situations in which the individual becomes inhibited and strives to avoid attention in order to become "unseen." The dissociation metabolic shut down state is a primary regulatory process by which the stressed individual passively disengages in order to conserve energies, foster survival by the risky posture or feigning death, and allow restitution of depleted resources by immobility. In this hypometabolic state heart rate, blood pressure, and respiration are decreased, while pain numbing and blunting endogenous opiates are elevated. This energy-conserving parasympathetic (vagal) mechanism mediates the "profound detachment" of dissociation. (Schore 2012)

62

When I analyzed my own thought patterns, I could relate this description of two distinct,

separate responses in brain activity to my own behavior and to the behavior that I observed in

my son during his early development. Sometimes, I can relate to a feeling of dissociation when I

just stop or freeze, while other times internal triggers enflame an emotional state. Possibly, what

I had experienced in the first story of this chapter when describing this topic to my significant

other was the hyperarousal state, during which my reaction was more dissociation. Let's explore

that later.

This second quote is the one that really goes to the heart of the chapter's topic. The description

of the two response patterns, hyperarousal and dissociation, was required to understand what

these responses do to the development of our brains. In the same reference, Dr. Schore

continues to explain:

> Currently, neurobiological data can be utilized to create models of the mechanism by
> which attachment trauma negatively affects the right brain. Adamec, Blundell, & Burton
> (2003) report experimental data that "implicate neuroplasticity in the right hemispheric
> limbic circuitry in mediating long-lasting changes in the negative affect following brief
> but severe stress" (p. 1264). According to Gadea, Gomez, Gonzalez-Bono, and Salvador
> (2005), mild to moderate negative affective experiences activate the right hemisphere,
> but an intense experience "might interfere with right hemisphere processing, with
> eventual damage if some critical point is reached" (p. 136). This damage is specifically
> hyperarousal-induced apoptotic cell death in the hypermetabolic right brain. (Schore
> 2012)

When I first read this section, I was not familiar with the word *apoptotic* in the context of

apoptotic cell death. After quickly looking it up, I found that if cells are no longer necessary, they commit suicide by activating an intracellular death program (Alberts, Johnson, Lewis, Raff, Roberts, & Walter 2002). This was very interesting because I had been looking for the reason I stopped thinking during certain thought patterns, and this revealed that adverse experiences might cause the brain cells used during that process essentially to commit suicide. What better way is there to set up a logical reaction to stimuli in a biological memory—in a brain? It appears possible that by killing the part of the brain that would have continued the logic to complete the process, our brains permanently stop the process they were performing when the stimulus was experienced.

Since my background is in computer engineering and cyber security, this functionality makes sense entirely. This is how we humans make software and machines complete the desired logical sequences. We discontinue operations based on a set of things that we restrict the machine from performing. In the case of machines, we have the ability to design conditions into the operation parameters. A logical sequence arrives at a set parameter, and based on the input of that parameter, the sequence moves in one logical direction or another, much like coming to a fork in a road where you have to go one direction or another.

When programming software for a computer, there are a few ways to look at the progression sequence of the commands. We can tell the computer that, if a certain condition occurs, then do a specific operation, or we can tell it that, if something wrong occurs, then recover and do something else. These two have subtle differences, mostly in the intent of the operation, so we want to deliberately decide each step of our program so it does not need to recover should everything else fail. Setting up deliberate positive control of the program is desirable because all the possible conditions are handled and the software will be less problematic. Well-written software is approached in this manner, and the process would follow a positive logical pattern.

64

On the other hand, exception-based software can also be written to catch problems when they occur and to recover by starting something else; this follows more of a negative logical pattern. The process takes on the appearance of stopping and recovering because everything else failed, following up with starting somewhere else. In well-developed software systems, both of these practices are done together, with all the positive conditions systematically resolved, but then should some case not be made, a negative logic stops everything and restarts the pattern. Anyone who has ever experienced the blue screen while using a computer with a Windows operating system has experienced the "everything else failed" situation.

Programming the Human Mind

Let's return to my second story about how I came to realize this topic. As I repeatedly retraced the thought process that had led to my own shutdowns, I realized I had reached a thought progression in which the next logical step would cross a belief that I had previously established. Thus, taking that next logical step was not permitted in my mind. I suddenly understood that a belief can be a logical thought we have programmed ourselves not to take. These are thought-process stoppers, possibly even involving physical brain damage because of an apoptotic cell death. The word *no* yelled at a child running toward traffic comes to mind. This nondescriptive, negative word tells us to discontinue, but it doesn't tell us what to discontinue. Our brains learn just to stop thinking when the next logical step crosses the thought-process stoppers we have placed in our minds.

In the growing baby's brain, experts have found that "brain development, or learning, is actually the process of creating, strengthening, and discarding connections among the neurons; these connections are called synapses. Synapses organize the brain by forming pathways that connect the parts of the brain governing everything we do" (Child Welfare Information Gateway, 2009).

Once again, look at programming in terms of how we create logic in computers. We use electrochemical reactions to create logical gates in silicone structures. Then we determine which of these gates to use and how to use them by programing code to make use of them with software.

Humans have learned not only how to program our next generation, but also how to set up a process of self-programming that is continued based on a firmly planted set of lower-level virtues established by negative programming logic. Each time continuous, nondescriptive negative versions of punishing events, which we may consider abuse, jolt our minds with hyperarousal, more and more apoptotic cell death occurs, causing more and more logical thought stoppers. These function similarly to the manufacturing process in which we create physical gates in silicone. We create our offspring's operational logic by burning into them logical thought stoppers for every instance in which a legitimate or falsely created hyperarousal condition occurs.

If this was a programming course, I would recommend against using negative logic unless all else fails. Any engineering practice would also recommend the use of positive logic at all costs. However, I have not read or observed any way to biochemically produce a positive logical pattern in our brains. We do not even seem to be equipped with a method for performing positive logic in our human brains. The only way to do so is by self-sequential logical thoughts that require the use of positive logic for each occurrence. The positive logic or software is now in the process we use inside our own minds as we self-explore.

Exploring Our Beliefs

What about other beliefs I had: were they all the same? Were they just logical thoughts that I would not move to the next logical step in the sequence? My beliefs said, "THIS IS IMPOSSIBLE." After all, beliefs are good things, right? Beliefs guide me to the moral upstanding behavior that is the fabric of my core, right? Determined to prove this theory wrong, I set out to find a positive belief, one that makes me move forward to a good logic in my mind. When evaluating every belief I could think of, I found that some thoughts from which my brain would not allow me to take the next logical step actually were what created each one. Wow, all beliefs are negative logic. This stopped me just as the original thought-stopper topic had. I did not believe it could be true. After returning several times to this logic, I just stopped thinking, often for days on end. Each time I revisited this, I came to the same logical progression, and my mind stopped me again. Beliefs are positive, right?

Later in the book, *The Science of the Art of Psychotherapy*, in the chapter entitled, "The Right Brain Affects Regulation," Dr. Schore states, "I will argue that the unconscious affects can be best understood as the repressed but dissociated affects, and the later-forming repression is associated with the left hemispheric inhibition of affects generated by the right brain, whereas early forming dissociation reflects a dysregulation of the affects resulting from the dis-integration of the right brain itself…. Although this topic has been controversial, neuroscience now demonstrates a 'right hemispheric dominance in the processing of unconscious negative emotion' (Sato & Aoki, 2006)" (Schore, 2012). This latest research leads to the same conclusion that I had reached in the evaluation of my own thought process. The right brain is able to connect the negative emotional triggers from past experiences to disengage the portions of the brain that provide logical thought operations.

In other studies that look at the brain activity of people subjected to abusive situations, researchers have found a correlation between the types of activity and the amount of development in the brain based on the number of continued negative experiences. For teens who have been abused, neglected, or traumatized, the researchers found that these youths have developed brains that focus on survival at the expense of the more advanced thinking that happens in the brain's cortex (Chamberlain, 2009). Therefore, as we gain more and more of these logical thought stoppers, we have more and more conditions and cases in which we do not use the higher thinking parts of our brains. The extreme cases of humans being exposed to these abuses or traumas become apparent in the overall cognitive development.

Researchers have found in the brain scans of three-year-old children that there are noticeable differences in the treatment of humans over extended periods based on the attention or neglect they receive. Children who were adopted from Romanian orphanages in the early 1990s were often considered to be globally neglected; they had little contact with caregivers and little to no stimulation from their environment—little of anything required for healthy development. One study found that these children had significantly smaller brains than the norm, suggesting decreased brain growth (Child Welfare Information Gateway, 2009). What I experience with the continued programing of my own thought processes that causes me to shut down thinking is the root behavioral cause of this. When logical thought stoppers of many different logical patterns cause me to stop contemplating entire topics, my extremely belief-oriented upbringing probably limits my overall brain activity. (not sure if this will stay)

After some time evaluating my own beliefs as well as other people's, each belief has been, in fact, a logical stopper. Even logical beliefs, such as the belief that you have to go to college in order to better your life, are logical stoppers programmed with the belief that you can't even think of not going to college. Going to college is not a single defined thing; it is a series of events or things in opposition to not going to college. If someone stands up in front of you and talks all day about things you have never heard before, but if each of these follows a logical progression

68

from one to the next, then you will follow each logical progression with that person until the single time when the next logical step crosses something you do not believe.

If presented with a logical thought process that does not go against our beliefs, we will follow it indefinitely. However, if a logical thought progression crosses a belief, we will immediately stop thinking. Therefore, the definition of a belief is a logical thought process or pattern that we will not allow ourselves to follow. If a belief is only negative, then should we have them at all? What value do they have? Is there anything good about them?

Now let's return to my first story, which I began when we started this chapter, where my explanation of this topic to another had caused such a violent reaction. The phrase I first said to trigger her first barrage of insults was, "I have found out in my research that all beliefs are actually negative in our minds. There is no such thing as a positive belief." My mistake was not to explain the logical-thought-stopper patterns or the nature of negative versus positive logic. In my mind, I was happily enlightening her to the exceptional progress I had made with reducing my own mental blocks. I wanted to share with her that, once I figured out that certain thoughts triggered me to stop thinking, my ability to self-explore and remove these blocks was exceptional, but in this case, going from A to C without explaining B actually triggered the process I was trying to describe to her.

After absorbing the first barrage of insults, I blurted out without thinking, which proved to be detrimental to my own relational harmony, "See, you stopped thinking because I triggered a belief in you." I continued with, "I didn't believe that beliefs were negative at first either." This second comment, which she later explained she received as, "Since she did not believe me, it was because she could not think properly," ignited her second barrage of even more pointed insults.

When I had time to think about this interaction and the responses we each had to the same conversation, I realized that I had definitely uncovered something there. We each definitely had an uncontrolled reaction to a belief trigger, but hers was different from mine. While I had been experiencing an internal process that made me stop thinking and that seemed to follow a *dissociation* pattern, her reaction was more in line with the *hyperarousal* pattern. What we had in common was that a belief trigger seemed to have programmed the pattern of biological disposition into us from earlier experiences, but my assessment is that under different circumstances we can be triggered to maintain control in these different states. Possibly, a biological trait leads some people to react one way, while others react the opposite way. This is something that I find interesting and that I will continue to explore; however, for the rest of this topic, I will refer to the logical thought stopper as stopping thought and redirecting to new logic afterwards and will not focus on the case in which a violent reaction may accompany it.

Because I Said So

When I was a child, I felt extreme confusion when hearing the phrase I so often received as an answer to so many of my questions. "Because I said so," was the answer, which is only designed to kill all logical progression of thoughts. Words and phrases like this are what I call nondescriptive negatives. With the exception of the word *no*, the phrase "because I said so" is the most commonly used nondescriptive negative. This phrase is an entirely overpowering statement that can only be used by those who have already established a dominating power over the target of their control. In order to get the power to use this phrase, individuals must first establish within the person whom they are targeting the belief that in any instance the controller knows better than the target. Parents who have this control over their children know instinctively it will not work on other children, so to sidestep this problem, they pull their children aside from a group in order to implement this control individually.

70

The establishment of the authoritative structure that allows parents to have this control over their children begins when the right brain is still developing in infants. Studies of developmental traumatology now assert that trauma affects the brain development of children (De Bellis et al., 1999). During the *Intergenerational transmission of attachment trauma* the infant is matching the rhythmic structures of the mothers's dysregulated arousal states. This Synchronization is registered in the firing patterns of the stress-sensitive corticolimbic regions of the right brain, dominant for coping with negative affects (Davidson, Ekman, Saron, Senulis, & Friesen, 1990; Schore, 2012).

The synchronization between the primary caretaker and the developing child results from biological responses that the child does not have conscious control over, which is why parents instinctively know only to attempt the "because I said so" phrase with their own children. As we looked at earlier, there appears to be a programming method for negative logic only in the human mind. Each time I have watched situations in which parents have exhibited this behavior, I have always noticed that both parent and child carry a negative overall feeling. This experience and other experiences of mine prompt me to propose that the method of setting up particular thought patterns has a direct connection to the emotional state that the human experiences when they return to the same thought pattern, which we will explore further in the chapter entitled, "Thought-Length Hierarchy."

I grew up in a family in which this dominating control was essential to maintain the way of life, and its practice was very wide-ranging. However, for some reason it did not take effect with me, as I never accepted this control within myself. Due to the unique set of circumstances with my parents, who were extremely busy, and with my older brother, who did not himself feel he had the right to impose this control but who still filled the role of my primary father figure, my parents missed their chance to impress this control upon me early enough for it to take hold.

71

However, I did see how effective it was as a tool for programming belief after belief in the people who were under the tight control of the religious circle in which my family was involved. Once parents had established that their child should remit all opinions and logical progressions to the parents' decision-making, the acceptance of new beliefs could be done by using this simple phrase: "because I said so." As you can imagine, other phrases and strong, overriding controls are also effective at setting beliefs, but they will all follow the pattern of causing controllees to discontinue their current logical progression when the controllers exercise these controlling phrases.

I have made it a point to never use this logic on my own son because of the experience I had watching it used as I grew up. In doing so, I realized that the early stages of childhood development were very difficult without the establishment of this control, but in my case it was not fully effective because, in the living situation of my divorced family, my son had enough other influences in his life that were setting up such controls. In many ways, it only served to have him effectively controlled by one parent who had no problem with such tactics. Often this enabled him to hurt me, as the other parent, with programming designed to be carried between homes, the only purpose of which was to disrupt the known, disliked traits in my home.

Being conscious of the use of nondescriptive negatives when addressing my son made me address things I was doing as well. As a parent, I now had to find a good reason for many of the things I used to do without having a reason. Often the conversation with my four year old would result in a progression of thought that led me to question why I was doing the activity I was trying to convince him to do. In general, if humans wish to develop as a species, we need to stop using nondescriptive negatives to train our next generation. The only things that these phrases and words do is serve to program beliefs and to stop us from continuing whatever logical process we are thinking of at the moment.

72

Do Other Intelligent Creatures Have Beliefs?

I have pondered the reason for these belief patterns, wondering what value they have. Do other animals have these types of behaviors? Predators will not kill more than they can eat. You can see large predators sitting and relaxing with a herd of prey in sight. They do not kill because they do not have a belief that they will not be able to find something to kill when they become hungry. In fact, any predator that may have acquired the belief to kill now to reserve for later may not have survived to reproduce for the next generation, because eating aged meats would have brought on sicknesses. Herbivores or plant eating mammals will not gather more than they need to consume in order to satisfy their needs for nourishment at any given time. They do not have a belief that there will not be food tomorrow, so they just exist in the instinctual region of thought of gathering what they need. I will address this more in the chapter on "Thought Length Hierarchy." Nevertheless, both the predator and the herbivore remain in a thought capability in which the highest level is to stay out of trouble. Thus, they don't need any thoughts of greater significance than those required to put multiple instinctual thoughts together to preempt danger.

Doing something twice when the second time does not serve any immediate purpose requires a belief that something available now will not be available in the future. Storing up resources for later, putting a second stone on top of the first one, and doing anything else a human does that is more than required to serve an immediate biological function, all require a belief.

Belief structures, the logical thought stoppers in our minds, are what make us different from animals. They are what make it possible to initiate thoughts that differentiate and individualize, because we all can have different beliefs programmed either by culture or by ourselves. These differences make us individuals who can be discerned from one another. The question of nature versus nurture is really the difference between whether beliefs are established by community control and programming or by the individuals themselves.

Beliefs make us able to continue work and able to think about illogical next steps. We decide not to follow a logical thought process, so we continue to repeat doing things that are illogical. Then out of this compilation of illogical piles of effort, another larger solution or greater purpose takes shape. If you take a computer chip out of your phone, the chip by itself is useless, yet it took hours of work and countless people to design, engineer, and manufacture that individual component. Still, it only has purpose in combination with all the other pieces of the device. At the same time, many devices were attempted that we will never hear about, and the same countless people and hours were put into even more efforts that entirely failed, efforts that have just been forgotten over time. Thomas Edison was quoted as saying that he found a hundred ways not to make a light bulb, but his logical patterns just kept moving on to the next possible solution because he did not have a belief that it was impossible. Thus, he had no thought stopper to stop his thought process.

Another feature hidden in these belief patterns is what they do to human behaviors that cause us to congregate in social groupings. For this example, let's think of watching a school of fish swim in harmonic uniformity. Each fish reacts to stimuli the same way with instinctive precision, which enables all of the fish to swim together in a school. This can be associated with a collective belief structure. If a group of people is doing any activity, the ones that are programmed with the same beliefs will react the same way to a given stimulus. Thus, they will naturally start to group together according to similar actions or thoughts. This is why people are comfortable in settings where others have the same programming. They feel relaxed and comforted when others act in the same manner in the same situation. The desire not to be alone is so strong in our species that, like schools of fish swimming in harmony, the programming of our beliefs draws us to each other.

Why Beliefs Are Required in Cultures

By combining the ability to make illogical next steps and the grouping of people into societies based on similar programming of belief structure, the greatness of human culture all comes together. Many people working together are more effective and productive than a single individual. To do this requires a social programming structure; beliefs are the phenomenon in human logic that makes this possible. As a human is developing through their lower cognitive capabilities when they are younger, we as a culture have learned to use negative thought-stopper programming to set up a control structure for each of us. Community programming is pressure placed on all of us until we develop the ability to understand, or to accept, their requirements. These actions are programmed to support society so that everyone knows the same basic set of involuntary thought stoppers (beliefs) that make up the requirements for all of us to harmonically interact.

When I first came to understand the paragraph above, another belief of mine was disrupted, one that stopped my thinking several times until I realized what was happening to me. To understand this concept is to understand that beliefs are in fact community controls. They are the things that have kept people working together instead of working on self-serving or self-satisfying activities, the things that have kept them programming the collective not to go against that which was found to disrupt communities, the things that have kept cultures growing and reproducing, and the things that have made people sacrifice themselves, their lives, and everything they had for the betterment of the community. If everyone is programmed with this same belief structure, then a community works.

Programming has a few phases. We all know these phases, as we all raise children, even if we don't actively interface with them or take part in their creation. The first phase is the recognition of undesired actions, followed by a repeated instructional phase. Reputation is the key to this second stage, repeatedly inflicting the same programming from a wide pool of environmental stimuli. The lyrics of Metallica's song, "Unforgiven," depict this process in the verse, "Through constant pained disgrace / The young boy learns their rules." Parents are not the only ones who do this. Everyone around each child in the entire culture imposes the belief structure, even if only through looks of disappointment and disapproval. Positive environments do not program negative thought process stoppers. You don't just learn to totally shut down a thought progression because someone says you should. Each instance needs something mentally disturbing to cause this. The third stage of setting up a belief structure, which results from the "constant pained disgrace," is the self-inflicting stage. Once individuals reach this stage, they continue to build the rest of their community's rules themselves, propagating the growing belief structure derived from the social cues of the collective around them. Upon reaching this stage, the individual becomes a part of the collective punishing body that punishes both themselves and the next generation.

What does it mean—and require—for an individual to be great? The greatest and most powerful leaders in the history of humankind have learned how this progression works and how to add a new belief into the culture to accomplish either a beneficial social survival control or a self-serving control. The most powerful and memorable have done both. The beneficial social survival control enabled them to build their society and to empower the people to feel positive about the collective, while the self-serving allowed them to produce the events and memorabilia that make their feats stand the test of time. In other words, they did things to leave their mark on the planet, and that is what we have in our history books today.

76

When someone becomes aware of the controlling structure that has been imposed upon them, the structure becomes less relevant. The reasons for the control are to guide and direct the younger or less cognitively capable in society to act correctly and react in a manner that supports the collective. Once you understand that the reasons for the moral base of beliefs is in fact to benefit the community, then you can change your focus to benefiting the community and loosen your repetitive stringency in blindly following the collective controls (beliefs). This is why we see that community leaders are given more leeway when the moral codes are broken or when they do things that are outside of rigid beliefs. The focus on the common good at the leadership level has to take more of an ends-justify-the-means approach than a strict belief structure. This is why we all cut the president slack on his moral decision to bomb a foreign country when he explains it as a tough decision that saved lives. We still entirely consider him a leading part of our religion, which instructs not to kill as a primary control, even though he commanded the killing of many people. However, a single person in the collective who makes the same unilateral decision should expect to have his existence ended by the same controlling structure that the president represents.

The Illogical Nature of Beliefs

Given that beliefs are necessary for community controls, individuals who sacrifice what is best for them or what they want for the betterment of the community require the joint knowledge that the collective is more important than the individual is. The youth need to know that their strength, skills, or fertility are for the community and need to concede that the value in the wise members of their society is more important than their own. Getting an entire collective to have that belief requires a progression of thought that is not logical in any way. For people to agree to this logic requires a belief that there is no way that they will be allowed to follow the logical thought process that this current life is the end of existence. I am not debating whether it is true or not, only that you cannot establish a common self-destructive (self-sacrificing) culture without this belief.

I have often heard ministers at churches walk through a logical progression relating something they want the listeners to accept. They know that people will follow their logic and agree with what they are saying, but then the ministers will come to a place where the next mental progression is an illogical thought that needs to be made to achieve their point. They want people to take the next thing on faith and just to follow them because people are programmed to do so. To program you to follow their next illogical progression, they open the Bible to John 20:29 and say, "blessed are those who have not seen and yet have believed." Their expectation is that people will believe the next thing that comes out of their mouths because going against the Bible is not a thought process their followers will take. This takes two stages of manipulation, as the belief in not going against the Bible first has to be programmed into listeners. Nevertheless, it is clear how they use one belief, with which people are already programmed, to stop people from thinking along a thought progression that runs counter to the new belief they are articulating, thereby programming an illogical belief. This belief programming structure is established in the entire community to maintain a back door into each person's psyche to program them continuously, even throughout their adult lives.

The entire community-controlled belief structure is based on being self-sacrificing and having a reference belief structure to enable the programing of illogical beliefs. If you do not have these two components, you cannot propagate the belief structure from one generation to the next. Though every religion in the world differs on the method of establishing these two components, all religions have them, for otherwise religions would not have stood the test of time.

Setting up Beliefs

Often, teachers know that what they are saying is not exactly true, and they sometimes even reveal when they are lying to you, but then they proceed by saying they are telling you what you need to know for now. What they are doing is acknowledging the fact that each human cognitive developmental stage has limits. We would not try to explain nuclear physics to a toddler because we understand this fact. Some people view the intelligence of an individual human being as analogous to a human's height, which leads to the conclusion that intelligence is essentially limited by biology. If intelligence is in fact limited by biology, then not everyone will achieve the ability to grow beyond the need for compliance with strict community controls. In fact, a bell curve of human cognitive abilities might suggest that a much larger percentage will not grow past the need for strict controls than those who will. I tend to believe that we can do a lot, within reason, to improve our own cognitive abilities. This has to start with setting up beliefs in our offspring and limiting the numbers of logical thought stoppers that we subconsciously give them

Research is finding that people who are raised with higher amounts of childhood trauma are statistically different from people who do not have as traumatic childhood experiences. The IQs of children ages 2–4 who were not spanked were 5 points higher four years later than the IQs of those who were spanked. The IQs of children ages 5–9 years old who were not spanked were 2.8 points higher four years later than the IQs of children the same age who were spanked (Straus, 2009). The same study also showed that not only the presence of the traumatic events but also "how often parents spanked made a difference. The more spanking, the slower the development of the child's mental ability, but even small amounts of spanking made a difference," (Straus, 2009). The more often these traumatic events occur naturally, the more places in biological memory (the brain) have holes from which logical blocks are sequentially removed.

From my experience, the effectiveness of being able to reprogram after the establishment of a belief does seem to be inversely related to the cognitive level of the individual. In other words, the higher the IQ, the more an individual seems to be able to use logic to think through the automatic reaction caused by beliefs shutting down a particular thought process. If this were not the case, it would be hard to account for the nature with which some very exceptional adults have had very difficult or abusive childhoods.

A belief formed during childhood appears to be more effective than one formed as an adult. A person seems to have a much more difficult time changing the involuntary thought-stopping process of beliefs programmed during childhood. Thus, beliefs established during the more impressionable times in the development of a human are more effectively ingrained into memory. Once again, this foreshadows the chapter, "Thought-Length Hierarchy," but it appears that thoughts set at times of lower thought capability are available in times of higher thought capability, but not the other way around. Even if a person logically makes a decision to break a belief pattern and logically understands the reason why they are no longer following the belief pattern, they may still involuntarily follow the same belief pattern when reacting instinctively.

The Power of Child Caretakers

As I evaluate my son's involuntary reactions to many things, I understand more and more the power a parent has in the life of an individual. Parents have the first shot at setting up beliefs within the child, so the more I am aware of this, the more I have remorse for some of the environments to which my son was exposed when in the care of others. Though I personally

80

employed the practice of not using nondescriptive negative programming, we placed him in day care when he was just under two years old. I remember that he had a difficult time with this, as I had been the stay-at-home parent up to that point in his life. The day-care staff thought it was humorous when my son wanted to hang out with the janitor—the only male in the entire building. I chalked this up to the fact that I, a male, had been his primary caretaker up until that point and inferred that he just wanted to be around another male for comfort. However, when I think about it now, the male janitor, with whom I had many conversations, was the only one not using an approach that relied on continuous nondescriptive negative programming. This is understandable because my son had not yet experienced human interaction infused with nondescriptive negative programming up to this point in his life.

The shocking thing for me is that the predominantly female-oriented childcare industry in general practices the most disturbing brand of culture-shock-inducing belief programming. I witnessed something that I would characterize as emotional terrorism when a friend from a love-and-logic class that my wife and I had taken asked me to help with a love-and-logic training session. This friend had an older boy and two younger girls, and while the boy was able to be very independent, when the girls had wandered out of the mother's sight, an example needed to be made. They were playing in the neighborhood and did not have a belief set up yet to make them stop thinking when their logic went in a direction that prompted them to wander away from their parents. At the same time, their mother did not have the belief that, if she could not see her children, she should stop thinking about whatever else she was doing and return to being able to monitor them. A half hour or more passed on this particular occasion before either the girls or their mother realized the situation, during which time the children had gone into a friend's home where the mother could not locate them. When the mother could not find the girls, she called the police, who issued an amber alert for the missing children.

Since this condition is unacceptable in a society in which bad things have occurred, especially to little girls who have been abducted, the collective knowledge from peers to the mother was that she needed to use a scare tactic to establish a control to prevent this from happening again. Since the father was away on business, she brought me in to assist with a love-and-logic intervention and to watch the girls while she implemented this control. It was one of the most disturbing things I have ever seen, and to this day, I am not sure how I feel about it. The mother informed the girls that she would be taken away to prison for letting her girls run off. Then she packed a bag and headed out the door. For my part, I was directed to pull the crying girls from their mother, their faces buried in each of their mother's legs and their arms wrapped so tightly around her legs that her skin was turning white.

Though the mother only stayed away long enough to let the girls experience the emotions of the situation and reach a calm state before she returned, the belief was effectively established by the emotional terror they endured. I watched their eyes as they clung to me the entire time, their pupils dilated, and they had glassy, empty looks of terror on their faces. This experience was extremely effective at achieving control, but at what cost? From that moment onward I observed both of these girls acquire a complete reluctance to wander outside the home. Literally, they both became comfortable enough to spend all their time in the home and stopped scheduling any outdoor activities at all. In my assessment, after this the children's outdoor activities when in the care of their mother reduced by over 50 percent. Both girls had been programmed with a belief forged in terror. You can almost see the recurrence of terror in their eyes during any remotely related incidents. Being outside or away from their mother in any way links to this emotional state, and any desire to take the logical path, down which they might consider wandering away, is entirely removed by entering this state.

In my experience, the physical overpowering of children has this same effect on younger, less cognitively capable children as they develop. As I myself was raised in a family in which overpowering was considered an accepted child-rearing style, I have experienced this personally. Stefan Molyneux, in many of his online podcasts, articulately discusses the non-aggression principle, which is something that I have followed for my entire adult life. Each occurrence of physical overpowering and punishment is effectively the same as the aforementioned situation involving the two missing girls who endured what I liken to emotional terrorism.

Considering the interrelations among beliefs, the more beliefs someone has, the more areas of their brain would be involuntarily shut down when a sense of this terror is accessed. This would effectively create holes in the brain's activity each time a situation involving physical or emotional terror was imposed upon a child. It makes sense that children who have been physically abused countless times over a prolonged period would have so many thought stoppers that they have an overall reduction in measurably noticeable brain activity.

In my case, the illogical thought patterns programmed into me as a child caused me to be in an extreme state of confusion regarding what I could logically rationalize versus what I was supposed to just accept. This confusion caused aggression, which was a way of reaching out to something that I could make sense of—the physical. Physical actions made sense and satisfied the need for logical progression in my mind. The more I found myself engaged in disallowed logical patterns, the more I needed to turn to the physical, which was controllable and made a logical progression. I believe that people's connection and need to reach out to the physical is inversely proportional to the number of illogical thought stoppers (beliefs) they have in their minds. This explains how physical punishment instills violence in people. Thus, as a society, forcing and overpowering people will only create the desire to use force in return.

I am in a complete state of awe as I close this section. If I had known what I have explored in this chapter as a younger person, my life would have been incredibly different. I now see that the only thing we can directly infuse into our offspring is negativity. We do this effectively and repeatedly, as is apparent from a cursory glance over the history of the human race. If we want to create a positively programmed next generation, the only way to do so is to promote self-exploration. Instilling self-exploration is much more difficult than programming beliefs, as it requires a higher-level of cognitive ability and emotional maturity from the parent. Unfortunately, even adults do not usually acquire these qualities until after their child-rearing years, so most of us will have to settle for reprogramming ourselves later in life after we become self-aware.

Breaking the Pattern of Beliefs

To begin to reprogram ourselves requires an understanding of what has happened and how we became programmed the way we are. If you are reading this book, you are at least on the right path. The first thing I determined that I needed for reprogramming myself was to recognize when my brain would shut down. Even though I am aware of the shutdown patterns and seek them out, they are still difficult to actually pinpoint. If your brain is shut down, you are not thinking about anything, so how would you recognize that you are not thinking if it requires thinking to recognize it? For myself, I found that noticing the redirection of thought to some other topic has been a good place to start. Though I may not recognize a thought stoppage, I can usually tell when I do start thinking again, and it is about an entirely different topic. It is like waking up and having gum stuck in your hair or to your face. You immediately realize that you must have fallen asleep chewing gum, even though you may not remember actually chewing it. I find right in front

84

of me the portions of what I was doing before the shutdown, even as I am thinking about another topic. As the first story in this chapter described, a more active or even violent reaction may occur when a logical thought stopper is triggered, so noticing these reactions in your own behavior might also be the beginning of the self-awareness to break such patterns.

After noticing the patterns comes the challenge of determining whether the particular beliefs are of value in your life and whether they limit you or support your productive life. The belief that you should not touch a red hot metal object (which is actually that you cannot entertain the thought of the next action after touching something that appears to be red hot) is an effective belief to maintain. As well, many beliefs actually aid you in being productive or socially successful. Determining which ones to keep and which ones to attempt to rewire may be a matter of being aware of your brain's natural progression in the questioning of beliefs. With this awareness, one can let the brain reset those that need to be eliminated when the situation occurs. Let's look at the progression of questioning the value of maintaining a belief.

When you were a child, society told you many white lies to aid in the enjoyment of holidays. These are so that children, who cannot understand the deeper meaning in emotionally or culturally significant events, can be impressed with the value of the festive time of year. A toddler does not understand someone who sacrificed life for the betterment of community because they don't have an understanding of death, but they do understand the value to themselves of a magical event-specific entity that can give them something enjoyable—they understand getting presents. However, at some point, each child starts to collect the environmental stimuli that surround the magical event. They begin to see that the magical nature of things does not fit their logical world. The logical patterns and events in their cognitive mind start to lead them to the realization that these white lies are myths.

I think of these natural thought patterns as if they act like the growth of a floret of broccoli. In your mind, you have a logical thought progression that proceeds from one logical conclusion to the next. The stem's edge represents a belief, the point at which you have programmed your thinking to stop should the next logical progression pass that point. Your brain looks for any other explanation. As long as you are not crossing your belief, you brain continues to function and branch out. This creates the logical pattern that looks like the stem. You will travel on a logical pattern as long as it progresses along your belief without crossing the line, so your thoughts will progress down the stem of the broccoli until you reach an area where you are allowed to branch out without crossing the belief. The florets are branches of logic you take that do not directly cross a belief, and you are able to take these logical branches because you brain does not shut down. When you have branched out multiple times, as the floret grows you will eventually come back to the stem's edge (belief line), but from the other side. One thought allows you to connect the floret's logical pattern to your stem, but it requires breaking the belief to do so. Letting yourself cross this line when the logic brings you there is how you realize a belief is no longer useful.

When I reach one of these thought patterns, I have learned to let myself explore the basis of the belief. Determining when and how I accepted the particular belief seems to be the best place to start. As I talked about in the section on reference belief programming, most beliefs I find in myself reference beliefs set up by another belief that I have often already discarded. For others, I have established the belief by watching someone else's action, usually someone from a previous generation, and whenever possible I often reach out to that person just to ask what the reason was for performing the observed action. If my reason is different from theirs or if theirs is something that relates to a non-belief or a previously discarded belief, I will adjust accordingly. For example, many cultures do not eat certain foods, but the reason was some historical epidemic or disease that caused problems in a less developed culture. We can choose to maintain or abandon the belief that such a food should not be eaten, but we should understand why the belief was established. If the epidemic has been eliminated, eliminating the belief could now aid in current or future survival, as the food may be plentiful in the future, and that belief based on past conditions could reduce the ability to sustain future generations.

Breaking Away From Unwanted Beliefs

As I wrap up this chapter, I will leave you with the largest reference programming belief that was programmed into me as a child. This one formed the basis of all the other programming of illogical beliefs. If one thing caused the most damage to me personally, this is it. The day I realized this, which was not until sometime in my mid-thirties, I was beyond much of my next-generation programming of my own child, and I was still very much reference programmable myself. The widespread use of this cultural-reference belief programming traces back to the dark ages, and according to my research, it is the control used most in society, the one used to control the most people in the Western world.

I was programmed to believe that the devil was in my brain, that someone else had control of my thought process. This belief becomes a process of examining each thought to determine if it crosses any of the random church lessons, parables, or historical accounts from the entire Bible. Any time a thought is out of line, then that thought should be stopped, and your mind should reset to logic that focuses on expelling this self-created foe. The power of the entire machine of human thought became wrapped in a circular process of examining what the process itself is doing and then of resetting to the beginning. A computer program with this logic would never accomplish anything except to continuously use up all the processing resources and burn up the hardware prematurely.

When I started to explore this belief, I found many opinions that link the existence of the Satan versus God contrast found in the Western world's primary religions to influences adopted from other religions. The concept of an afterlife comprised of heaven and hell, as well as the Satan versus God conflict, are said not to be found at the beginning of the Bible, but actually appear later, as its authors were exposed to other religions.

Whether the belief that some external force has access to an individual's thoughts is possible or not is not something about which I am willing to speculate; however, I will say that its effect on human thought processes are the most detrimental thing I am aware of. In my opinion, the adoption of, or increased focus on, this by the Catholic Church was most likely a key determining doctrine that contributed to the reduced human cognitive states of the dark ages in general. My assessment is that this is the root of negative programming to the offspring of each generation. Society received its largest negative infusion from this one influence of the world's predominant structure of social control. Once I rewired my personal beliefs to exclude this belief, my cognitive abilities exploded in every area. The ability to achieve what you are reading in this book was only possible after this conscious personal change.

88

As unfortunate as it may be, this same structure, which is most destructive to the individual, was the most important and necessary aspect of building Western religions into what they are today. Stopping any thought process that may be against doctrine is as effective as a ruler killing anyone who verbalizes anything negative about them or their tactics. If nobody exists in opposition to them, then no influence can change the thoughts or ideals of others. Ignorance and negative programming feed the continuation of violence as well as the same ignorant patterns in the next generation.

Now for the disappointing news, I do not believe—I cannot even conceive—that it is possible to change in my lifetime this social structure of negative programming. My opinion is that the social control offered by the Western world's predominant religions is required for a society in which the majority of individuals will never gain the cognitive ability to rise above the need for such controls. Since this is actually the majority of the population, these reactionary controls are the only way to keep from creating a generation with widespread sociopathic behavior. Since we cannot predict that an individual will gain consciousness, we are best off continuing to program each offspring with a base level of reactionary moral beliefs.

References

Adamec, R. E., Blundell, J., & Burton, P. (2003) Phosphorylated cyclic AMP response element bonding protein expression induced in the periaqueductal gray by predator stress; its relationship to the stress experience, behavior, and limbic neural plasticity. Progress in Neuro-Psychopharmacology & Biological Psychiatry, 27 1234-1267

Chamberlain, L. B. (2009). The amazing teen brain: What every child advocate needs to know. *Child Law Practice*, 28(2), 1-2, 22-24.

Child Welfare Information Gateway, (2009), Understanding the Effects of Maltreatment on Brain Development, www.childwelfare.gov

Davidson, R. J., Ekman, P., Saron, C., Senulis, J., & Friesen, W.V., (1990). Approach/Withdraw and cerebral asymmetry; 1. Emotional expression and brain physiology. Journal of Personality and Social Psychology, 58, 330-341.

De Bellis, M. D., Baum, A. S., Birmaher, B., Keshavan, M. S., Eccard, C. H., Boing, A. M., et al. (1999) Developmental traumatology: Part 1 Biological stress systems. Biological Psychiatry, 45, 1259-1270.

Gadea, M., Gomez, C., Gonzalez-Bono, R. E., & Salvador, A. (2005). Increased cortisol and decreased right ear advantage (REA) in Dichotic listening following a negative mood induction. Psychoneuroendocrinology, 30, 129-138

Keenan, J. P., Gallup, G. G., & Falk, D. (2003) The Face in the Mirror: The search for the origins of consciousness. New York: Harper Collins.

Sato, W., & Aoki, S., (2006) Right Hemisphere dominance in processing unconscious emotion. Brain and Cognition, 62, 261-266

Schore, A. N. (2001) The Effects of relational trauma no the right brain development affect regulation, and infant mental health. Infant Mental Health Journal, 22, 201 - 269

Schore, A. N. (2002c) Dysregulation of the right brain: A fundamental mechanism o traumatic attachment and the psychopathogenesis of posttraumatic stress disorder. Australian & New Zealand Journal of Psychiatry, 36 9 -30

Schore, A. N. (2012) The Science of the Art of Psychotherapy: W.W. Norton & Company, Inc. 500 Fifth Avenue, New York, N.Y. 10110, 61 - 63

Straus, M. (2009), Children Who Are Spanked Have Lower IQs, New Research Finds, UNH Family Research Laboratory

Alberts, B., Johnson, A., Lewis, J., Raff, M., Roberts, K., & Walter, P. (2002) Molecular Biology of the Cell. 4th edition. Programmed Cell Death (Apoptosis).

http://www.ncbi.nlm.nih.gov/books/NBK26873/

Chapter V

How to Fail

For us to start redirecting our lives in a positive direction, we have to understand what we do not do well and the obstacles to our achievement. Removing obstacles is a precursor to positively engineering our lives. The sooner you identify obstacles, the sooner you will be able to build successfully and consistently over time. The greatest hindrance for people is not that they cannot move in a positive direction, but that they enter cycles in which they move in a positive direction then slide into a negative direction. The problem for most people who repeatedly fail to live productive lives is that the negative slides exceed the positive movements.

Learn to take advantage of the lessons of other people's failures and mistakes. This chapter is a list of the various categories of the many times I fell short in my own life. Being prepared for these to occur and knowing how to identify them before they consume you is vital. Resistance to support from others is the primary reason people fall into problematic periods of their lives, which are so obvious that others want to scream at them. The fact that these situations are so obvious is often the very reason that some people do not recognize the situation. The most successful people often have an instinctive reaction to others telling them how to run their lives. They will shut out advice just because of the source of the advice. I am guilty of this more than most.

My decision that I should not respect in any way the opinions of certain people stems from my earliest decision, which I describe in the chapter, "Building Blocks of a Person's Core." This trait has been invaluable at times and my largest obstacle at others. Either way, this trait comprises my first self-programming event leading to self-awareness and is now inseparably linked to my personality, so the question is not whether I should start listening to every opinion, but rather how I should go about setting up my list of valued opinions and invaluable resources.

Now that I often find myself in the role of mentor, I see these blocking triggers in others. People will hear advice that may be very good for them from a source that they do not respect; by rejecting the advice, they place themselves in terrible situations that they sustain for long periods. Just having another person who they do not resist recommend the same or similar advice will make them consider its value. At the same time, in other areas of my life I find myself being the person who is blocked. Often in competitive relationships, the closer two people are in their personal lives, the higher their resistance to input from each other. My advice as a neutral party is often the same as what they have heard before, but received better from someone else.

Follow with me as I give you some of the categories of the many difficult times that I, or others with whom my research has led me to interact, have experienced. I hope that you can identify or learn from these and start the path of positively engineering your life by becoming aware of how you fail.

Can't Maintain

Often, people who have achieved exceptional accomplishments at some point in their lives have done so to prove something to themselves or others. In so doing, they pushed well beyond the bounds of what humans can maintain indefinitely. What happens when they cannot maintain that level of achievement? One of the three basic requirements for self-fulfillment is the need to maintain a healthy environment. When someone cannot maintain such an environment, one of these three basic needs is unmet.

There are many other reasons for not being able to maintain an exceptional level of achievement. The health of someone important to you could be declining. Or situations beyond your control, such as the economy or market trends, could affect your ability to maintain the level of achievement. In any case, what people do to adjust for this is important and can make the difference in their overall paths through life.

In order to adjust to be able to maintain an exceptional level of achievement, you must adjust your expectations and your scope. Offsetting in this area also can be done for a while to compensate, but eventually maintenance must come into balance before you can move ahead. The sooner this is addressed, the more quickly recovery can begin.

Can't Transition

Why can't people transition to moving in a positive direction? In my experience, it is because they have made a goal to get to a certain point and then achieved that goal. That should be a good thing, right? Not so much—when the goal is achieved, the human mentality is to take a break, relax, celebrate, and enjoy the victory. Nevertheless, in pursuit of the goal, people establish set habits that help them attain that goal. Those habits do not go away; they continue or sometimes refocus inadvertently to something else. When the habitual trait continues to focus on something that was already achieved, depending on the goal, it can become futile.

When it redirects inadvertently, it can change to become a directionless, obsessive, or simply annoying personality trait.

When the exceptional habits you've gained become associated with negativity, it changes how that goal and achievement is viewed in retrospect. With a negative perception of the previously achieved goal, the transition to another goal becomes difficult because the brain has been programmed with this success-to-negativity cycle. At the same time, the focus and the new inadvertent goal develop in order to stop the habits from the last. To stop a habit, a person needs to have something with which to replace it. It is a hundred times more difficult to stop a habit than to replace it with a new one.

In order to transition you need to break out of this trend and escape the pattern of your primary goal being to stop working on the things that let you reach your last goal.

Bite Off Too Much

Too much on your plate is not necessarily a bad thing when properly managed and when expectations are reasonably set. In many cases, though, people find themselves failing because they take on more than they can handle. This occurs when the project or task someone undertakes should be considered more of a path.

Breaking an objective down to manageable portions starts with setting personal expectations and then managing the relay of those reasonable expectations to others. The others who become involved are an even larger portion of the expected path for people who bite off too much. Managing what can be managed of how others are involved can variously be an emotionally, comparatively, competitively, or collaboratively important component. This management falls into the categories of 1) setting expectations, 2) isolating, 3) reducing, and 4) abstaining. For the most part, these will focus on how to avoid involving people in the first place.

Emotionally Involved People

Your family often fits into this category. When you tell your children that you are going to rope the moon, they will become emotionally involved with your efforts. At first, they may think you can actually do this, and then they watch you work, while their expectations change as they assess your abilities. This emotional connection can lead you to become frantic in trying to meet an unrealistic expectation; after some time, it affects your mindset as well as theirs. Setting a more realistic expectation from the beginning would have mitigated the negative aspects of their involvement.

Comparatively Involved People

This category involves comparisons with one's peers. I would use the old saying that "a prophet is never accepted in his own town" to explain this. People who were your peers at one level will, with few exceptions, have a lingering desire to see you fail at any endeavor you undertake that they did not or that they feel they could do better at themselves. They compare their success to yours, and since they made the decision not to attempt what you attempted believing their way to be the right approach, your failure is, to them, proof that they are more successful. Once again, setting expectations with this group can be done at first, but for the most part, this problem with comparison will have to be overcome by using isolation more than setting expectations.

Competitively Involved People

96

This category encompasses an interaction that often leads in a direction that you do not choose. Competitive paths are sometimes profitable and validating to your efforts because, if someone else is competing to achieve the same goal, then the goal must be a good one. Competitively involved people can cause interactions that become more of a personal failure than something that the community considers a failure. This particular involvement can lead to changes in the direction of your overall path.

Collaboratively Involved People

People you feel you need to bring in to help you characterize this category. They will each have different expectations for your time together, but all will believe that your time with them is more important than your time with others. A collaborative person who understands the value of each person's time in the collaboration is the most effective for the effort. This type of involvement can get out of hand very quickly. The more successful the effort and the more valuable the end path, the more risk this involvement will have.

I have found that most often, when people fail from biting off too much, they usually do so because they have overcommitted in a social manner, either by not being realistic with themselves and leading others to have unrealistic expectations or by allowing others' expectations to drive the scale of their effort out of their control. Intentional efforts 1) to manage your interactions with people, 2) to abstain from interacting with groups, and 3) to isolate oneself from the people to whom one should reduce one's exposure will help to control this aspect.

Setting expectations for what is realistic to anyone with whom you do interface is important because everyone who becomes aware of your effort has some influence on you whether you are consciously aware of their effect or not.

Wrong Life Phase

People expect a certain amount of activity at their current level before they can move on to the next level in their minds. Let's explore why this is.

Many employers will expect the average person to work for 3-5 years in a position before receiving a promotion to the next level. Jobs in organizations like government agencies, the armed forces, and large corporations have policies that mandate the minimum amount of time on the job before an employee can apply for a promotion to another position.

Often, if you believe that you are better at your boss's job than he is, you are correct. However, if the management above him made such a change to promote you early, the entire organization would feel repercussions that stem from jealousy, claims of unfair treatment, or even feelings of superiority over the boss or over you, so in that case many people would share the same view.

Exceptional people often have the most difficult time because the expectation is that everyone is average and the same and thus exceptional ability is bred out of people by the pressure to conform to a standard of expected talent or skills.

Until you step back from this desire to replace the person ahead of you and look at the things that took them to that next level, you will be stuck in the wrong life phase and feel discontented, and that personality trait always shows. The best leaders and managers are often the ones who have given up the desire to advance.

Once you see that each life stage is at the level that it is because of the mindset of the average individual who is at that stage, the level starts to be less important, and working toward the mindset is the defining direction or path for which one should strive.

Achieving and moving to the next level is a goal-oriented approach. As this goal is achieved, one has to redefine the next level and set a new goal. Often the new goal is to do a good job at this new position. This new goal requires an entirely different focus than the goal of achieving the position in the first place. The change in focus takes time and a redirection of primary effort. Then once the goal-oriented person feels that they have achieved the goal and done a good job at the newly gained position, they again change focus to attain the next higher position, and so the progression continues.

When the progression of the goal changes from attaining to maintaining, it positions the individual on a timeline that requires an average amount of time in each of these phases. Since the average person in society goes through these same progressive, goal-oriented cycles, all of these like-minded people gain a perspective that progression through life has the same expected timelines.

To step out of this mold requires a path-oriented approach with self-directed, continuous redefinition and process improvement. In some cases, a promotion becomes a delay on your path, as responsibility to perform outside of your own direction is often required in the new position. However, you were chosen for the position because you are self-directed and your path is well defined. Management wants the portion of the company for which they have given you responsibility to be managed as your life is. Your achievements will also stand out to your peers, and you will not have large issues or discontent. Your subordinates will have mixed feelings about your selection, which sets up more of a leadership than management environment. At the same time, your mindset is one of reluctance and caution, which makes you more objective and less emotionally connected to the position. The position becomes less something you achieve and more a burden you bear.

Emotionally Overwhelmed

Emotional maturity is the aspect with which I struggle the most. It would appear that the ability to be subjected to emotional distress and to recover from it is vastly different from one person to the next. To be emotionally overwhelmed is a condition that I would describe as patterns in which the mindset's position on the emotional chart rapidly transitions downward, followed by slow transitions upwards. Sometimes I have the ability to bounce right back, while other people may move upward faster than downward, but when I become emotionally overwhelmed, I move downward rapidly.

During these times, I have devoted considerable focus to what types of things enable me to elevate my mindset slowly up the emotional chart. Usually these times, during which I have previously not focused on things, bring back a recurring affirmation, and thus I have had a lack of praise for or affirmation of my efforts.

Combating emotional, overwhelming situations is actually an effort that requires repeated tasks to set your emotional response to stimuli in the future. In such cases, your emotional maturity is actually something you have a lot of control over with the actions you do to affect similar future circumstances. This is something that I will talk about in more detail, especially with regard to how to control the outcome by affecting the three components of your life cycle. The chapter, "Setting up Success," will continue this topic.

Belief Sets a Poisonous Path

At times in my life, I have found myself interacting with a group of people who caused me to gain or act on beliefs that were common to that group. Sometimes I did not even truly agree that those particular beliefs were the best for me, but I had simply become complacent in interacting with the people around me. Meanwhile, the same group condemned traits that I had previously displayed. After taking on this belief pattern and moving away from previous traits, I found that my adoption or removal of the set of traits made me less productive.

While striving to make those in my environment happy, I came to believe that my traits were bad. This was a poisonous influence in my life because the people on whom I was relying to influence my belief patterns were extremely unproductive and unsuccessful in their own lives. Over time, I realized why this was the case: they actually made fun of the traits I possessed that made me successful. Once I adopted their belief structure and eliminated those traits, I found that I became just as unproductive as they were. I found that the traits I had eliminated had in fact made me the productive performer I had been my entire life.

Poisoning the Process

The examples in this book of how to fail are just from my lifetime. I have failed a lot, but I am sure you can define many of these on your own. In fact, just as there are hundreds of ways to fail at making a light bulb, there are also infinite ways to fail at life. I will not spend much time on the ways to research these, but I will tell you that, in order to fail, you will always find something that is poisoning the process of life engineering. Determining the source of this is critical to adjusting your path.

If you enjoy helping people, working somewhere that puts profit over people could be a major poison to your life cycle. If you enjoy the feeling of self-betterment, then a person who convinces you that your efforts at self-bettering are hurting you could be poisonous. If people tell you that education makes you unable to relate to people, then your process of acquiring education may be poisoned. If you are convinced that working out makes you threatening to others who then avoid you, it may poison your enjoyment of working out.

An entire path can be poisoned as well. When you are working on a path and that path is involuntarily removed from your life, or when the path becomes something that is bypassed, this is also a poison to your life cycle. For example, if a person is working toward becoming Mr. Universe and his life path is to be physically fit, and then if he breaks his back, his entire path is poisoned. We often see this with athletes whose entire lives center on the sport they pursue, but then at some point in their lives, they will ultimately no longer be able to perform the sport, at least competitively. This poison to their path often leaves them mired in uncertainty until they find a new path—for example, in politics, executive management, or sales.

Poisons can affect all three areas of your life cycle: people, situations, and mindset. Often, they will be in some area where you are not meeting human needs. When this is the case, you may not even know what the problem is. For example, if you do not have enough iron in your diet, it can cause physical problems and poison your mindset, but you are not aware without medical analysis that this problem exists. In a culture that praises the denial of self and the mantra, "no pain no gain," this is a large area where we often see poisons to our life cycle. In my opinion, examination of human needs is the first step to take when trying to identify poisons to your life cycle. In fact, nearly every other area we discuss in this book could be thought of as an extension of this area. Engineering your life to be effective, some may claim, is entirely about meeting all of your needs so you can be in top-performance condition.

Chapter VI

The Practice of Life Engineering

When I was in the process of evaluating which years of my life had stood out in my memory as the best and the worst, I realized when I ranked them in my mind that three areas gave me measurable fulfillment. As I talked about in the first chapter, they seemed to fulfill a human need for tasks in which I could have an initial scurry, be able to maintain my environment, and could feel that I was continuously marching forward. With this realization, I developed a theory to practice on myself, as well as a few other volunteer test cases, to try to proactively set up a life environment in which I controlled these three areas. The fact that this theory was successfully applied to a few people showed that I was not alone in the need for balance in these three areas of my life. Let's look at these three areas in detail and talk about the things that comprise each of them.

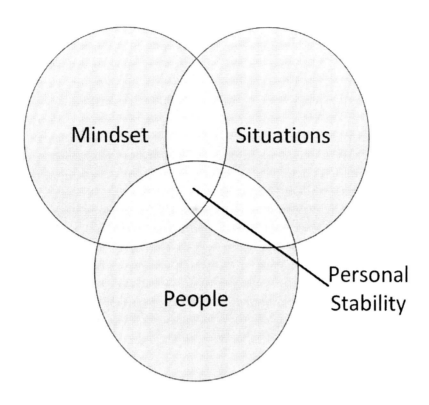

Maintenance

I begin with maintenance because this has been the most important to me and has seemed to resonate with everyone else I have worked with. Maintenance, in general, means to be able to keep any achievements that the other two areas yield. Human nature is in opposition to this in many ways. The first way is that people are never content with what they have. They collect new things every day and pack them away into some space out of sight. Most of us have no idea what we have unless we are prompted to do an inventory. People who move often realize this, as they find they usually have more possessions or things than initially realized.

Moving companies make fortunes on this fact of human nature by bidding too low to be profitable based on the weight of goods that people think they have. However, their service's total cost is based on an added price based on a per-weight increment above the initial amount of goods the customer thought they had. If you have ever been in this situation, you know what I

105

mean. The final bill ended up being double the price you expected to pay. Whether you just stared at the bill with a hint of anger or even if you took your frustration out on the poor moving guy, you eventually concluded that you did it to yourself. Meanwhile, moving companies expect this and even create their business model around it.

Since we're not addressing why people collect things for now, let's look at the ability to maintain as a basic need that humans have. Like taking a bite of food that can be reasonably chewed and swallowed, people need to be able to keep achievements or progress that they have made, at least for a time. Since we can collect for our entire lives, however, we make some concessions to this, much as we do for personal space. Our need for maintenance has spatial and chronological aspects associated with it. This is analogous to nesting birds who can return to the same rock ledge each year and build upon the previous year's nest without caring about the base sticks at the bottom of the pile, which they started five years ago, as long as they can build on top of the remnants of previous nests and customize the entire nest to conform to their bodies. The most important portion immediately surrounds and conforms to their bodies. The further away from this conformation to your individual needs, the less important and out of mind these parts become. Having moved nearly as many times in my life as the years I have lived has made me see this relevance to my own maintenance. It has come to the point that I now have a rule that, if I have moved something twice and have not utilized or even unpacked that Item, I will not move it a third time. Over time, I have determined that any item I have moved twice without using is obviously beyond the scope of my maintenance needs, either spatially or chronologically.

As you may be able to see from my examples, maintenance is not really about physical things, but about the perceived progress you have made in your life. Physical conditioning and fitness is a prominent example of this. Self-esteem closely relates to the maintenance aspect, and a person's self-esteem will slip directly in step with the degradation of or the ability to maintain the most relevant portions of their lives.

Of the three areas of fulfillment, maintenance is the one that is the most easily affected by us. Thus, it is the one that people will hold onto the tightest when they sense in their lives a slipping of the control of their mindsets or situations. I have seen this in myself when I feel out of control of my own life. Keeping my environment, like my nest, just the way I want it, which for me means as organized as possible, is much more important at these times than when the other aspects of my life are clicking. I can almost tell when I meet someone if they are in a phase in which they are very demanding of their surrounding environment (nest) because they are feeling out of balance with the other aspects of their life. This causes them to hold on tighter to the things that they *do* perceive they can influence or have control over.

Fulfillment Projects

Being able to have the feeling of accomplishment is very important to human peace of mind and to one's sense of internal worth or value. A big portion of what this does is to set up a positive feedback schedule for self-worth and value. If you have a project that you know you can accomplish and that takes about a month, you have now set up a self "pat on the back" in one month's time. The more value this has to others who recognize and praise this accomplishment, the larger the effect there will be for you from this effort. This is why it is very important to set up projects that you know you can accomplish versus only setting long-term goals. In fact, I will talk about goal setting quite bit, and my opinion is that setting goals is not a good thing to do if you are engineering your life for success.

These self-fulfillment projects (tasks) should always be endeavors you know you can achieve and do well. Granted, not everything in life can be a success, and you cannot always know ahead of time that you will hit a grand slam on something you have never tried before, though you can break it down into the pieces that you *can* knock out of the park while the ones that are larger get pushed off in the long-term direction. By looking at them a little differently, we can then work on our own self-motivation if we only set out to do fulfillment projects that work toward a long-term direction. The point I will make repeatedly is that it is all about how you feel inside about your own performance. Your perception of success or failure is entirely controllable within your own mind.

Long-Term Direction

This area of human nature is defined more by what is *not* a fulfillment project or maintenance. It is the rest of how you perceive your efforts in life. Having a long-term direction is very different from having long-term goals, mainly because a direction is never achievable. This area of people's needs is the key defining aspect of human behavior that is not displayed in any other species on the planet. If you have a goal to travel to a city, once you have reached your destination, you stop to reassess what the next thing is. If your direction is to head west and visit new cities that you have not been to before, you will never reach any endgame. Your focus then changes to adjusting the path, which doesn't mean that you will never go the same place twice, but the second time you are there you will be on a path through it, on the way to a city that you have not yet visited. This long-term direction is constantly assessed by always looking at the next day heading west but also by adjusting what you are heading toward next.

Balancing Your Life

108

This drawing, which I titled "Life Balance Diagram," is a common engineering tool that shows the relationships between several systems focusing on how they relate to each other. I think this is fitting for several reasons, but mostly because it shows that life is a balancing act that must be changed in small increments in order to maintain its delicate balance. Anyone who tells you to change everything at the same time is just sending you into disaster. At the same time, any of the components of life left unchecked for a long period will cause an out-of-balance situation from which it may be difficult to recover. The thing to take most note of on the diagram is that the people, situations, and mindset portions of your life are entirely contained in the ability to maintain. You cannot begin to have a direction in life or make progress toward things you consciously desire unless you can maintain the things that make up your stability.

The most significant out-of-balance conditions I see are where the people involved are unable to maintain all the situations and people they have added in their lives. Their mindsets and stability first suffer while blowing the ability to maintain sections so large that their progress on life's direction and achievable projects are entirely lost. The people and situations drive them in every area, leaving nothing, as the top two circles are lost from their lives. They begin to feel that they are stuck in their lives after having no progress for a prolonged period. The balance portion goes away and they even lose sight of their personal stability. When all of these overlaps go away, they are often headed for collapse, but usually they will experience shortsightedness and an extremely out-of-control feeling.

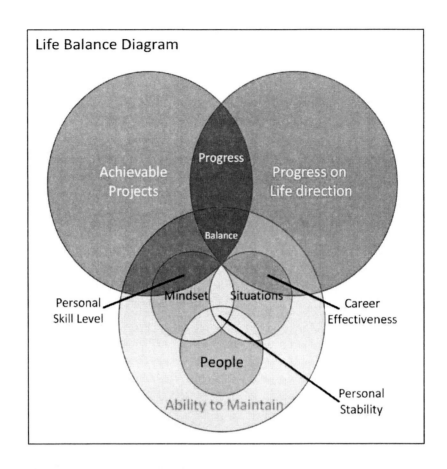

Life Balance Diagram

Achievable Projects

Progress

Progress on Life direction

Balance

Personal Skill Level

Mindset   Situations

Career Effectiveness

People

Ability to Maintain

Personal Stability

Controlling Life Direction

Long-term direction, something we will spend a lot of time discussing, relates to the path in life that everyone determines consciously or subconsciously—or by reflexively letting random events in life determine. Many of us end up letting the random events of life determine our path. Ask yourself, "Am I in the place that twenty years ago I thought I would be now?" Granted, we always look back and say, "Twenty years ago, I did not know what I do now, or else I would have thought those expectations were not realistic and would have set my expectations differently." How differently would you have set those expectations? Should you have lowered the bar and expected less? Should we tell the people in our lives who are twenty years our minor to set their expectations to the "lower level" to which we should have set ours?

When I think back to twenty years ago, I remember those people who were telling me to set my expectations lower. I remember how my opinion of them was that they were pathetic, destroyed by life, and bitter people. I am sure they thought they were helping me or protecting me from disappointment. Let's think for a minute about what would happen if we took the opposite approach when talking to those who are our minors, if we were to tell them, "Set your expectations much higher to be able to achieve even more than I did." When I was a younger version of myself, I remember hearing advice to set my expectations lower, and within myself, I changed that self-talk to say, "I have to double my efforts to shoot for further than I expect instead of lowering my expectations of the outcome." Working harder was the only thing that I knew to try to throw at it. I assumed that working twice as hard as everyone around me was the only way to avoid reaching the point at which I was destroyed by life.

Though brute-force effort and work ethic have defined me in almost every aspect of my life, the information I am going to give you now is what would have helped me the most. Yes, the combination of my exceptional work ethic and my learning to control the direction of my life has made me the person I am today. In fact, knowing how to engineer success would have made the required effort much less or driven me much further with the same amount of effort. Nevertheless, for much of my working career, I engaged in many of these practices subconsciously without really knowing that I was applying them or having much thought about how I was doing it. I just repeated the things that worked previously and reduced my effort in the areas that had less favorable outcomes.

When I took some time to think about how I would repeat my successes and eliminate my failures, I found that many of the traits and practices I had instinctively exhibited in my life were actually things I had a great deal of control over. I compared many times in my life when I had worked incredibly hard and had achieved results beyond anything I had expected in order to determine what these times had in common. I wanted to know: "Is this something I could reproduce?" and "Is this something I could help to reproduce in others?" I also wanted to answer a question that has often crossed my mind: "Can anyone do these things, or does it take someone special?"

Analyzing Past Success

I first understood the process that created success by looking at the successes I have had in my own life and finding similarities that were crucial to the creation of each.

My first monumental success came when I was twelve years old. Though it would not rank on any list of successful events now, it was monumental to me at the time. Deer hunting was the most important activity in my immediate and extended families, from my earliest memory until I left that environment to pursue my career. Every year's activities and calendar centered on the various seasons for hunting different types of game. Even before I was of legal age to have my own hunting license, I used to get up before dawn and trudge out into the wild with members of the family to support their efforts. By the time I was old enough to obtain a hunting license, I already knew the lingo, the techniques, the strategies, and the locations. When I set out to go hunting on my own, I knew when and where to go. I was so eager that I bowhunted in the early season in preparation for the later seasons to find out where the deer were running and to determine their behavior.

The outcome is still the subject of legend in my family. Since my family lived for hunting, I remember hearing story after story, year after year, about the nervousness that caused everyone to miss their opportunities. The entire group trudging out into the wild had brought successful hunts every few years for the more skilled individuals, but mostly we returned only with stories of how the big one got away. While I was "enjoying the process" of finding and locating the deer and determining the best approach for attempting a successful hunt, I found that when I was enjoying the process and not focusing on the goal of taking the wild game, my judgment was not clouded when the game was in front of me, which made me natural under pressure. When the deer stepped out in sight of my tree stand, my focus clinched. My aim and execution were right on. I had landed the most exceptional trophy buck yet in my family's history.

Though I was bursting with pride in my accomplishment, my euphoric feeling wore off quickly when I came to the realization that I had achieved a goal. Now hunting was over for the year. The actual completion of the goal hindered my path. Something I had anticipated as long as I could remember came to an anti-climactic end. The rest of the year, though, my family expressed congratulations with a hint of jealousy due to my age, so I felt disappointment. The anticipation of the process was hindered by the "achievement of the goal."

What defined the outcome: 1) I "enjoyed the process" of hunting. 2) I had "a path laid out for the season." 3) I was "working past the present task" (season), using it to gain knowledge for the upcoming seasons. 4) Achieving a goal hindered my progress.

After thinking about my hunting experience, I looked at the next monumental accomplishment in my life. This occurred when I had ventured out on my own to join the United States Navy. Since I struggled through high school with problems focusing, I had not achieved the most desirable educational outcome. Moreover, I had become an underachiever, but when I took the entry test for the military, I did fairly well. To this day, I believe an element of guessing on the placement exam graciously benefited my score. In fact, the outcome of the placement exam was that I had the lowest possible score that would allow me to enter the career field I ultimately decided to pursue in the Navy.

The promise of a bonus that was more than I had ever considered and the ability to thumb my nose at an institution that would let someone as dumb as me get into this program intrigued me enough to start a career in nuclear engineering, which I never believed I would actually complete. Another determining factor that aided my decision was that my brother had looked into the same program. My family was under the impression that he was so much smarter because on average he achieved two letter grades better than I did. In addition, it gave me the ability, even if just for a while, to push back in the face of all the people who had said with conviction that I would never amount to anything. Thus, off I went on what I saw as the first ship out of hell, with no expectation of returning, without any real understanding of what I had signed up for, and with no confidence that I would be able to complete the program.

Something the recruiter does not tell you about programs in the military, such as this nuclear engineering program, is that they have a 95 percent dropout rate. They basically take anyone with a score high enough to demonstrate that that person is an above average high school student, then they use the 95 percent of dropouts to fill other, less desirable jobs. With this trend, they know not to pay out the promised bonus immediately but instead make it based on each student's progress in the program. At the end of the first of three schools, everyone who

114

completed them, which was usually 40-50 percent of students, would advance to the higher rank, which the recruiter told me would happen immediately. Then the promised bonus was paid out in increments based on a proportional increment for each week the student lasted into the second school.

Since I determined that I could not pass the program, I still knew what I could control and became determined to be the hardest worker in the group. I vowed always to put in more time and effort than anyone else did. Since the time spent studying was monitored by the program, this also had a secondary purpose: to give me the satisfaction of showing them that, when I failed and when they finally kicked me out, they would be losing the hardest worker they had. Each week I stayed in the program was a game and became another week of me thumbing my nose at the institution. I took more of their money and documented more of what a good worker they would be losing. I made a game of it so that I could actually enjoy the weekly challenge of staying in the program. Since they told us that our effort and their recommendations influenced where we would wind up if we washed out, my constant reevaluation of the possibilities based on how long I stayed at the school also drove me to try to achieve my seat in the best possible alternate job once I eventually washed out.

The outcome was once again of legendary proportion. Not only did I keep pace with the school week to week, just taking it one day at a time—like a sports team down three games in a best-of-seven series playing every minute as if it could be the last—I also did not step back to see what the outcome had become. Then all at once, I realized that the school was on its last week, and then it was over. I was shocked! When I looked at the final tally of those remaining along with me, out of the fifty-six people who had started the program from boot camp, only three of us had completed it.

Unknown to me, this school's graduation was a very big production, and in the departing class of nearly 400 graduates, there I stood, one member of the large group in uniform still in awe of what the heck just happened. Thousands attended the graduation ceremony. I had been concentrating so hard that I did not realize I had just completed a school that the Navy considers its flagship equivalent to the Naval Academy, one that even some officers and academy graduates wash out of. During the graduation ceremony, the formality of the Navy brought us from anticipation to a slight boredom as they announced the valedictorian and other special recognition, including of a few children of admirals and generals who were in the graduating class, followed by a general and a few elected officals making long, drawn-out pitches that were sure to get them reelected. As you can see, I don't even remember the details.

Then something unexpected happened. They ended the program with what they called "an unknowing candidate," which was someone who exemplified the most exceptional value and work ethic and who had been chosen for the highest honor of the class. I didn't even know what was said because I had no reason to be thinking about anything. My mind was on how soon I needed to get all the items out of my barracks. In the midst of listening to a Charlie Brown teacher voice from the badly tuned speaker system, my name had been called, and the two people on either side of me were pushing me, which was not allowed in formation. After a quiet moment, I moved to the front where I proceeded to receive the award and recognition.

What defined the outcome: 1) I made a game of thumbing my nose for one more week and enjoyed showing harder effort than anyone else 2) I worked for each next week to take a larger portion of the promised bonus. 3) I had a path where I looked at better jobs that I could achieve after the school. 4) Completing the goal to finish had no path beyond the school.

My next monumental achievement was the first that takes on the role of building my reputation and building value in my life's work. During my time in the Navy, we were out to sea a good portion of each year, and I had a lot of time to be the hardest worker again. For the most part, just out of pure boredom, I took the opportunity to mentally absorb the things that were going on around me. In the military, you need to put in certain amounts of time at each level in order to be considered ready for the next. I am sure this is because the average learning curve for people takes a relatively similar period of active participation. On the other hand, I had just gone from being the underachiever in high school to excelling on par with peers who had successfully engaged throughout high school. I had made up for four years of educational neglect, learned how to study and focus, and learned all the information necessary to graduate from the hardest school in the Navy, all in a matter of months. I had engaged myself and improved my cognitive ability exponentially.

Much like a muscle that you work out as hard as possible without injuring it, my brain had been flexed repeatedly for two years, and it not only needed to continue its growth, but also to accelerate. On top of that, my desire to put in more hours than everyone else continued, and I became a learning machine (and a stress time bomb, but that is a topic for another section). I absorbed how to do my job and how to do the tasks done around me. In fact, I did it so well that years before my time, I was provided the opportunity to reach the supervisor qualification level of jobs. As this happened over a span of time, I did not actually take a step back to see what had been accomplished. My attitude was nonconformist, and much of my direction was based on being better at performing my job and my tasks than anyone around me was.

This was not because I was playing nice with everyone, but because I enjoyed the get-out-of-jail card that this hard work yielded. By always taking on so many things, I gained some freedom from the hassles of the conformity expected within the ranks. I made it a point not to salute, took every opportunity to mouth off to those outside of my organization, and watched as my commanding officers gave me the flexibility to do it. I enjoyed once again being able to thumb my nose at the formality and structure of the military institution. I was given all of the less than desirable people on my shift, and although they were considered outcasts, we were the best-performing team onboard. I was assigned this team mostly because people who outranked me refused to be placed under me on a shift. However, when I gave them the respect that they were not getting in the military structure, they worked harder than ever. We all took pride in this fact and in the ability to thumb our noses at the emotionless military structure.

I did not fully appreciate my achievement there until just a few weeks before I got out of the Navy, when one of the people who determined job placements within the Navy showed up from Washington, D.C., to talk to me. He was trying to convince me not to leave the military and had several desirable jobs to offer me as an incentive. I was bitter toward the military structure, mostly because of the excessive time at sea and the perception that I had lost some of the best years of my life in the process. I did not choose to stay in the Navy, but I realized what an accomplishment it was when he informed me that I was the only person in the entire Navy at my low E-5 rank that held this qualification. This monumental accomplishment, which I achieved by breaking the rules, started to show me a pattern of my capabilities, and the reproducibility of patterns made this possible.

What defined the outcome: 1) I made a game of being better at performing my job and completing my tasks than anyone around me, and I enjoyed the flexibility that learning and achieving gave me in the rank structure. 2) I was thinking about my path after exiting the military. 3) I always worked on defining the next level of jobs and defining what others were doing. 4) Completing the goal led to the loss of the continued path.

118

A Process to Repeat Monumental Accomplishments

From this point on, I found that I was able to readily repeat these types of accomplishments, which showed me not that it takes remarkable people to accomplish remarkable tasks, but that it takes a repeatable process that leads to others perceiving that the set of manageable tasks are remarkable. I started on my next set of accomplishments, which were first to build my body to a level suitable for bodybuilding competitions, while I also continued to move forward with my hard work, working unreal hours to provide my wife's college tuition.

Once this was accomplished and after some other life changes, which I will talk about in the next chapter, I turned to pursuing my own education. I went to work on my bachelor's degree, with a graduate degree and possibly doctorate "in my path." I had to find a new reason to push into each class, as I was learning for myself now and not to prove something to the Navy or others. I had to find a new method of "enjoying the process" of learning. After a bit of searching for my enjoyment, I found that I enjoyed when I drilled the teachers so much that they were almost frustrated. I enjoyed the other students looking at their watches and sighing that the class was not going to get out early, and I liked to hear the instructor say, "We will cover that later." Above all, I "enjoyed" understanding every topic, statement, and concept that came out of the teacher's mouth. I found that if I understood—or stopped the instructor until I understood—I did not have to spend a lot of time studying, and I was able to put all the concepts together at the end of the course. I made a "game of this." For two hours, you can focus on such processes and "enjoy the accomplishment" of it at the end of the class. It gave me measurable success and gratification of that success. I now understood what I was doing to succeed a little better. This stage involved setting up achievable tasks so that I could feel accomplished.

Along with setting up tasks to feel accomplished and enjoying the process whether I failed or not, completing college was not something that even seemed feasible, so much so that when I finished my bachelor's degree, I had overlapped into my first master's degree. Consequently, there was no sense in going to graduation, as I was simply enjoying what had just become a part of my life. As the process moved on, I decided I enjoyed the graduate business classes better than the technical classes, so midway through the graduate degree I had begun in computer engineering, I started taking classes for a master's of business administration. The ease with which I made this switch showed me yet another factor in engineering success. I switched to a different branch on my path without any self-punishment or resentment at all. The fact that a certain degree was not a goal allowed me to shift when something a little different suited me more. This actually benefited me again when I completed the MBA degree. I immediately picked back up on classes toward the computer engineering master's I had started out with, but after a few classes, I saw that my path had shifted in my career at work and that a different graduate degree made more sense. At that point two classes from completing a master's of computer engineering, I shifted to a master's of computer system security.

By the time I had completed the second master's degree, I found that I had begun to enjoy work that related to defining future industry needs for the security industry more than I enjoyed the process of interfacing and learning from university instructors. In part, this was because I had reached a level at which these instructors often were less advanced in their careers than I was, but also because I enjoyed thinking about undeveloped things more than learning about things that were better defined. My life was onto the path of defining an industry. My path had extended, and the need for this current master's degree in computer system security was just something I needed to get out of the way to free up my time. Because my path had adjusted to bigger things, all three of my degrees were mailed to me, and I never attended a graduation ceremony.

What defined the outcome: 1) The achievable tasks became the processes I enjoyed. 2) Milestones became unimportant, as I was thinking well past them when they were achieved. 3) The path was able to change without an entire life change 4) Life work and path became full of items that could never be completed in a lifetime.

When I quit even setting goals and just set up a way to enjoy the process that led me down my path, these successes in my life become less meaningful than just living and enjoying what I am doing at the time. The next phase of my life moved me on a path away from university learning, and the largest reason for this is something that we have all have experienced but that most of us don't realize. When you were a child, you played with some toy that held your attention entirely. At some point, however, you knew everything there was to know about that toy, and you had played with it in every manner possible. Even though you still liked the toy just as much, the process of playing with it became less exciting because it was familiar. It was the process not being enjoyable anymore that made you stop playing with the toy. What happened is just that I lost my enjoyment in the reasons I was going to university classes.

I was now enjoying the process of thinking and defining things that nobody had ever thought about before. Learning and drilling teachers was not providing the same enjoyment as this newfound interest. Without realizing it again, I had moved my path to a new branch that extended to working past my education. This further defined that engineering success needed a reason to finish the immediate thing in your path because you had something on your future path for which you were defining the requirements.

The next phase of my life and accomplishments were the result of a major change in life, which I will talk about more in the next chapter. Still, the process with which I achieved success followed the same exact repeatable process. I defined the path of my work, which took on more of an idealistic nature at this point in my life. My newly discovered direction is something I view as not at all achievable, but since I have not set goals in many years, that fact now does not deter me from following such a path. I found ways to enjoy the process, which mostly involved identifying whom I could help at a given time as well as seeing how far my reach extended, which social media enabled greatly.

I had spent many years flexing my brain, growing it like a muscle. Now like a Mr. Universe contestant who picks up the back of his automobile to slide it out of a tight parking spot while also having a conversation about his dog (without any awareness that passersby are shocked), tasks that required using cognitive ability took on a different light. I actually spend a lot of time trying to conceal this and hiding the same thing I had been developing for so many years. Any accomplishments that I have from this point on, though they may be even more monumental than past life events that stand out with such vigor in my mind, all fit in a compartment related to how I felt about the process that accompanied each.

For technical releases, this was how many people gave comments that the material had helped them. For education and course material, it was how many feedback items I received that could go back into the next version to make it better. In general, it became the social media and circulation reach for each release: how many views and shares. This told me something new about my behavior—and human nature in general. I see nearly every person in the media age striving for what people need—recurring praise. Setting up recurring praise is something we all do whether we are conscious of it or not. I will talk about this more in later discussions about working past where you are.

122

What defined the outcome: 1) The achievable tasks became therapeutic to self-fulfillment. 2) Milestones became a recurring affirmation of progress 3) Life work and path became return of effort to the beginning of the next life cycle path for the next generation.

The accomplishment of this phase of my life once again reached a level beyond what I would have expected a poor, dumb country boy could ever have achieved. I say that with a hint of sarcasm mostly because, no matter what I have accomplished in my life, I feel that I am still that same person. Thinking back to the second chapter, in my mind I am still the person that I was for the first number of perspective lifetimes, which in my perception are more relevant than the measurably longer ones of my later years.

Life Engineering Practice Areas

After examining all of my major accomplishments throughout the course of my life, I realized that the same very simple process had made all of them possible. It was not a matter of superhuman feats or impossible accomplishments but a series of the same things I desired to do because I enjoyed something about doing them. Once I followed the process of collecting everything I knew and grouping the things I could file into similar patterns, I boiled them down to the following areas:

I. Determine a path for your life

- Do not set goals—the enjoyment process is often hindered by the accomplishment of a goal

- Determine how you want to interact with surroundings and people

- Switch to a different branch on your path without self-punishment

II. Work past where you are

- Define the phase in your path that is past the current area you are actively working on

- Modify tasks in the current phase that lead to benefit tasks of the next phase

- Allow the relevance of current tasks (or path) to change as the next phase is defined

III. Find ways to enjoy the process

- Set up ways to feel accomplished

- Do things that return recurring praise

- Meet your human needs

IV. Persistence, Persistence, Persistence

In my life, the largest strength I possessed was not intelligence, coordination, or any physical attributes. It was persistence, yet as valuable as that was, unguided persistence was not useful to me. Not until I started to put together the other practice areas that had made the various times successful for me did I start to be able to repeat successful accomplishments. If I had had the information that you will gain from the rest of this book at an earlier point in my life, things would have been much less difficult for me.

Breaking Work Into Achievable Tasks

You have already seen me recommend several times not to set goals but instead to break your workload up into achievable tasks. So, what is an achievable task? Achievable tasks are things we instinctively create for ourselves for anything we do, but we may not be consciously aware of the process we use to do so. We do not set out to spend our evening. Instead, we think about making dinner when we get home and plan the components of the dinner. Whether to cook or to stop and pick up something, it involves multiple steps. Then we plan for how we will eat—utensils, plates, and a beverage to accompany the meal. Afterwards, there is an effort to clean up, and then we move onto the next thing on our agenda for the evening, which may include a social event. If so, then this involves the preparation task, the travel task, the activity, and the return travel task. We think in terms of what we can achieve, and we know the steps for the common things we do without making a conscious plan to do so.

In terms of tasks around the house, we know that it takes us 2–4 hours once a week to complete lawn work (cutting grass, trimming, etc.). We may have to spend four hours once a summer to prune shrubs, two hours to clean windows, or one hour to pull weeds around the seasonal flowers. We also know that it takes thirty minutes to vacuum the house, twenty minutes to water the grass, and ten minutes to sweep the outside patio. We instinctively relate how often we and others around us perform these tasks to the standard of living we desire for ourselves, so we know how the reward metrics for performing tasks of routine housework relate to our reward of self-image in our surroundings. The metrics for tasks involving the routine cleanliness of our surroundings set us apart and separate the demographics we relate to the various classes of people in various environments.

It would not be effective to set a goal to have a high-end home or yard in the most prestigious neighborhood without knowing the tasks, steps, and recurrence of these events that yield this result, so the metrics related to achievable tasks are what set apart the different results that could be achieved. If you cut the grass once a month then clean windows, prune shrubs, and pull weeds once every three years, your environment will look different from the same tasks done on a weekly basis. Thus, achievement of a result is more about the metrics than desire or goals.

If you want to save for a large purchase, you can set a goal to achieve it in a two-year period. However, what will get you to the purchase result is both the desire to have the object and the task of saving one amount on a recurring basis (metric) that will then add up to the amount required for the purchase. If we rely on desire only, the immediate desire will always outweigh the long-term desire. So making immediate desires correspond to long-term desires is what helps us reach them. The metric and recognition of progress can become an immediate reward. If I save a small amount using a metric of twice a week, then doing so three times a week will give me the reward of being ahead on my progress. In addition, you can use a small incentive reward for yourself along with the metric. For instance, I will reward myself with my favorite candy, coffee, or ice cream, but only after making the small contribution. Games, rewards, and progress then make us enjoy the immediate process of performing the tasks that lead to achievement. What will happen is that by the time you have enough money saved for the thing you desire, you will have set up a fun game of making progress, which will continue, instead of end, with the achievement of the goal.

Breaking Down Large Projects

The practice of project management is about creating, scheduling, and monitoring achievable tasks. Though I am not recreating any practice material for project management here, I will use some project management principles to help you understand how to create achievable tasks in your life. If you are doing a larger home project—say, finishing a basement—and if it is only you performing the work, then you would have to break down what you are going to perform into achievable tasks. You can count the number of straight wall segments to determine the cost and work required for doing just one. In doing so, you may find that there are fifteen to twenty wall segments and that the cost for one is $80 and takes about six hours of work. Though your schedule is full, you can set aside six hours and $80 every 1-4 weeks, and today you will start the first one. From this point on, the metric for how many you can do in each period is just added into your schedule. Now use this task as a physical thing to do when you may be frustrated with something at work or with a social situation. Allow yourself to take out your physical frustration with pounding, carrying material, and the physical aspects of the task. Don't try to schedule this task, but let it be a release for your human emotional needs.

Major achievements such as a college degree are easily broken down into tasks because learning institutions are designed around this strategy. We schedule classes on certain days of the week and add them to our schedule. These achievable tasks now need to be accompanied by enjoying some aspect of each task's completion. If a student only focuses on the end of a course or the completion of a degree, they will be overwhelmed and will often fail at the completion of this accomplishment. Rewarding yourself on completion of each achievable task (class in this case) can make all the difference. For example, you may stop for ice cream after each class, and over time, the memory of a pleasurable experience at the end will add to the anticipation of the task itself. Students that integrated each class into their social support or that found a feature of each course that they enjoyed and eagerly anticipated will find themselves working past the end of the degree in order to keep enjoying the same process as they work on the next.

Life-directional items that are less definable, such as the achievement of a status, are also just a compilation of achievable tasks. When we look at what makes someone reach the level of a political official, famous celebrity, or industry expert, it is not because of large, exceptional feats that nobody else could have achieved. Often the combination of a lifelong list of small achievable tasks reaches the awareness of more people with each performance of the same task. If you consider what makes you believe an individual is famous, important, or an expert, it will not be an understanding of what they do. It is a combination of the number of items they have completed within a given period and the extent of their reach. In short, it is the self-directed metric, which anyone can achieve.

Scheduling Metrics into Your Life

When we think about performing these achievable tasks, it is important to have lists of reserve tasks lined up that we can then fit into our schedule as we have availability. For this, my recommendation is to have a few categories of tasks identified by the effort and resources required for the tasks. I very rarely run into tasks that could not be divided into increments of four hours, two hours, twenty minutes, or five minutes. If a task does not fit into one of these at first, I will subdivide it until its components can be reduced to one of these durations. Then I look at my day and weeks in terms of these blocks of time. I do so in the same manner that someone would fill a jar with different-sized stones: first, add the larger stones, and then fill in the spaces

128

with smaller stones that fit between the larger stones and the container; lastly, fill in the rest of the empty space with sand.

A schedule for the week should have no more than five four-hour blocks that can be effectively scheduled. This equates to approximately half the week, most of which should fall into times of productive focus (reference "Enjoying the Process: Weekly Patterns"). Then add no more than four two-hour blocks, which will fall into slots for which part of a four-hour slot was used on some smaller tasks. Next, schedule times of 30-60 minutes to be filled up with five-minute tasks. These will usually be at the beginning or end of work shifts, since the nature of these tasks are often scheduling or social interfacing. It is important not to let the five-minute tasks take over and fill up your entire day, but rather to discontinue these at the end of the allotted time and come back to them at the next scheduled time. Lastly, fill in any remaining time with the twenty-minute tasks. For the most part, an endless list of tasks will be tasks of twenty minutes in length, and because twenty minutes is very nonthreatening and thus easily started, people do not have a negative anticipation of tasks of this length. In my opinion, if every larger block could be subdivided into twenty-minute tasks, it would be optimal for reducing the anxiety surrounding work in general.

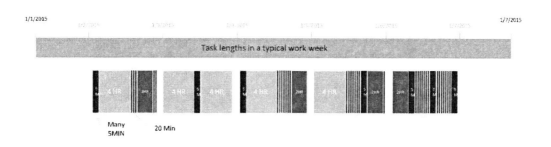

Remember that keeping up the progress over time on any metric requires feeling good about that process. This is something we will look at in depth in the chapter, "Enjoying the Process." In general, though, while still using metrics and not setting goals, follow that up with playing a game with yourself, rewarding yourself, and enjoying the return of results from the process. Be careful, though, not to punish yourself for failing to meet a desire metric. There is no better way to remove your enjoyment of pursuing a particular aspect of your life than to self-punish.

Chapter VII

Thought-Length Hierarchy

As I will reference this concept throughout my work, I thought it best to take a chapter to describe and define the concepts and contexts in which I will use them. My career has spanned nearly every aspect of computer growth. I have likened the various stages—generations—of computer development as they relate to watching my son develop. Derived from my studies of computer and software engineering, this analogy also correlates with the length of commands, processes, data sizes, and application operations. The first generations of systems could only run three-letter commands, which were called assembly code. The power of these systems was adequate for the operation that interfaced with the physical operation of electrical switching that triggered mechanical actions. Human interaction was text-based and not appealing to the average human interfacing with the systems.

Each generation of new physical computer equipment brings with it the shrinking of the last generation to half of its last size, then the doubling of the number of new circuits in the same external size of packaging. Many remember the doubling of resources for each new generation that resulted from repeatedly performing this shrink-and-double cycle. On an operational basis, the next generation could always handle everything from the previous, but if you tried to use new software on machine that was a few generations older, it would not be successful. Much like a child not understanding college physics, the basic capabilities of the older system could not support the new software.

As children grow like new generations of computer systems, they exponentially expand their operational capabilities. Each new exponential growth brings the capability to handle multiple instances of the same cognitive activity that had to be done one at a time before. The first computers had to load one process at a time and then stop that process before starting the next, but now look at how many processes are running in the background on your one computer system. These background processes become involuntary and subconscious in humans— processes that we simply lump in with instincts. Still, while watching my son in his first perspective lifetime, I saw what appeared to be a conscious thought behind his breathing. When some other stimulus happened, such as a bowel movement, I watched his focus shift, and his breathing would actually stop monetarily while his focus returned to the next breath. It appeared to me that not even breathing was involuntary, but rather an action he consciously did to relieve his discomfort. I would equate this to learning that the beginning phase of involuntary relief from the discomfort of low oxygen was to flex the diaphragm that brought air into the lungs and relieved the discomfort. My assessment was that he had learned to do this repeatedly until it was involuntary.

After later stages of exponential growth, you can watch as a two year old, who is eating, practices basic problem solving. They learn what to eat and in what sequences to lessen the discomfort of the process in general. I have seen a child this old know to reach for his mother's water cup when he had milk in his, because he had eaten a lemon that had curdled the milk. He knew to reach for a piece of fruit when the eggs were too hot, causing discomfort in his mouth. He wanted to add jam to his bread to reduce its dryness and improve its flavor. The curiosity that the parent saw as annoying is a form of repeated problem solving that they are learning by combining multiple thoughts of avoiding discomfort and then predicting favorable outcomes.

In any case, you can see that as the brain grows with each perspective lifetime, the pattern of a multitude of the previous cognitive capabilities seems to ensue with each new growth phase. Neuroscience tells us that this development is actually the process of different portions of the brain being enabled and expanded into (ZERO TO THREE, 2006). Consequently, the activity of different portions of the brain will be like keeping the earlier generation of computer, but expanding by adding a later-generation version with exponentially more capability. Thus, these portions from earlier growth will always exist and be accessible later in our lives. In this chapter, we will explore how we may return to earlier states of emotion and brain activity later in life or even in the course of normal, day-to-day behaviors.

The Lengths of Our Thoughts

The basis for this work is an understanding of how my own mind works. My theory was designed after pondering how at various times in my life I had been capable of deeper thought that tended to lead me to a higher level of performance, while at other times I had been mired in performance levels that anyone would consider subpar. I first considered whether humans could possibly have times in their lives when their intelligence levels biologically changed and when their cognitive abilities then followed this biological change. The other alternative was to look at possible rhythmic changes in aspects of my (or any individual's) life that related to the changes I had experienced in cognitive ability.

Having already made the connection between my own life cycle, my people-situation mindsets, and the logical thought stoppers that become the subconscious programming features in my mind, I started looking at all of these in search of a correlation to the cyclical cognitive phases I had experienced. In my case, each of these times was directly related to periods of distress in my overall life cycle. Sometimes a connection to the situation was a factor in previous mindsets. Other times they were a factor in my current mindset, due to an overwhelming amount of contact with the people aspect for prolonged periods. Still other times, the reduced cognitive capabilities were a collapse of desire during an impending situation in which I felt trapped.

What they all had in common was a progression, a process that had triggered them. This was a progression that I could track and recall happening over time. I took an analytical approach and started writing down the steps that I could remember for each time this happened and compared these steps with the other times. Presto, a pattern started to emerge with some stages I could logically group together. This pattern showed that I had adapted to my new, current, people-situation mindsets and had begun to place new logical thought stoppers in place to adapt to these new sets of stimuli.

After reviewing what at first looked like stages, I determined that it lacked the traditional defining points of a staged approach. Much like everything I talk about in this book, it was more of a progression or process. Like the logical thought stoppers, these are the hardest for people to see from within the situation they are experiencing. This is why people do not realize what has happened until they have gone way too far. This gradual progression of mindset change in me was something I detected only after feeling that I had been in this place before. This time, however, I endeavored to figure out how I got here and determined that I could affect its progression in a positive way.

My cognitive ability had followed a pattern that I could relate to my improved performance in periods when my life cycle was stable, but also to my adverse regression of mindset in times of imbalance. If left unguided, the pattern followed the stimulus of the situation portion of the life

134

cycle. How could I categorize these? My ability to think about things that required deeper contemplation was the thing that changed. During some periods I was able to think deeply, while during others I only seemed to be able to think about shallow topics. The times when I could only think about shallow topics were not noticeable during that particular period or frame of mind, but then when I entered the next period, when I was able to think more deeply, I could see the shallower time clearly. Often those shallow times felt like wasted or lost time in retrospect.

As with the development of computers, I had become a lesser machine, incapable of more complex processing and operational thought-length structures. Cognitive ability seems to follow the trend that people have that determines how long a thought they can support before their minds change focus. In the Master Key System, several exercises are designed to practice prolonging mental focus. Even at the turn of the 20th century, exceptional thinkers realized that performance was linked to being able to think more clearly and deeply about a topic. (Haanel, 1916)

In the development of infants, experts relate the caretaker and infant in terms of a dialogic process between the two that enables the infant's right brain to develop by watching the caretaker's facial cues, similar to looking into a mirror. Experts say that, in the dialogic process, the more the mother constantly tunes her activity level to the infant during periods of social engagement, the more their engagement affects synchrony, and then the "pair are in affective resonance…. Thus, emotion is initially regulated by others, but then over the course of the infancy, it becomes increasingly self-regulated" (Schore, 2012).

The current knowledge of infant cognitive development shows that operations of the human brain seem to support that emotional state and thought-length correlate. The difficulties we are experiencing in computer engineering are often the interconnection of older and new generations of systems. Synchronization between systems requires the newer system to shorten to the older command lengths, processes, and operations to match the older. I speculate that at different times in our lives a biological event occurs in the mind that effects a change in chemistry that actually shortens or lengthens a person's thought process. The dialogic development of an infant human that I observed while raising my son was the child watching and following the caretaker's facial cues, which show how long the caretaker thinks about each topic before moving on to the next.

I had a good friend who had experienced a traumatic brain injury, and I observed that when interfacing with this friend, he had a noticeably difficult time maintaining a single thought for more than a few seconds. Then again, this feature of his personality made him extremely personable and approachable; he was like a conversation magnet. People he had never met before felt entirely comfortable approaching him. Why was this? I studied him and saw that the length of his thoughts was extremely apparent on his face and in his body language. We see the length of someone's thoughts on their face as they change their focus, move, shift their eyes, or change their body motions with jerking actions. Someone with long thought lengths is more focused—they don't shift their eyes or change focus, sometimes for long periods.

Young children link facial cues to when and how they can approach and interact with people. In his book, *The Science of the Art of Psychotherapy*, Dr. Schore explains his work with infants and states, "Through visual-facial, auditory-prosodic, and tactile-gestural communication, caregiver and infant learn the rhythmic stricture of the other and modify their behavior to fit that structure, thereby co-creating a 'specifically fitted interaction'"(Schore, 2012). Elsewhere, he later states, "Via this contingent responsivity, the mother appraises the nonverbal expressions of her infant's internal arousal and affective states, regulates them, and communicates them back to the infant. To accomplish this, the mother must successfully modulate non-optimal high *or*

136

non-optimal low levels of stimulation, which would induce supra-heightened or extremely low levels of arousal in the infant" (Schore, 2012). Nonverbal communication is expressed by these facial movements, which I propose match our thought lengths, which in turn match our emotional state. The universal signal to a child indicating whether one is serious or not is the bouncing of one's facial features. Displaying quick jumpy facial movement to them means you are not focused or serious and are thus approachable.

I have also often thought about why people who have had near death experiences say their lives passed before their eyes. Some chemical trigger makes the brain capable of the longest possible length of thought, opening up pathways that allow instant access to any or all content available. Though this is a bit off topic for my work, I believe there must be a way to sustain this state in the human brain all the time. These times of clarity, when people are exposed to the possibility of their lives ending, allow them to jump to the highest state of thought length and cognitive ability, but then when the situation is over, they regress to a lesser pattern of thought-length capability.

Psychology counselors that are involved in clinical work with PTSD and other later-life patients have found "the evolution of...developmentally impaired regulatory system[s] over all stages of life" (Schore, 2012). I relate my own reduced cognitive periods, when I reentered a short thought-length capability as an adult, to this impaired state, but as I found out when I was within the shorter thought-length times, I was unable to characterize or access the things from the times when I was capable of longer thought processes. In my case, anything experienced in those longer-thought periods was perceived as if from a dream state. This explains, in my view, the occurrence of or the perception of supernatural experiences that people often proclaim they have had after near death experiences.

What are these lengths of thought and how can we relate them to human activities? Let's look at what we know about people's behavior and what activities they seem to support in different emotional conditions. Let's look at a diagram I put together with a list of thought types correlated to length of thoughts. This chart shows the thought length in which I would assess a typical human spends the majority of their time.

Thought length progression	%
Ascending	0.01%
Self-Enlightening	0.04%
Revolutionizing	0.10%
Utilitarian	0.30%
Hypothesizing	0.65%
Compiling and correlating	0.80%
Replicative	1.40%
Exploring/Expanding	3.00%
Conceptualizing	4.00%
Organizational	8.00%
Individualizing	17.00%
Distinguishing	20.00%
Brevity and Fun	19.00%
Interactive-reproductive	16.00%
Staying out of trouble	6.00%
Instinctual	2.00%
Survival	1.00%
Physically Sustaining	0.50%
Involuntary	0.20%

I am sure that many of us could add more categories of thoughts into this list; my point is not to make the list all-encompassing, but to show that these thoughts are grouped according to the length of brainpower spent on a single thought. As a person changes how long they spend thinking, their minds shift back and forth as if between older and newer generation computer

138

systems with less or more capabilities. I have read psychology counselors use a term called "transference," which is explained as "an established pattern of relating and emotional corresponding that is cued by something in the present, but often calls up both an affective state and thoughts that may have more to do with past experiences than present ones" (Maroda, 2005, p. 137). This transference, like the computer shift, also links emotional stimuli and situational operations from the current time in life to an earlier time when the less capable components of the brain were developed. Thus, a human's emotional state externally appears to have this strong connection to their current average length of thoughts.

When I explored my own patterns, I realized that when I am in a particular emotional state, I usually have the same or similar thoughts, and by consciously thinking longer or shorter, I can adjust myself. Most people, on average, without attempting to control their thought length, fall into the percentages in the color-coded table above. An examination of how these affect me personally revealed that I can affect these thoughts and actually determine, with practice, which type of thought I put myself in by controlling how long I think about one single topic. Years of attending university had this effect on me by practicing the process of lengthened thoughts over time.

Wow, what a revelation this is! If I can just sit and think about the same thing for a longer period of time, I will start to go through this table in an upward direction. My practice starts with slowing down the stimuli that change my focus. Then I start to think about a topic, first distinguishing what the topic is, then identifying individual components, and finally moving on to organizing the components. Next, I continue to think about the topic, determining and understanding the concepts that make the organization of its components possible. After that, I explore possibilities, either similarities within this topic or other topics that relate to this one. At this level, I replicate this to other topics, while each is compiled and correlates to the outcomes of previous thoughts. If you followed this, you are using my same process.

Involuntary Actions of Humans

Let's add in a theory to practice applying: look around now and find the most attractive person of the other sex in the room. Quickly compare this individual in your mind against your own list of people who you would consider the most attractive people you have ever seen in your life. Who comes to mind? Are they a sensual, soft figure, a rugged and virile person, or a compassionate person? Are they well formed with a visibly attractive figure? Now think back to the last paragraph. Do you remember anything we were discussing? Does the topic of the last few paragraphs feel like a déjà vu? Take a minute. The suggestion of a topic that lowered your thought process to the "interactive-reproductive" level shortened your thought capability. All thoughts of the higher level require a longer thought length and now seem like a dream or surreal past experience.

If the last paragraph successfully caused you to have images or thoughts of an interactive-reproductive nature (sexual nature), then the change in thought length would bring you, as a reader, to a shorter thought length. This relation would then shift the operation of your brain, more or less shutting off portions with longer thought-length capabilities and enabling only more primitive capabilities. When raising my son, I would spend a lot of time talking to him in what some people thought were far too advanced conversations. For example, one person was frustrated with me when they found me explaining the grouping of toys into multiplication tables when he was six months old or so. Even though at the time I was only following an instinct I had for child rearing, which I did not entirely understand until putting together my thought for this

140

chapter, what I was doing was letting his thought length expand as far as he could continue his thoughts.

I felt out my son's interest in continuing to think about a topic and then continued myself as long as he did, even if it appeared way beyond his capability. I was practicing leading him through these longer thought lengths, progressively moving him up this chain. The list of these thought lengths seemed to fit into a progression, which I have listed below. This progression relates to the development of computer systems and the way the logic of each layer of technology has developed. When watching his abilities progress, I could find a parallel for each stage of my son's development with multiple combinations of each single action from the capability base below:

Involuntary Thoughts

Each living creature has involuntary thoughts. We do not seem to have much conscious control over the things that occur in our bodies, such as the heart beating, the eyes blinking, and digestion. Some part of our existence knows that if these are not done continuously, we cease to exist. Thus, it is not an option for us to change these thoughts.

Physically Sustaining

Thoughts that enable us to be physically sustained are things like sucking, chewing, and swallowing that we learn at young ages and that enable us to survive. They are obviously not involuntary, though they could be instinctual, but if so, then they are on a very low level of survival instincts. These thoughts do not need to react to a set of inputs, but only react to a single input. These actions are multiple combinations of involuntary thoughts that combine to reduce discomfort. Examples of this include a cow taking a bite of grass from a readily available field or a predator that has to kill its food prior to eating. This series of multiple thoughts is how I make this differentiation.

Survival and Instinctual

Though here could be difficulty distinguishing between survival actions and instinctual actions, when it comes to thought processes, the fight-or-flight, reflex-driven responses to survival stimuli require less thought length. Instinctual actions do not include the chemical reaction of life or death, as with survival, and they are less traumatic. Instinctual thoughts, in my view, are a combination of several survival thoughts with the capability to plan ways to possibly eliminate the survival condition in the first place. From my research in neuroscience, these thoughts are the first to include the human response system, which includes hyperarousal and dissociation.

Staying Out of Trouble

This is a big category of thought lengths, as it is still relevant in modern social interactions and still causes repercussions for each of us. Thought levels that are optimized for keeping us out of trouble are things that we all return to subconsciously each day. These thoughts are the first that have a logical component whose purpose is to determine how to minimize the effects of involuntary hyperarousal and dissociation.

Interactive-Reproductive

This thought-length category also defines much of our human society in one way or another. In fact, this underlying level of thought may be the most important in our biological structure and the only reason for the higher levels to exist at all. In some way or another, cultures or people with the ability to reach higher levels only survived the test of time because of the ability of the higher-level traits to affect this lower level. If that higher level of thinking made them more valuable to reproduce, we have them on this planet today, but if it did not benefit reproduction, the culture with those traits may no longer exist on this planet.

Brevity and Fun Thoughts

The next level of thought lengths above the interactive-reproductive category is probably the most important to the lower-level interactive-reproductive thought lengths. These thoughts support having fun and are obviously the most enjoyable. They feature the optimum length of thought for the human mind. Every derivation or progression of thought length from this natural state eventually returns to this optimum level. In my assessment, humans as a species are on average just moving above this level. The more people differentiate and individualize, the more they pair off and connect with others, which is necessary to bring them back to the interactive-reproductive level.

Individualizing and Distinguishing

As people evolve as a species, they are only able to have longer thought processes because it is desirable to do so, and so they practice lengthening their thoughts regularly. This regular practice of lengthening, like flexing a muscle, is what in fact makes them able to do so more effectively. The combination of unique or distinctive ways of combining multiple brief thoughts is the first way people become unique. The need to distinguish ourselves from other people and then define our individuality, make us more likely to reach an interactive-reproductive pairing. You could also make the argument that any levels above this continue the individualizing thought process, just at varying levels.

Organizational Thoughts

The ability to see all of the individuals and the uniqueness of those individuals in a society requires a thought process that is a bit longer than that required to organize within one individual. This level of thought length is able to gather multiple lower-level individualizing thoughts, so the length of thoughts required to organize is on the next level. These thoughts are larger than the thoughts of the previous category on a linear level. The more individual components of an organization there are, the more thought is required to keep track of them at the same level of growth. As this is a linear growth of the thought process, the growth of these sorts of thoughts takes a different pattern from those above this level. Skills at this level may depart from those of the next longer length.

Conceptualizing Thoughts

This level of thought requires the next longer length of thoughts beyond those required for organizational thoughts. This requirement is not because of the addition of more repetition, but because of the addition of infinite levels of capabilities. These capabilities are unrelated to the individual's growth, but are related to the growth of possibilities that correspond to overcoming the organizations at the previous level of thoughts. The possible outcomes or scenarios connect those organized components. This level of thoughts reaches exponential growth in comparison to the individualizing and distinguishing thought lengths.

Exploring and Expanding

This is the thought length required to begin to encompass and embrace more than one grouping of conceptual organizations. This level, like the organizational level, is linear and grows with the exploration of new levels of conceptualization groupings of the capabilities for the interactions of organized groups.

Replicative Thoughts

This level of thought at the next length of thought capability starts to enable the relation and reproduction of more than one conceptual thought. We start to see that there may be more conceptualizations in existence, as we discovered in our exploring and expanding stage, and we need the thought-length capability to replicate our impression of the world as we knew prior to this expansion of capability, with equal weight given to what we already had a conceptualized understanding of prior to this replication.

Compiling and Correlating

At this level, multiple replicated thoughts converge. Thought length is required for compiling and comparing the large level of replicated thoughts from the previous level. The magnitude of replication at this level depends on the intensity of the outreach and detail of the exploration of the last two levels in the replication of thoughts.

Hypothesizing

Thoughts of this length pull together the organized replicated concepts and correlate their similarities in order to bridge the gap to a desired result. Thoughts at this level require the development of possible solutions and methods of bridging the compiled and correlated material to the solution.

Utilitarian Thoughts

These thoughts take what was gained from compiling and correlating the processes and from determining possible hypotheses (approaches) in order to separate and determine the best for everyone involved. Thoughts on this level begin to diverge from any correlation to the individualizing and distinguishing level.

Revolutionizing Thoughts

These thoughts take the best hypothesis from the utilitarian level and push them forward by linking all components involved to provide a direction and implementation for the last level.

Self-Enlightening

Thoughts at this level work on and above the level of revolutionizing thoughts solely to benefit the individual's purpose.

Ascending

This level of thoughts works at correlating and building self-enlightening activities. Granted, this category is a catch-all that signifies that the larger groupings may have a use, but I was unable to distinguish the nature of that use.

Relating to Human Needs

I have adopted some of the structure of this organization from Maslow's Hierarchy of Needs, which I believe shows the human needs that cause us to go through these levels of thought-length abilities (Maslow, 1943). People can have these needs met at one time in their lives, while at another their life cycle may become out of balance, rendering them unable to meet the same needs later. This imbalance leads to reduced thought lengths and then to collapse when individuals are unable to meet their needs from the previous level of Maslow's Hierarchy. As we move down the thought-length capability table, during the turmoil of unbalanced life cycles, we also have limits on our ability to attain certain levels of Maslow's needs due to corresponding cognitive changes.

The good thing is that we are able to affect this balance when we understand it. We can transcend up and down the thought-length hierarchy as we affect, with positive control, our overall length of thoughts. There are times when shorter thought lengths are beneficial and times when it is desirable to lengthen thoughts. Some tasks and jobs are served well by shorter lengths and others by longer. Positive control comes from the knowledge of how to affect aspects of yourself, and engineering your future will require setting this aspect as needed for your success.

Thought-Length Trends and Capabilities in People

If we think about the average person spending the majority of their time at thought lengths in accordance with my table above, we see that they spend their days mostly interacting with others and individualizing themselves. About 70-75 percent of the time, people inhabit the social arena of thought length more than any other does, but this should not be surprising because people are in general social creatures. What you also saw, as we went through our example of shortening your thoughts using an interactive-reproductive distraction, is that the length of thought is continuously adjusted. A person can change from one moment to the next; however, it happens more easily on the down side than the upward side. What does this mean for us?

If we can change and adjust thought lengths subconsciously, then we can certainly do the same consciously, by design, to fit our needs. We just need to be aware of ourselves and know how to engineer this control into our lives.

We also need to recognize that thought length is transferable from person to person. If someone in a close proximity to you has a trigger that shortens their thought process, then the changes in breathing, speaking patterns, shortness of movements, and number of activities in a period, all will be noticeable, even if only on a subconscious level. Dogs and lie detectors, for example, are able to detect people who appear to be afraid—or who seem to be in a mindset of avoiding trouble—by catching all of these subtle components.

Figure: Average Person's Thought-Length Patterns

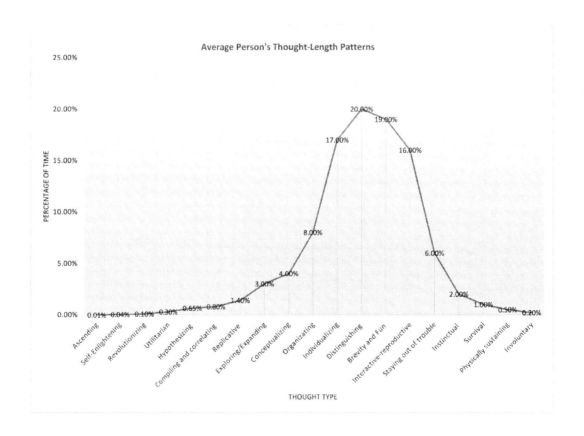

Since this is the average time spent by a person at a particular thought length, it means some people are higher and some lower, but each one of us is also sometimes below average and sometimes above. In fact, as I began by discussing at the beginning of the chapter, this changes day-to-day, hour-to-hour, and even cyclically. At times in my life I have found myself below this average for such extended periods that I believed I was incapable of little more, but as I mentioned previously, by building and flexing this ability like a physical muscle it can be developed over time. Though there may be some biological predispositions limiting how far individuals can expand their cognitive abilities, anyone can improve this in oneself just as people can improve their physical bodies. The person I started out as is the same person I am now. Any difference is the result of my continued flexing in this area.

By practicing the lengthening of thoughts repeatedly, not only will you accomplish more progress on your life path, you will also improve your cognitive ability over time. In the figure, "Expanding Thought-Length Capability," you can see if someone who spends a large part of their day working a professional job that requires continuous thought may find that their distribution looks more like one of the following. They are continuously moving their thoughts toward their need for longer concentration on work tasks. It is not that people are born with or without cognitive ability; it is the nature of how they utilize the tools they have.

Figure: Expanding Thought-Length Capability

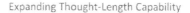

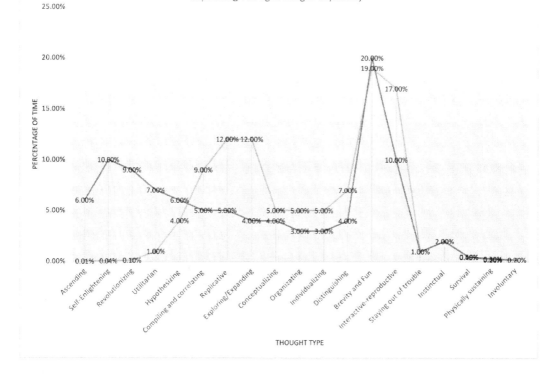

Expanding Thought-Length Capability

THOUGHT TYPE

Often, I will hear people explain how they are not the type of person who can be an intellectual, how they could never be on the same level as someone to whom they compare themselves and whom they perceive as highly educated, but length of thought is not a level. If you can guide yourself just once a day to think about something long enough to go through a process of comparing and contrasting, grouping like components, and so on, while moving up the list of the different thought lengths found on the table, "Thought Length Progression," you will exercise your cognitive capability. Remember, Mr. Universe did not become Mr. Universe in the seventh grade, when he picked up the 250-pound dumbbells to show off his muscles, just because he was born at that level. We see how physical ability is developed because we see the movement that causes muscles to build and the progression that follows, but the cognitive development is done exactly the same way. We all are born with thought-length patterns looking like those on the chart, "Average Person's Thought-Length Pattern."

150

In the graph, "Expanding Thought-Length Capability," I have shown how a person can shift their average time spent at different thought lengths by engineering patterns and behaviors into their lives. The important thing you will notice in each of these graphs is that the normal, most natural human state—brevity and fun thoughts—remains the same. Maintaining this state of brevity and fun thoughts is required for any human to remain balanced. Think of this state as if it were an unstretched rubber band. If a person attempts to remove or minimize this relaxed state, their stress level will increase until they become imbalanced. Stress and anxiety are the visible result of this. In fact, as a person moves further up the thought-length table, they will actually require more of this relaxed state. Moreover, when we engineer our lives, we look for ways to integrate this state into the processes that advance us on our chosen life paths. We will explore this in more detail in the chapter "Enjoying the Process."

Shortening Thought Processes

In the same manner that we can all practice lengthening our thought processes, we can also artificially shorten them in the same way. With the continued input of shorter length durations, we can inadvertently reduce our thought processes to a very low level. I have seen this occur in particular in the social media era. People have continuous input from thousands of sources, all of which serve to stimulate them on a regular basis, never giving them a chance to reach the longer thought lengths. Jobs that require multitasking or that have continuous interruptions in the work environment will also keep people in those situations at the thought lengths required to survive and excel. In many cases, people in these environments will skip a particular length—or several—on the "Thought Length Progression" table. While many project managers spend all their time at the organizational thought level, they need to compile and correlate for their environment, so they will skip the thought-length levels of conceptualizing, exploring and expanding, and replicative thoughts. They will insert the compiling and correlating level of thought length appropriate to their smaller realm of knowledge—the scope required for their organization—into the shorter length of thought characteristic of the conceptualizing level. This allows them to progress in thought length and fulfill their personal development within the reduced scope of their perception of the world.

I am not sure how future generations will assess what is also happening along this same perception-based adjustment of thought length. As we talked about with the shortening of thoughts by the constant bombardment of social media, these messages have become shorter and shorter as the magnitude increases. Twitter is limited to 140 characters, and it is difficult to get successful interest in posts that are long enough to reach the full maximum length. People are trained to read more and more, and they skip over the ones that appear to be longer than the others are. This constant bombardment registers below the organizational thought length. As the posts are continuously random, there is no reason to organize them. Rarely do people distinguish among who sent which tweet or post, with the exception of very popular or trendy posters. By my assessment, these constant short thoughts, multitasked into our brains, are straddling the state of brevity and fun thoughts and the state of individualizing and distinguishing thought lengths in our minds. Interestingly, the great power of our brains takes all of these into a continuously growing collage of thoughts and then jumps straight to the compiling and correlating state followed soon thereafter by another jump to the hypothesizing level of thought length. I have studied this with some interest, as the younger generation, which has grown up in this constant media generation, possesses a new skill set that does not mesh with the rest of the business world. It presents as these people enter the work force with skills that appear to be equally matched to a seasoned manager; however, they lack the progression of all the phases of growth in between. They have placed this high thought-length capability into shortened thought-length brackets in their minds. This may be a new skill requirement for this new age and could be the next progression of the evolution of our brains, but only time will tell.

Active Case Studies:

When following a few case studies of people who spent exceptional amounts of time absorbing the short content posts of social media, I observed that the thought lengths these individuals exhibited were shorter than those needed to reach the organizational thought length were. Thus, the people in the case study seemed to lose the ability to assess how much time had passed. A comparison of elapsed time and productivity required them to think at organizational thought lengths, but forcefully keeping the length of thoughts short did not allow these thoughts. Thus, unknown and unrealized time intervals were continuously expressed after social media engagement periods. This often resulted in remorse afterwards when the individual realized the extent of the time lost. As you can imagine, this becomes a large productivity loss as well, since these shorter thought lengths are more closely aligned with the thought-length level of brevity and fun thoughts or with individualizing and distinguishing thought lengths, both of which were difficult to link to productivity.

Biological Science Connection

Previously, we looked at transference, which is when the emotion involved in a particular situation "calls up both an affective state and thoughts that may have more to do with past experiences" (Maroda, 2005, p. 137). When we use outside influence to continually shorten or lengthen our thought process, we may also push ourselves toward an emotional state and mindset for which we are not consciously striving. At the same time, the process of purposefully stretching or compressing thoughts, for which the expectations would be a different thought length for a given situation, will also cause reactions in people that lead them or draw them to a desired emotional state. Famous people have used this to bend and set the outcome of people's interactions. In the book, *48 Laws of Power*, the author gives several of these examples:

> Rhythm and timing are critical. One of the most important elements in the rhythm of drama is suspense Houdini for instance, could sometimes complete his escape acts in seconds—but he drew the act out to minutes, to make the audience sweat. The key to keeping the audience on the edge of their seats is letting events unfold slowly, then speeding them up at the right moment, according to a pattern and tempo that you control. Great rulers from Napoleon to Mao Tse-tung have used theatrical timing to surprise and divert their public. Franklin Delano Roosevelt understood the importance of staging political events in a particular order and rhythm. (Green, Elfers, 2000)

Maybe you wondered how groups of people could be influenced to the point of anger, apathy, sadness, etc. It is easy to see that the one thing we can transfer from one person to another is the length of time they think about something before changing to a new thought. Any time individuals speak out in public—and others listen to them and contemplate what they are saying—this process is in play. Before I explored this area, I often wondered why I could sit in a church and watch everyone reaching emotional pinnacles together while I could not. How did they all become saddened or excited at the same time? Because I was watching with an analytical approach, my mind was not following the progression of thought that was being publicly relayed to each other person. I had set my own thought length, and so my emotional state was not tuned to everyone else's.

Immediate Jumps Caused by Regressive Thought

We explored this area earlier when we talked about visualizing an attractive person. Your mind can immediately shorten thought process based on a biological response. We must anticipate and understand this involuntary survival thought-length function, which we do not have much control over, in order to master its occurrence in ourselves. The first step is to be aware of them and of what triggers their occurrence in us. Let's look at and define a few of them.

Social Interruptions

Interruptions by outside stimuli are the most common, which I classify as social interruptions, and though I often relate them to social media, they are really any outside influence that brings us back to the individualizing and distinguishing level. These happen all the time and are the most common in our lives, but they are also the easiest to prevent from affecting us. The boss has a big corner office with a closed door. He is removing social interruptions. We can put our phones on silent mode, close our social media pages, or check our email less often, and you can imagine many other ways to minimize these distractions.

Sexual Triggers

Stimuli, which include interactive-reproductive-level stimuli, are also reducible in many ways; however, many of us choose not to reduce them. The reason for this is biological. As stated earlier, without this driver, which is often subconscious, we would not exist. We all know this at some level, and for this reason, it is and will be the purpose for all the other thought-length interactions that follow. If you shut this off with social requirements and punishments, it will come out in another area.

Staying out of Trouble

The next lower level of thought-regression stimuli is getting in trouble. We instinctively react to the threat of trouble, which we were programmed to do at the age when our thoughts were just reaching the ability to be long enough to understand socially expected behavior. People in a situation in which they are triggered with the thought of getting in trouble enter a thought length in which they are no longer able to resolve anything but discontinuing the situation that presents potential trouble. They will shed moral, social, and intellectual restrictions and make decisions that only support this shortened thought length. When this is triggered in them, they will often look back with a deep level of regret at the decisions made in this state. Shows like *Cops* like to display this aspect of human nature so the world can gain some amusement from the natural, human state triggered by these situations. Unfortunately, the use of drugs and other lifestyles in which some underprivileged people find themselves artificially stimulate people to remain in these thought-length states for such extended periods that it often defines their entire existence.

Survival Regression

Survival triggers are not very often experienced in the Western world. Shortening the thought process to this level may happen for a moment in a situation like an impending accident, for example. Still, many of us may never have experienced this length of thoughts. I have been in a few life-threatening situations where I felt that, in this shortened thought-length pattern, something else was obviously going on in my mind. I liken the difference between normal thought-length patterns and these instinctual activities to the difference between my thoughts normally seeming like a single lane road across the Atlantic Ocean to Europe and my survival thoughts seeming like a 50-lane highway between two cities that are within viewing distance.

156

Something changes in those split seconds to allow nearly infinite pathways to locally access the information in my mind.

Humans can also find themselves locked into this shortened thought length, which supports thinking only related to survival for long periods. I experienced this once when I was in the Navy. We were picking up destitute people who were risking their lives attempting to escape the island of Cuba. They had placed themselves in rafts made of whatever buoyant material they could find, and they set out in the direction of land north of their island. When we picked these people up, they had no physical possessions. Most were male, but we also pulled a few women and even children out of these makeshift rafts. The behavior I witnessed still haunts me today. Riots over food were common at mealtimes, especially when many new people had been picked up. We stood ready with fire hoses to break this up. We had to have all outside doors on the ship under lock and key with armed guards. All women were watched constantly. After several gang rapes started right in front of hundreds of people, we used the same fire hose spraying method to break those up as well. Children had to be fed their rations of food in watched areas, as mothers had been found ducking out of sight and consuming the children's rations. Even though we had set up restrooms, after each load was dropped off the ship we had to clean countless piles of feces that were deposited right where they slept and ate, as if they were saving these piles up for some future need. The regression of people in this state still makes me sick to the stomach when I think about it.

Visibility to Self-Cognitive Capability

As I continued to self-explore, I found another aspect of the human psyche that seemed to have a large effect on me personally. I refer to this as a limit to my own cognitive self-image in my memory. I remember my capability for thought and my ability to perform mentally challenging activities for only a set amount of time in the past. To explain, if I am very mentally capable and if my mind just seems to be on the spot for the months of January and February, then for the month of March, I will be very confident in my abilities and will feel as if I can sit on a panel of international scientists as an equal. In contrast, if in March I begin to interface for the purpose of marketing my products and if I then spend the months of March and April writing and reading social media posts and promoting changes to my self-image with humorous content, then by May and June my memory of the last two months will solidify my cognitive self-image, and I will no longer associate with the ability to be a leading scientist anymore. I will now feel that I am capable of bridging and organizing groups and able to have light, friendly conversations with many people, and I will now have a difficult time remembering that I was that other person. My confidence in this ability to have sustained, longer thought lengths, which was very high just a few months prior, no longer seems like much of a reality. I have often gone back to read my previous work and felt like I could not even have done this. The memory of the state I was comfortable in just a few months prior diminishes because I can only remember my cognitive ability for a set amount of time in the past.

What Makes a Memory?

What makes us store something in our memory? If we think back to what portions of any event we remember, it is never an entire span of time that we were doing an activity. What makes us store one part of a situation and not another? Storing memory seems to involve a chemical combination in our minds that includes the emotional condition we find ourselves in. Many people in the same situation will remember (thus their brain stores) entirely different portions of the same event. Triggers that mostly involve movement are what prompt me to store memories. When I walk through an open field for a long period, I will only remember the short periods when motion occurred, the rabbit that ran in front of me, or the brightly colored cricket that jumped at my feet. The rest of the walk may have been very long, but the two periods of fifteen seconds of motion are all that my brain stored in memory.

Other people in the same situation may store different portions of the same trip or the same events, but each does this because of a predisposition to a type of events they store based on a biological reaction in their own minds. Since the storage or each of these remembered events was prompted by emotional (biological) triggers, they also have the aspect of the person's emotional state at the time that they were stored attached to them like metadata to the memory. This emotional aspect, stored over a length of time along with my memories, makes me feel positive or negative about that span of time (memories). This topic is something I have looked at in more detail, but it will not be included in this book. However, the point I will make is that the memory of emotion over time is accessible to a person and becomes a part of that person's self-cognitive ability when looked at in retrospect.

Cognitive Self-image—Case Study

A case study of a friend, whom I have followed extensively, involves a time when she went through a low point in her life, during which her thought-length capability became extremely shortened over a long period. Previously in her life she had been an international model. Life had stood still when she was in the room. Unfortunately, everyone reaches certain ages in life when others do not elicit the same behavior that they did before. The world now stopped when the new, next-generation model walked into the room behind her. She indicated to me that these lyrics from the Coldplay song, "Viva La Vida," best expressed how she felt:

I used to rule the world

Seas would rise when I gave the word

Now in the morning I sleep alone

Sweep the streets I used to own

I used to roll the dice

Feel the fear in my enemy's eyes

Listen as the crowd would sing

"Now the old king is dead! Long live the king!"

One minute I held the key

Next the walls were closed on me

And I discovered that my castles stand

Upon pillars of salt and pillars of sand

I hear Jerusalem bells are ringing

Roman Cavalry choirs are singing

Be my mirror, my sword and shield

My missionaries in a foreign field

For some reason I can't explain

Once you're gone there was never

Never an honest word

But that was when I ruled the world

(Coldplay – "Viva La Vida" Lyrics)

When I met her, she was in the aftermath of the reduction in her abilities. In her case, this was both cognitive and physical. I saw her struggle to understand who she was now. The residual self-image of previous capability was still very fresh in her mind but did not seem achievable anymore. As I watched over a few years, the memory of this previous ability became less bright in her mind, and only the realization of the current state remained recognizable to her.

What to Take from Her Case

The fact that our abilities are time dependent can be good and bad, depending on how we address or use this aspect of own behavior to adjust ourselves. We all know someone who was exceptional at one time, only to fall apart entirely later. We also all know someone who has gone through a bankruptcy or through credit problems, and their credit score became so bad that they were not able to get any credit at all. Like a credit score, your cognitive capability is recoverable no matter how low it gets or for how long. When you are in this reduced cognitive state, you will not be able to remember ever being more capable; however, when you finally get back to the higher cognitive state you will look back and wonder how it was possible to be so low.

Because of her desire to retrieve a past feeling of validity, she became increasingly intent on exploring the numerous connections that social media platforms like Facebook could bring her. On top of achieving a lower thought-length capability from the emotional state her declining life cycle had caused, she was artificially shortening it even more with the continued bombardment of short messages from the social media platform. This fed on itself with the loss of the ability to realize how much time was spent on these social media platforms.

The visibility of self-cognitive capability is a factor in being at a particular thought length for a prolonged period. As I explained earlier in the chapter, when you are in the lower cognitive state, thoughts that were stored in your memory at longer thought lengths will appear at the reduced state to be déjà vu. They will feel outside of reality or unreasonable because they are just too long to process in your current state of mind. Conversely, when you are in a higher cognitive state, you will be able to access the shorter thoughts you created in lesser cognitive states.

When I think about these times of reduced cognitive ability in my own life, my natural tendency is to feel a bit of embarrassment and shame. However, the thing I have learned is that no matter what state I find myself in now, I can easily return to a reduced cognitive state. In truth, I will most likely have these lesser times again. It is part of being human to have them; however, those who understand their own weaknesses are able to recognize these times, turn the corner, and stand out from the crowd. These people have been immortalized in our literature and history books throughout the history of our species.

References

Coldplay, (2008) "Viva La Vida," (Lyrics) Copyright: Universal Music Publishing Mgb Ltd.

Haanel, C.F., (1916), The Master Key System, Psychology Publishing, St. Louis and The Master Key Institute, New York.

Green, R., Elfers, J., (2000) 48 Laws of Power, Penguin Books, New York, NY

Maslow, A., (1943) A Theory of Human Motivation. Psychological Review, 50(4), 370-96.

Maroda, K. J., (2005) Show some emotion: Completing the cycle of affective communication. In L. Aron & A. Harris (Eds.) *Revolutionary connections*. Relational psychoanalysis: Vol. II. *Innovation and expansion* (pp. 121-142). Hillsdale, NJ: Analytic Press.

Schore, A. N. (2012) The Science of the Art of Psychotherapy: W.W. Norton & Company, Inc. 500 Fifth Avenue, New York, N.Y. 10110, 61 - 63

ZERO TO THREE, (2006) BrainWonders, a collaborative project (1998-2001) between Boston University School of Medicine, Erikson Institute, and ZERO TO THREE

Chapter VIII

Working Through Plateaus

Many times, people have plateaus in their lives when they just feel they cannot work past a certain point. They feel that they have been stuck in one place for too long, that they have not progressed in their jobs, or that they are not moving past a feeling they have that their needs are not being met by those close to them—or many more things that make people feel stuck.

Plateaus at Lifetime-Defining Points

These feelings often begin when you enter a defining point of your life, as I discussed in the chapter, "An Eternity Followed by Twelve Lifetimes." Since you personally experience these defining points, even the people close to you in life do not share them. In fact, the people closest to you usually do not want you to push through the plateau, and often those people are a part of the feeling of being stuck. The people closest to you are accustomed to how you interface with them; they enjoy the way you are because the situations you create work for them.

I can think of two times when I have been very much at a plateau, and each time the dynamic caused by the romantic relationship I was in at the time directly contributed to this period of non-progression. In both cases, the other person had been very content with the way things held steady in the relationship, and in the first case, the other person appeared to be at the beginning stage of the lifetime I was leaving. The second time involved a very large age difference. I found that, after an initially fun time with someone much younger, the gap in our perspective lifetimes was closer to a two-lifetime difference. In this instance, I could see us continuing if she could reach the point where she entered at least the lifetime that I was exiting. However, my pushing

for that did achieve something that is very likely common in cases such as this. She actually

seemed to have determined that she would regress to a lower lifetime, so she began looking for

the opposite end of the spectrum in her next relationship.

It is very important to have a way to address these times in a relationship with a significant other.

I believe this is one of the two key reasons for divorce, as people reach defining points at

different times in their lives. When one person in the relationship is solidly in the middle of one

of their perspective lifetimes, they will be very content with the current status quo. If the other

person in the relationship has turned a corner and moved on to the next and if the other

person's values, thought processes, and desires have migrated, then the two of them will have

difficulty seeing eye to eye. Relationships can also be stressful in this way when both people

reach a defining point. Even if they reach it together, they could both decide to handle the

change to the next in different ways. Having been married and divorced two times, I can tell you

that I directly attribute one of my divorces to both of us reaching a defining point at the same

time. The defining point was the birth of a first child, and we both handled it in such different

manners that there was no longer common ground.

Plateaus at Peer- or Self-Defining Points

To understand these defining points, we need to understand the common management concepts

that Abraham Maslow initially described in 1943 when he produced a theory of human

motivation. For this, he produced a model of evolving human needs that he placed into a

triangle. Maslow's groupings are described by the terms Physiological, Safety, Belonging/Love,

Esteem, and Self-Actualization/Self-Transcendence. These were related to the patterns that

human motivations generally move through from the lowest to highest respectively (Maslow,

1943). The image below is a recreation of the triangle model that Maslow used to describe this level of human motivation (Maslow, 1943). In order to progress to meet the next higher category of motivation, an individual must feel secure in the aspects of the level below.

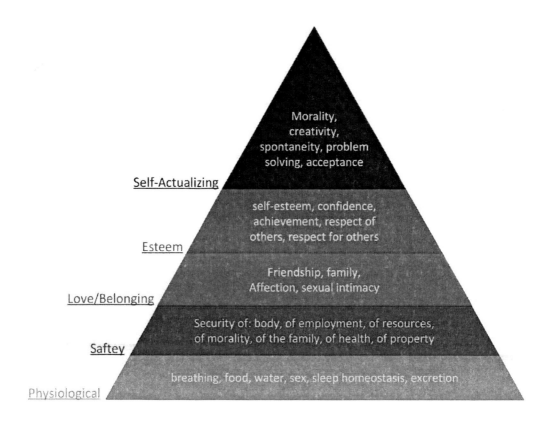

Often, people will find themselves at plateaus when they are at the point of bridging from one level of this hierarchy of needs to the next. These could correspond to life-defining points or could just be a natural progression of self-development. When younger people are in between living at their parents' houses and moving on to start their lives, they may find themselves at a level where up to that point all of their safety needs have been met by their parents. However, they feel the need to break away from their parents and move to a life situation where not all of their safety needs may be met anymore. This regression of the needs hierarchy can cause a prolonged plateau to which most of us can relate.

I see that, with the onset of social media, younger people are starting their own families later in life because their belonging needs are met by this interaction. In past years, when a person exited the high school environment, they lost a large portion of their social structure and often chose to start their families earlier in order to achieve this love/belonging level. As social media fills these needs, much of this generation finds themselves at a plateau with regard to the continuation of this level. The longer they remain at this level, the larger a regression they will experience before they become able to make a change into the next era of their lives, and the plateau or stuck feeling will continue to become more and more difficult to see past. The bridge between those has risen on social media, and the next generation seems to be mired in this dynamic.

Later in life, when a person has a family and obtains comfort in the love and belonging level for a prolonged period, they may feel they are at a plateau when they desire to do something different with their career or living environment. This need to pursue esteem and to differentiate from peers is a natural progression. However, this can cause a plateau again if some other aspect of life keeps them from working towards the desired next level. Likewise, several times people can find themselves desiring to work on self-actualization and can find other aspects of their lives that hold them back and that make them feel as if they are hitting a plateau. One example of this was an individual I spoke with who was interested in working toward a doctorate after his children had started to move out of the house, but then he found that his wife had become pregnant.

Plateaus Caused by Life Cycle Imbalances

Some of the other reasons I have defined in the chapter, "How to Fail," look at things that have plagued me in my life. In terms of life cycles, any time I was in a deadlock, one or two of the people, situations, or mindset were locked into an intermittent gaining and declining cycle. You may feel a plateau if you cannot move past it after a considerable amount of time. In this case, you will need to adjust your life cycle in a proactive manner to tip the balance in a positive direction. Often this will require small adjustments to your life cycle. Start with adjusting your mindset, as this is the easiest. Attending training sessions, conferences, seminars, or motivational speaking events will often be of great help. Situations are also something you can begin to slowly adjust by making better decisions in your current environment. Exposure to people in your life can also be done with small modifications. You will often do so when making changes to the situational aspect of your life cycle.

If one of the three aspects of the life cycle—people, situations, or mindset—is being poisoned, then a drastic, abrupt approach may be necessary to jump-start part of your path. At times, I have had to make drastic and abrupt changes in all three areas. I will give some examples of each.

Ejecting the People Poison

In the process of my second key lifetime accomplishment, which was during my Navy school, I had chosen a close friend, who was very motivated, to work out with me in the gym each day. We were thick as thieves for some time and always together before class, after class, and during breaks. This individual and I clicked in every aspect, and he would have fit right in with any of my best friends growing up, even though we had only met a few months prior. Unfortunately, this was not a good thing. I had typically aligned myself with mostly underachievers and people with a negative outlook on education. This challenging school environment was not navigable with such influences. When we started the training program, the two of us were hanging out continuously, and my grades were a constant 2.8—the lowest passing level. Both of us used to

168

make light of how close we were to failing and joke about the teachers, the counselors, and the school in general.

It hit me one time after he and I had stayed in the restroom well past the designed study break. In fact, we had done so to the point that the next break was going to start, and we were debating whether to just stay there until the next break or not. At that point, something clicked in me. I knew if I continued on this path that it was just a matter of time before I washed out of that program, so I walked out of the restroom and left him there, saying only, "No, I need to refocus, and hanging around you is not allowing me to do that." I went back to studying, and within ten minutes, I started to focus my social interaction by engaging with another student whom I had known to be very positive, even though it brought me many sneers and remarks from my previous partner in crime. From that moment on, I only greeted him in passing. I had removed that influence from my life. He ended up failing out shortly thereafter anyway, which was no surprise to me.

People often relate interfaces with a particular individual to an emotional state, and the interaction always seems to be the same for each interaction. When this has taken on a negative energy, something needs to be done to change the dynamic. If you wish to keep this person as part of your life, it is up to you to remove the poison; however, the only things you have control over and thus can change are inside of you. Two things you can do to change this dynamic both require some time and effort. This person could be choosing to interact with you because you are their method of resolving the negative mindset. If this is the case, then you need to take control of the timing of your meetings and set the interaction time only for when they are not in the negative mindset. If the mindset is a mixture of both of your input and develops out of the interaction, then you need to take control of setting the interaction situation and only interact with them in predetermined situations when and where the undesirable mindset is not possible.

The meetings between the two of you then have to take on this new, intentionally set mindset for a long enough time that you both lose the negative association feeling you have to each other in your minds.

Ejecting the Situation Poison

Changing a situation poison can be challenging because once again we associate emotional state, thought length, and beliefs with locations, places, or the occurrence of events that make up these situations. Understand which emotional states make you choose situations, and then predetermine the action you will take next time. Many people become alcoholics because they use a group of alcohol drinking friends at the local bar to help them forget a problem. They learn to associate this situation with the relief of stress or discomfort. The person could choose to go to yoga to remove the emotional state and could choose to drink alcohol only when they are in a happy mindset, and then they would probably never acquire lifelong problems with alcohol. Though gradual changes to a situation are possible that over time will remove situational poison, sometimes a change of environment is the best or only way.

For example, in my own life I knew that the moment I turned 18, I had to eject the situational poison from my life. Though I had been attempting the slow process of adjusting my situation while I was growing up, I knew it would never change without some distance. I had researched military branches and spoken to recruiters from all four branches well before my 18th birthday. This was not something I had discussed with anyone other than a few friends at school who I knew were evaluating a military direction for their lives as well. Without any discussion or consent from my family at all, I enlisted just a few days after my birthday. This started me down not only an independent path but also one that I had desired for as long as I could remember. Additionally, it was in conflict with my family's beliefs in many ways. I was shipping off to become

170

self-independent in pursuit of a technical engineering vocation. There were only two outcomes for this path change: one was complete failure and having to return to beg for redemption, while the other was success on my own terms.

Ejecting the Mindset Poison

Changing the mindset often takes a renewal of perspective that is brought on by getting a new perspective or opinion from someone else. In many of your cases, this is the reason you are reading this book, which I hope is helping you. If you are at a plateau, I hope I can give you a perspective that will jump-start you through this by enabling a mindset change. Mindset poisons include negativity, complacency, or just not knowing how to approach a positive change in your life.

I had reached a point a few years ago where several changes in my life affected my mindset in a way that I never would have anticipated. I had finished my second master's degree and gone to work for a career opportunity that appeared to be the next stage in progression of my life. This involved considerably more travel, but gave me the opportunity to build a group for a company that expressed interest in moving into the market on which I had centered my career for the previous several years. As you can see, I did not start with the fact that I would be making significantly more money, which I considered a bonus but not something that personally motivated me to make the career change. However, this aspect would be the central determining factor in the disastrous aftermath of this change.

The considerably more money, which I had resolved to put aside to invest in my son's future, became the target of discontent that I attribute to a mindset shift from several different independent forces in my life. The first was a change in the girl I had been dating who previously seemed to view our involvement as a temporary phase. She overheard a phone call with my mortgage agent, during which I talked about income, which then changed her entire outlook on our involvement. The light, uncommitted relationship started to involve long talks about having children. The second thing was that my son's mother, who had been receiving regimented child support for the preceding five or so years, was immediately interested in a higher level of support. Lastly, the company I had joined was not aligned with my goals. I was interested in the challenge of growing and developing a market for them, but their view of this arrangement was that I should grow their sales at the expense of developing the market. Their business model, I later discovered, was revenue growth above all.

Money, money, money—it was not on my list of importance entirely, but it became the plague of my existence. The mindset of my life came to revolve around the following three things. 1) I had to figure out how to appease the girl I was dating with a house purchase that would meet her approval and the expectations of her immediate family. 2) I had to participate in court filings, which were designed to cause me to spend money on attorneys, in order to withstand the onslaught of someone who was unprofessionally representing herself. On this issue, rather than attempting to achieve anything in a ruling, the agenda of this unemployed person seemed to be to spend the equivalent of a full-time job filing items that I had to address with a costly attorney. 3) My goals for business development were twofold: to find full-time project work after they lost the project that I was hired to start and to book five million dollars of new business by the end of the first year.

My life and mindset became about money, which essentially poisoned everything about me. I bought a house that was much bigger than what I set out to buy in order to make woman number one satisfied that there was enough space for her and our expected offspring. This made me the target of jealous woman number two, who was able to achieve a nearly threefold

172

increase of my monthly child support while causing me to rack up $20,000 of fees for attorneys and court costs, all in a single year. The result of this obviously stressful situation was that woman number one became disinterested in the aforementioned opportunity and living environment. All of this caused countless hours away from work, including the restructuring of several work travel arrangements for the court proceedings. In all the chaos, my objectives for the monetarily focused employer were not very effectively pursued.

I contracted to work for two years at this new company, and at the end of that time, we parted ways, neither of us happy with the results. I needed to do something to get me out of a world so focused on money. I had to remove this mindset poison from my life. I was totally burned out, and the mindset had taken a toll on my health. I felt like another health disaster was looming. Staying in a mindset that was so much in opposition to my motivating drivers in life eventually caused me to work myself to a point where my health was affected, and entirely ejecting from this situation was the only way I saw to get out of this money-centric world.

Jumping Past Plateaus

In general, how do we tip the balance to work past a plateau? Although the process of engineering your life and continuously shifting your path should set up a day-to-day effort to progress continuously along your path, sometimes you need to provide influences that with any luck will jump-start your progress and propel you past a plateau. Either the current level of needs of your life or the path you have chosen for yourself will determine what is needed to get past a plateau. Attending a motivational conference is one of the influences I suggested earlier, and I recommend scheduling activities like this on a regular basis.

In many cases, the normal process of working past where you are, which I describe in the chapter of the same name, will enable you to start moving past your plateaus. The entire design of the approach to engineering your life is to be continuously in the process of progressing down the path. When you look at defining the next level of the path beyond where you are, the plateau will show up as a branch to your direction. A redirection of your path to include the next level of items in the hierarchy of needs or a change to a life cycle element may help to break the plateau. Many of you are addressing such a point in your life now by reading this book, and I congratulate you for taking this step toward revolutionizing your life.

Recreating Positive Energy

Creating the feeling of positive energy is most important to working through plateaus. First, remember you are human; most of us treat ourselves worse than we ever would anyone around us. If we practiced our own self-talk on others, they would never want to be around us. You can never build positive energy with such self-talk. Instead, work on small things that make you feel accomplished today. Moving forward, improving your mindset, or just making a good decision for your situation today makes you feel like you are accomplished. Feeling accomplished multiple days in a row feels like progress. Just saying that today is better than yesterday can be enough to build the positive energy needed to feel progress. Spending time to balance your life today will also add positive energy.

Removing the influences of negative energy will also add positive energy. Make a commitment to excuse yourself from interactions with people who are hopeless about themselves, who are argumentative, or who have self-destructive behaviors. Choose more activities with people (even the same people) that are building, improving themselves, or grouping together for happy or exciting events. I have thousands of connections on social media, most of whom I know little about. People have often addressed something I do with a corrective or condescending comment. In the past, I tried to appease them by sending emails explaining myself, and I would feel rotten overall on those days. One day, after a few such interfaces back and forth with an individual, I stopped and stared at their profile and thought, "I have no idea who this person is, but I have let them give me a negative energy trend for three entire days now."

I had recently read a message describing how LinkedIn had added a block contact function, and when I clicked on the name, there it was. As I reluctantly clicked my first block, my anxiety slid away. Why had I spent so much energy on this person I did not even know? Treat yourself to some respect. In my new, revised opinion, there is no reason to have anyone who reaches out through social media for any reason who is not positive to both parties. Since I have made this decision, I have greatly improved my own satisfaction and positive energy. Though online interaction is widespread, it is also the least personal. Don't let these interactions give you one day of negative interaction.

In our day-to-day lives in the real world, we make decisions that affect our situations each day. These decisions then influence the people around you and your mindset at the time. People have often asked for examples of how they can make a positive choice in day-to-day situations.

Here is an example of two possible choices of directions: everyone has those days when they find themselves in a foul mindset. For whatever reason, it may be that someone sent you hate mail on social media or that someone made extra work for you with a bad decision at the office. Now that we are past the event, we have the residual effects of a bad mood. Thus, you could come home and call your bad news friend, who will be happy to have you join them at the local pub,

175

where the two of you can exchange miserable experiences and console each other. You could close the place down feeling the turn of your foul mood to the feeling of irritated drunkenness. You could then get to relieve some steam by insulting a local. You may find yourself with one more person that dislikes you and may even take a swing if they had a similar day. You and your new friend could then take a trip to the local jail, where you will get to spend some of your future hard-earned money on an attorney while adding the stress of a new pastime: learning necessary litigation.

Now let's rewind to the place where you had the initial control of the situation after your bad day. You could have come home and called your bad news friend, but instead of the drinking buddy, let's say you called the person who enjoys a yoga workout after a stressful day. The two of you could let out steam while meeting a neighbor who turned out to be friends with the local police chief. The new friend and you may choose to go out for a coffee after yoga, where you spend some time with a few members of the police force, who in turn introduce you to your newly elected state representative. Now when the police get called away to break up a fight at the local bar, where a few of your high school buddies happened to be intoxicated from venting because one of them had a bad day at work, your conversation with the state representative leads to a new pastime: learning the necessary skill of aiding the representative's upcoming campaign for governor.

The choice of situation, no matter what mindset you are in, is always yours. There are always several options for each mindset, but what makes the difference is determining which choice you will make. Make a list of whom you can call and what activities you can do relative to identified mindsets. Especially identify your individual problematic mindsets, know them ahead of time, and plan what you will do to address weaknesses or problematic moments in your life.

Surround Yourself with Like-Minded People

As we discussed in the last section, you have a choice over the situations you enter. Choosing situations with like-minded people will help you to improve yourself by engineering your surroundings. It doesn't matter who you are. If you choose to stand on a street in the ghetto, then after prolonged exposure, you are not going to feel positive about life. At the same time, your mindset is also not going to be improved by surrounding yourself with closed-minded people or stressed-out workaholics either. Balance is vital. If we think back to the chapter "Thought-Length Hierarchy," each of our minds have a comfort level with a certain length of thoughts. Finding environments where you are comfortable with the thought length of the people around you is as important as surrounding yourself with people focused on success.

Surrounding yourself with success-minded people creates a positive influence on productivity in several ways. The first, and arguably most important, is the motivational factor. When you see others achieving, you understand that such accomplishments are possible, even if it is only a subconscious understanding. Moreover, just being around productive people creates interfaces and associations that directly enable you to build interactions in business and commerce. In this case, the association with others, who are busy and who themselves are achieving, yields the awareness of opportunities or business needs.

The need for comfortable thought-length interactions in your surroundings is also very important when choosing with whom you surround yourself. It is my opinion that the length of thoughts is relayed between people, and it causes them to synchronize and be more or less comfortable with each other. We showed this same phenomenon in the graph, "Average Person's Thought-

Length Patterns," from the chapter, "Thought-Length Hierarchy," which represents the average person's thought length over a period. All of us have an average thought length that represents a combination of our cognitive abilities and the thought-requiring activities that occupy our time. People performing the same or similar lengths of thought activities interface more successfully because they do not have to change thought patterns or focus to interface with each other.

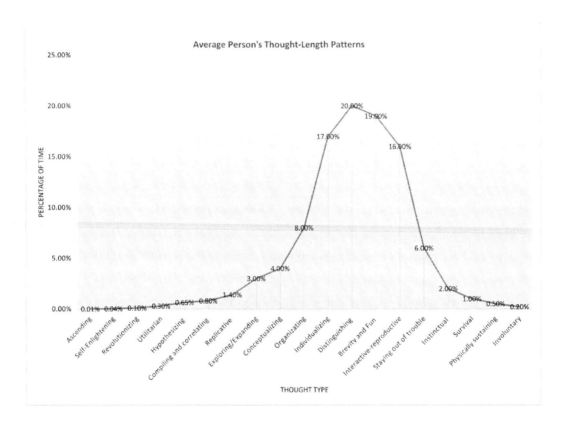

It would not be beneficial for a company to place an engineering team in an open work area with call center people interfacing all around them, in the same way that it would not be productive for a researcher to work at a reception desk where they would be subject to answering phones all the time. When people verbalize what is on their minds, anyone within hearing distance can be synchronized to the thought length of the individuals verbalizing those thoughts. This is why

178

people learn differently when listening versus when reading. The verbal speech-listening transaction adds to the ability to set one's emotional state based on thought length.

When choosing the environment and people to surround you, this thought length from the speech-listening interface is important to consider. The environment must fit your needs for productivity. I have been in working environments where the physical working environment was not conducive to accomplishing the job I was assigned to do. I was expending many work cycles and was busy all day each day, but the work from my assigned task list still went unaccomplished. For one company my job had a few facets, one of which was to design software that was released in support of new products, but others revolved around marketing and customer support. The engineering work for software required longer thought lengths and focus on deeper concepts to achieve any progress, but my phone would ring all day with requests from customers about marketing or product development. Any time my thought length shifted to answering shorter topics during the brief disruption of the phone calls, my ability to shift back to the software development work in between the interruptions would diminish. The work environment and tasks were not conducive to accomplishing the other assigned tasks. This contradiction created a continuous deadlock of my productivity.

Since everyone in our group was plagued by the same work conditions, it made us all unproductive, and it rendered the business overall less effective, even though a comparison between employees showed everyone with similar levels of productivity. In this example, the overall productivity was affected even though individuals were not being penalized. It is important to look at the thought length of the average surroundings. It is not as important to have everyone doing the exact same work or working together on the same tasks as it is to have similar thought lengths in the ambient energy around the worker.

For example, having all project managers work together, even though they may be working on different projects, will be more effective than having the project manager work in the room where a deeper thinking team is working, even on the same project. All the project managers together will support the organization's thought length, which each of them will sustain for the type of work they are doing. If the project manager were side by side with an engineering team, his constant shorter thoughts while performing tasks and his calls to organize aspects of the work would only disrupt the longer thought length required by engineering thought processes. At the same time, the project manager would lose effectiveness in multitasking if they were continuously overhearing longer conceptual thoughts from the project engineers.

Surrounding yourself with like-minded people also requires the adjustment of removing the people who are not like-minded. This would include reducing the influence from others who fit some of these categories: they themselves have plateaued; they exude negative energy; they are frequently on a disruptive thought length; or they are people who do not desire to grow personally.

Environmental Conditions Contribute

Often, things outside of yourself create these plateau conditions. These environmental factors may be addressed by modifying the situation, but they also may be the result of factors that limit your life situation. I have experienced some of these in my life, and I feel that they had an impact on my environment.

Economic Conditions Lead to Larger Trends for Many People

The more productive I have been in my life, the less that economic conditions have affected me, with one exception. For much of my life, as I practiced the life-engineering concepts that I am giving you in this book, my value to my employers was much higher than the average employee. In many cases, I could directly measure my productive contribution to an organization with metrics that displayed 2-3 times that of the average employee in the same performance category and same organization. With my performance metrics at these levels, I had no expectations when difficult economic times arose that I would be in any way considered for downsizing. The one exception occurred later in life when my value as an employee reached a level of compensation that was 2-3 times the cost of a new hire. As you can see if you do the math, my value and my cost had equalized by this point.

This was a very difficult time for me as far as self-image, but as a business leader, the necessity of these decisions and the value to the company were something I understood. This is the largest period of plateau in my life, and reaching past this one has required adjustment in all three of my life cycle areas. Much of this experience, in fact, is why I am sitting here today, reaching for the next phase in my life—the phase of redistribution of lifetime knowledge, instead of the one who implements my own story.

Industry Shifts—People Are Shifting Towards Alternate Products

The nature of markets shows that certain items, products, or services become less relevant than they were in the past. Entire industries have to adjust for this and reinvent themselves at times. In my risk management training sessions, I have often discussed how the largest risk to businesses is caused by growth. This risk has crippled companies on both the up and the down side. If you can't meet growing demand, the market will shift to producers that can. If you do not identify shifts toward negative growth and transfer effort to alternate products that have growing trends, you will be locked in a continuous downsizing and in the negative energy produced by the reduced trend.

With this in mind, note that positioning and aligning your efforts with growth trends is, in my experience, an essential part of your life cycle. If you choose a career or hold employment with a company in a declining industry, you will position yourself with people who are not thinking in a progressive manner. In fact, they will be very accepting of stagnant conditions, and arguably, all persons in that industry are in a constant plateau situation. By the nature of the environment, advancement is limited and continuously decreasing. An example of this in the paper industry, in the early 2000's, I was offered a great position at a check printing company. They were the best remaining company in an industry that was reducing by 10 percent a year. The directive for the job I was offered was to use technology to become more efficient. They had accepted the constant reduction with the expectations that it could never go entirely to zero, so at some point growth would balance out. The mentality of the co-workers was extremely hopeless and negative. Yes, someone needs to ride this product to zero, but the effects on personal productivity were dismal.

Think about this environment in terms of your life cycle. The situation is such that everyone knows that next year you have to increase productivity by 10 percent in order to break even. The people all have the knowledge that reductions will be made every year and that productivity increases will further reduce the number of people, so their primary work objective is in opposition to their—or one of their co-workers'—continued employment. This brings on a mindset of continued defeating efforts, bitterness, or hopelessness within the employees. The nature of humans is that, if you are not growing your social control structure, you are not going to feel empowered or productive.

You Are in Between Identifiable Status Groups

Throughout the stages of your life, as you progress through your perspective lifetimes, social and cognitive limiting factors will create environmental limiting conditions. Both social and cognitive factors have been equally limiting to my progression and have created plateaus for me. In my life, I have spent most of my time either advancing or at a plateau, mostly because I do not accept a regressing feeling for myself. I feel productive when I am advancing, but as soon as my productivity slows down, the feeling that most would associate with plateau for me feels as unacceptable as declining. I would imagine this is why the few declining portions of my life I felt an exceptional feeling of instability.

Earlier I used the example that nothing goes up forever, and no matter how talented a person is at their employment or within their social organization, if they have been elevated in stature this year, they are not going to—nor should they—expect to be elevated next year. The collective of many people who surround you has input into your identifiable status groups. You cannot become more senior in someone else's mind without taking the steps that the majority of people making up the status group expect someone to have taken. An example of this is that if you get a promotion at work where you have a new group of peers, each of which has defined achievement at that level, you will not get another promotion next year based on the previous level of achievement. You will need to distinguish your achievements at the newly promoted level before any higher level of achievement is possible.

Being in between identifiable status groups could also be specific and unique to an individual. If we think back to earlier discussions on human needs, some ascending levels of meeting your personal needs are very identifiable but still unique to each person. Often in life, individuals need something for themselves that limits their ability to internally progress to the next level. Think back to Maslow's Hierarchy of human needs. There are defining points where people have to feel fulfilled in the lower level of human needs prior to being able to work on the next higher level. Sometimes only one thing is missing for people to feel fulfilled at their current level, but it entirely prevents them from even starting to increase thought length at the next level of cognitive activity, which will allow them to start concentrating on the next level of needs.

Unmaintainable Conditions Exist When Something Is Declining and You Have No Control

Many events that are out of our control occur in life, and so do these. Broken relationships, failing health, or just the reoccurrence of negative situations involving others, all affect either social or physical stability. I will not focus on these much here, except to let you know I have not been immune to them, as you will read about extensively in the next chapter on "Thriving at the Low Points of Our Lives."

References

Maslow, A., (1943) A Theory of Human Motivation. Psychological Review, 50(4), 370-96.

Chapter IX

Thriving at the Low Points of Our Lives

When I began to compose this chapter, an emotional influx hit me like a bag of hammers tossed over a fence. Even though I knew exactly what the content would be, and I had already written many of the pages, the moments from my past that I will revisit in this chapter are the hardest to recount. For men in this world, such memories and the feelings they evoke are not supposed to have an effect. We are taught to lock them away and go watch sports, such as football. Doing such manly activities and letting time pass will make it all better. Right? If you are a man for whom that has worked, please come see me and let me know how you did it, because I want to understand where I have gone wrong.

Granted, some of the manly distractions I was advised to pursue actually helped, mostly because they coincidentally set in motion some of the positive events I will tell you about in this chapter. Nevertheless, I have not pulled through the hard times in my life because I am such an exceptional person. I have had more than my fair share of hard times, which proves that I am not exceptional. Had I been exceptional, perhaps I would have learned to avoid at least some of them. However, I have learned how to pull through hard times because I have had practice, and my persistence—at finding the one approach that works after many attempts—has paid off. The approaches that enable people to move past low points in their lives and come out better on the other side are identifiable and reproducible. They can be planned and engineered into your life.

I remember when I was young hearing about adults who were going through very difficult times. The phrase "nervous breakdown" was often thrown around. When people talked about others in such situations, I heard pity, condescension, and even barbs thrown out of a sense of superiority. The tone itself often located the person under the boot heels of society. The social pressure that we should never "be this type of person" and never be susceptible to the condescension of others is programmed into many of our psyches at a young age. Nevertheless, everyone will experience these indignities at some point in their lives. How you handle these situations and how you ultimately emerge from them will depend on how much you know about your own behavior and the inner workings of your mind.

To deny that you could ever suffer a mental collapse, or to think that you are not the weak-minded type of person who risks such a collapse, will land you there quicker than those who understand and address the fragility of their own human existence. The human mind is capable of great things; however, it is also capable of all sorts of collapse. The difference between the president of the United States and a homeless person living under a bridge is all within the realm of the human mind.

Turning Collapse to Triumph

Anyone who is in the midst of a collapse or has suffered from one wants to know how to turn failure into triumph. How can a process of life engineering lift you up from rock bottom to a level that could be envied? To begin such a process, you first have to know the important commonalities in the lives of people who are at their low points. What is happening to them? What are they going through in their minds versus what others see? What social effects are aligning to improve the situation, and what powers of perception does this time afford to the person who is suffering?

Identifying Where You Are

Unless you have previously been at rock bottom, how can you identify where you are? How is this different from just another difficult time you need to work through? Your determination at rock bottom is something that only you can make for yourself. Often you are not aware of it until much later. I would define rock bottom as the decision point at which you make changes that move you forward when the only other alternative is not to continue at all.

Only someone who has been there can fully understand. It comes with the knowledge that you could not have continued to exist had you not made the decision that you made. At the time, you no doubt debated, "Does it matter which way I decide?" In terms of thought process, you shortened your thought capability to the point that involuntary thoughts were almost impossible to sustain. You may or may not have realized that it mattered. Either of those decisions may have seemed irrelevant at the time, but for some reason, you decided to continue and took a step toward a longer thought process, which allowed involuntary functions, like your heart beating, to continue. The ones who made the other decision are the subjects of news columns, long or short, on the front page or in the obituaries. I am sure that you can find them if you look.

The decision that you made defines you from that point on. You now realize that life paths, or directions, are choices—even the choice to be alive—and that our surroundings do not impose them upon us. You made the choice to continue. Whether or not you are still debating if it was worth it, you know that you made the choice. Having made it, you need to have a direction, which includes at least the next few steps to move you to a point where you can come up with your own path.

When you are at such a point, I recommend finding someone you can hide beside for a while, someone who can redirect the focus away from you. Unfortunately, this needs to be someone removed from the situation. It needs to be someone that is neutral and not emotionally involved, as sometimes people involved in the situation are quite vulnerable. This is why people see counselors during these times, and I too would recommend doing that. I recommend taking a personality test so that you can seek out compatible people. The neutral person must understand and be able to guide you in the lengthening of thoughts and support you in achieving self-assessment. As we discussed in the chapter on "Thought-Length Hierarchy," when you are in a lower position in the hierarchy, you will not be able to perceive things from higher levels that enable you to understand the shortened thought-length condition in which you may find yourself.

The Difference Between What You See and What Everyone Else Sees

During these times of distress, people's perception shrinks. They can't see beyond the situation they're in because the state of reduced thought-length has decreased their ability to process and understand what happened during previous periods of longer thought-lengths when they were more balanced. How many times have people talked about the world collapsing around them? This feeling comes from the perceptions shaped by only being able to understand the shorter thoughts and memories in their minds. You will keep circling back to the thoughts in your mind that you can understand, the length that fits your processing capability, and they will correspond to other, similar times in your existence. What fits the same length of thoughts that you can process are 1) thoughts produced under the same emotional state, 2) thoughts from a younger age when you were incapable of longer thoughts, and 3) a combination of lower-level thoughts that may be unrelated. Inside, you are reaching for what you understand from your own perception because that is all you have.

People you were involved with before the onset of your crisis have difficulty relating to your reduced thought-length capability, so they disengage. While their disengagement is mostly subconscious on their parts, it happens just when you want more involvement from them. You see and feel isolated. New people you meet react to you differently than the way you remember people used to react to you in the past when you first met them. Granted, you have become different. You know you feel different, and people treat you differently. As a whole, you start to feel something is wrong with you, which leads to social anxiety and internal conflict, which adds to the social triggers affecting the process.

Other people see the external effects of this internal struggle—the frustration and anger that you have toward yourself. They see someone who has regressed since they last saw you. If you have just met, they see someone who does not fit their expectation of thought-length capability for someone with your status in life. I have observed that no one contacted me in these times of my life. Though I admit that this may have been as much my perception as reality, inside I felt abandoned. Bitterness, frustration, and anger are what people saw from the outside.

I remember the day that I got a call from a friend's mother asking if I would talk to my friend when she was going through a divorce. Since I had been in that situation, she thought I might be able to help, or at least understand, her situation. Excited, I picked up the phone and immediately called this friend with the hope that I could help her feel better in the situation. After two minutes on the phone with her, I felt like I was talking to someone who hated me. I was a man, and the unloading of stored up negative emotion toward men came across as if primarily directed at me. As bad as I felt about the situation, I was unable to speak with her. I

189

realized from this experience what had most likely happened in my own case to foster my perception that I was alone in the hardest times of my life.

In retrospect, this Isolation had benefits as well, as it allowed me to easily exclude from my new life path the toxic environments of the earlier times in my life. Others' responses to your mindset can initiate a progression that will skyrocket you past all of your expectations. At difficult times, I use this motto to motivate me: "I will be silent and out of sight until one day when you notice the castle that I have erected in the shadows of your party." Every time I have had a life-changing situation, I have used this motto. I have taken those opportunities to begin something of epic proportions. Let me teach you how to do this as well.

No One Expects Anything From You

The most powerful thing about these times in people's lives is that "no one expects anything from you, so use that to your advantage." The times that challenge us the most are always a factor of all three components of the life cycle. The situations are overwhelming to us, which affects our mindset, and the people in our lives have not supported—or negatively affect—our cycle. This means that you cannot pick yourself back up into any of these three areas, and others who were previously in this cycle participate significantly in the outcome and are aware of the situation. In fact, one thing that defines the realization of a rock bottom point in your life is that everyone has entirely disengaged and given up on you. This actually becomes the final progression of the situation. In my experience, the change for the better cannot occur without the trigger of the last person giving up on you.

Let's discover how to use this to your advantage. Remember when I said that some of the advice I was given, such as to lock away my feelings and go watch sports, had actually helped? It was

190

because they inadvertently set in motion a path to recovery. For starters, when following the advice helped, it broke the chain of events that had led to the situation and gave me some time to think about and resolve things for myself. However, following such advice did not take full advantage of the situation, which can provide a free pass to build the greatest stage of one's life. When I took the advice, it helped me to resolve the feelings, lose the emotions, and unexceptionally emerge from the situation. Let me give an example from an economic standpoint. When a war mostly destroys a region and then a peaceful period enables the rebuilding of the region's infrastructure, the latest and greatest infrastructure is erected, and the entire area skyrockets to the most modernized level of productivity. It's the same when people rebuild themselves from the ground up. This is especially powerful because no one expects anything from you.

Framework for Rebuilding

Breaking the chain of events that you were previously in is the most important thing to start with. If you were stuck in a situation in which you felt like the bad person, or you were abused or manipulated into doing things that made you feel out of control, or you were overstressed, then simply don't return to that situations. Avoid the people, the places, and the conversations, but do remember that you have a past. Begin with managing your maintenance. When you can effectively manage your maintenance, you can start to assess your diminished cognitive condition and begin to move in a positive direction.

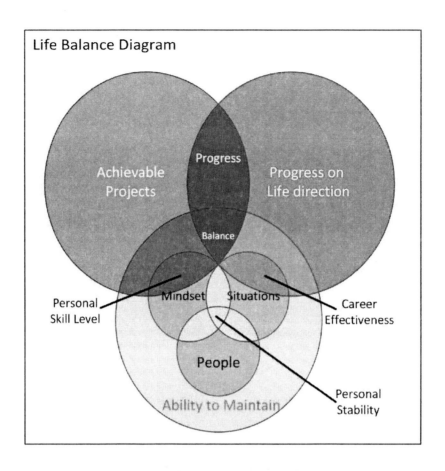

Life Balance Diagram

Achievable Projects

Progress

Progress on Life direction

Balance

Personal Skill Level

Mindset

Situations

Career Effectiveness

People

Personal Stability

Ability to Maintain

The Life Balance Diagram above shows the interaction between the components of the life cycle and the components of life engineering. To begin recovering, we must first find what makes us stable. Using this as an anchor, we can start to move toward a life balance. The first thing to notice about the Life Balance Diagram is that working from bottom to top constitutes a positive progression. The ability to maintain key elements of our lives is central to our core stability. What gives us this ability is the balance of the life cycle. When progressing out of a time of collapse, the first areas in the life cycle to address are the ones that affect your life cycle balance. We will begin by discussing those items and work through the rest of the framework.

Maintenance

If you can't maintain key elements of your life, you can't achieve balance and move forward. When a collapse occurs in your life, you are at a reduced capability because of the persistent triggers that shorten your thought length, and when these triggers persist over a long period, your memories of being any different fade. Meanwhile, you cannot see a way out of the collapse. In fact, you will have some long-term damage, similar to when professional athletes have an injury that sidelines them for an entire season. They often try to return too soon and find they are no longer at the same skill level. In fact, they often reinjure themselves by returning too soon, or they lose confidence that they can reach their past levels. Either of these can end their entire careers. In any case, the first thing that needs to happen with respect to maintenance is to reduce the scope of what you are maintaining to what you can manage. Only you know what you can manage, and it is important to be realistic and honest in making an assessment.

For the purposes of maintenance, you will have to start with the physical and reduce the number of things around you. Humans by nature are pack rats; we gather and store things for which we will never have any use. As I mentioned in an earlier chapter, having frequently moved from one home to another, I have a rule that if I have moved something twice and not touched it, I must sell it or give it away instead of moving it a third time. This has kept my footprint relatively small and has made this aspect of my recovery less difficult. I have seen people return repeatedly to collapse situations because they return to unmaintainable physical surroundings.

Projects

Start by working on your knowledge and skills. If you don't have the ability to think in a stable manner about your life, then the best thing to do is to start doing something that will lead you in a positive direction. At this point, I will not tell you to start the plan of your life path all over again. Yes, that will come, and you will naturally want to pull it together when you are ready. For now, we can start with something that guides you in a direction that matches the ability of your thought lengths to process. In my earlier example of the advice to hide emotional dysfunction and go watch sports such as football, the outcome should naturally be that the individual builds an exceptional knowledge of football. Whatever you turn to for escape at this stage imprints on your mind because of your diminished cognitive capability, much like memories, skills, and fears from childhood imprint on your personality. You will find people all the time who possess extreme, almost obsessive, knowledge of subjects like football, religion, or any other area that seems out of place, and if you look at their past, you can find an instance when they rebuilt from a collapse just by losing themselves in this chosen activity.

Since this devotion to a particular activity is a natural response after a collapse, it will help you to be proactive when choosing the activity. To do this, I want you to make two lists: a list of things that you are good at and a list of things that you enjoy. Then make a third list of just the items that are in both of the first two lists. If the third list needs refinement, determine which of its items will best help you sustain yourself. Ask yourself which of the items might lead to making money. This last question could affect the rest of your life. You have been triggered into a childlike state in which you can learn in an exceptional way. Take advantage of it.

The next step is to "get up and show up." Keep yourself busy by working from your list. Make starting work and looking prepared your top priority each day.

Direction

Once you make starting the work a habit (remember, habits take about thirty days to form), be open to seeking direction. The euphoric moments and the ways that society comes together for the benefit of all can become a bridge toward making the next phase of your life the best it can be. Look for something to spark your enthusiasm.

If you are carrying your momentum forward into the next phase because you are at a point of collapse, then planning your direction and life path may not be the best use of your time at this point. But after a few months of building your knowledge and skills, the next chapter, "Determining a Path," will further guide you in planning the direction you take during your recovery.

How to Balance Your Life

Shifting back to the Life Balance Diagram, we see that the maintenance portion, which is the most foundational, contains the life cycle aspects of people, situation, and mindset. Balancing this portion of your life will enable you to grow. You can obtain balance and feel in control of your life by making it maintainable for your current state, regardless of your current level or capabilities. In the most vulnerable portion of my life, I sat on the floor and sorted through piles and piles of possessions, which I had previously spent valuable resources to purchase. But at that point, I viewed them as junk. Until I could throw out enough items to make sense of them, and until I could reduce the scope to what fit within my then-limited mental capability and thought lengths, I could never move forward. All three areas of your life cycle need to be balanced within in this new limited scope.

People

The people portion of the life cycle is always the hardest to adjust and is going to be difficult to change for many of us. For me, breaking codependent patterns has been the most liberating change—when I was finally able to do so.

One day, I tried to assess what value I had in a particular person's life and why the person continually wanted to engage with me, even though the person seemed to dislike me a great deal. I came to realize that we had different expectations about each other's role in the relationship. The other person and I saw my contribution to the relationship differently. I assumed that somehow the other person must derive some value from my actions with respect to the relationship. In fact, the person didn't want me to do what I kept doing, which irritated them. They just wanted me to be there, to be the thing they wanted me to be. While pondering this, I found that in most of my relationships, past and present, I could categorize this same sort of dynamic. People view others as either having something or being something. I classify these people into two types: "has a" and "is a."

A company can want a particular employee because that person has a (has a) master's degree or because he or she is very experienced (is a) at the particular skill set required to accomplish the work. A woman may be interested in a man with a (has a) successful, high-paying business or someone who is an expert attorney (is a). One can be interested in someone of the opposite sex because they are attractive (has a) or because of their virtues (is a).

Although these relationship categories affect many other dynamics, this is a good tool to use to evaluate the people aspect of your life cycle when at a point of collapse in your life. Look at the people who have influential roles in your life. Think about these relationships from the

196

perspective of what type of person they are to you. Are they in your life because they have (has a) something that benefits you or that is important to you, or does the relationship continue because they are (is a) something you desire in your life. Now think about the same relationship, but reverse the role. Does the other person stay around you because you have something to offer them and because of something they need (has a), or are they interested in your virtues (is a)?

As you evaluate your relationships through these lenses, you will probably find that most of your relationships are with people who want something from you. Thus, they view you as a "has a," and you view them in the opposite light, as an "is a." How did I know this? It's because those who are reading this book want to better themselves. These types of people usually are in a collapse situation only because they are caretakers who find themselves overwhelmed by too many relationships in which they are the provider of resources or energy. People flock to the caretaker to get resources, but the caretaker usually enters this role with people from whom they desire a particular personality trait (is a) in return. If you were a person in collapse looking for the next "has a" provider, self-improvement books for that personality would have content different from anything you will find in this book.

What does this evaluation do for you? In my case, just going through the process of identifying how people viewed me—versus my perception of why I was in those relationships—made it clear how each relationship would continue. Some relationships I built upon when possible, while others I gradually eased out of or stopped actively pursuing, and still others I severed altogether. Since I was always in a provider role, though, I found that all the people who viewed me as a "has a" had removed themselves anyway during my periods of collapse because I no longer had what interested them. The decision in these cases becomes whom to let back in when you eventually become capable of caretaker activities again, because these people always come back as soon as you are able to resume being their "has a" person.

Situations

Your current situation will affect your ability to recover after a collapse. I have always liked the song, "Name," by the Goo-Goo Dolls. When I found myself in a situation of collapse, I wanted someone to mask me, someone to "hide beside," as the song's lyrics say. This did not need to be another caretaker person because I had reduced the things to maintain in my life to the point at which I was able to sustain what I had, but I needed someone to mask me from the world when it came to social interactions and personality. Though this crosses into the people section, the need for someone to be a situational masker is something I think belongs in this section. People will always have a situational masker, and the selection of this individual could be extremely beneficial or detrimental depending on the personality of the person.

When choosing your situational masker, I recommend that you follow these guidelines:

1) Do not choose someone of the opposite sex to whom you are attracted—or whom you attract—because if you choose someone such as this, the relationship can often turn to romantic involvement, which people in this situation are not ready for.

2) Do not use your spouse or someone with whom you are already in a romantic relationship.

3) Do not get financially involved with this person.

4) Do not live with this person.

5) Do not try to attach to their social media network, at least until you no longer need them as a situational masker.

198

6) Have a pact that, if you behave badly, such as inflicting any physical or emotional trauma, you will release them from this role and leave them alone afterwards.

To be a great situational masker, the person must be able to be neutral and objective in social situations. Many relationships will begin to change in this period, and the person recovering from collapse will become entirely emotionally dependent on the masker. This is natural for a time. A good masker, however, will know how and when to gracefully remove this dependency. These will become the most long-lasting relationships you will both form, but they can also become a disaster if one person is much more dependent on the other emotionally, and the dependence becomes a source of control.

Therefore, whether you choose a situational masker or not, you will next need to start to improve the situation aspect of your life cycle. How do you accomplish this? First, know that your emotional state will slip toward the shorter thought-length conditions quicker than the average person's will, and they will improve more slowly as well. Others will see this and relate it subconsciously to your emotional maturity. The situations you choose at these times will define you for a good while, but some—or many—of them will not be the best decisions in retrospect.

Don't beat yourself up too much over this. Remember how we talked about no one expecting anything from you at these times. From experience, we know that people in a condition of reduced emotional maturity make bad decisions. You are going to make some choices that seem entirely reasonable during these times that won't hold up later upon reflection. What matters is your current set of attributes and capabilities relative to what you had before. So let's start working on those.

Put yourself in situations in which you can add value to your post-recovery self. Start to build something that takes some time. I recommend retooling your mind and finding a subject to study. Not only will others see this, but it will become a way for you to define yourself and build self-confidence. Persistence is the key to continuing, but your recurring selection of situation has the biggest impact on your ability to be persistent and to keep returning to the activities you have chosen to build your self-confidence. To do this, knowing yourself is once again important. You need to know which emotional states leave you most vulnerable and which are your most productive, and you have to determine how to react in each emotional state in a beneficial manner. I will talk about mapping your emotional states more in the chapter, "Reevaluating Your Path," but it is appropriate to mention here. For each identifiable state you find yourself in, know what decision you can make to place yourself in a positive situation.

If you get upset and are often out of control, and you are someone for whom eating something cold will help calm you. Then get yourself a punching bag and keep a pint of ice cream in the garage. Allow yourself to lose control in that environment while enjoying your favorite flavor of Ben and Jerry's. This begins the system of "Enjoying the Process," which is also the title of chapter twelve of this book. Let yourself get mad. Enjoy eating your ice cream and smashing your fists into whatever you imagine the bag to be. For now, it is especially important after collapse to know your emotional states and to determine a set of situations to place yourself in for each state. This includes having a vice, while also remaining in a controllable environment.

The second step in improving the situational aspect of your life cycle is to add a control to your emotional states and vices. For this, you need to know which types of activities or sets of surroundings take you from one undesired mindset to another, more beneficial one. If you use drinking alcohol to make you happy and if it works for a while, but if you then want to fight when you get drunk, then you go from being sad to going to jail—and entering whatever mindset

200

accompanies the situation of being in jail. Another selection may be to sit in a crowded coffee shop, which also has the same effect of making you less sad, but it places you in a social mindset. Once again, knowing yourself and a few things about what gets you to a better place within yourself is the key.

Mindset

I used the example earlier of how, after a collapse, people told me to watch sports and not think about my predicament. During that time, the first few relationships I turned to with situational maskers were short-lived because they were entirely centered around sports and drinking. I could very easily have followed a path while hiding beside that personality, and today I would be the best fantasy football and beer pong player in my league. This is because of what I mentioned earlier: what we turn to at times of reduced thought length is akin to what educates us during early childhood development. It becomes imprinted on us, as if a subconscious thought, because it was digested and stored in portions of the brain that we developed as children. These memories are accessible more often because we do not have to use higher-level cognition or longer thought-length patterns to access them and especially because we access these thoughts at extremely emotional times.

This is why situation is so vital to mindset during these points of collapse in your life. It has a larger effect on mindset during extremely emotional periods than it does during more stable times in your life. Just making a decision to place yourself in an environment where people are constantly learning or developing in any way will benefit you immensely. You will absorb what is going on around you and subconsciously adapt it to your mindset. Determining your situation best affects your mindset. Go sit at a university library, a crowded gymnasium, or a community center on a regular basis, and you will eventually catch up on whatever is happening. Your mindset will match your surroundings.

Think about what will help you in general and especially in this weakened cognitive condition. First, before you start to think that you are incapable of a particular activity or that you lack certain abilities, know that a person is never just naturally good—or not good—at something. People have varying levels of interest and focus, which affects their abilities. If you are not interested in something, and if you spend less time and effort on it than others have, then naturally you will not be as practiced at it as they are. If you think about life in these terms, you can do anything you have the interest to do. I have met people who had obvious ADHD and who spent their lives trying to change their tendency. In order to maintain self-control, they medicated and constantly worked harder than others did. Other people with the same tendencies picked up a ball and repeatedly fetched, threw, passed, and hit relentlessly. With the same predisposition in two different people, one an exceptional accountant who continuously controlled their natural disposition and the other a professional baseball player who embraced it, each of these persons can be successful, work hard, and have passion to become the top in their field.

When people are in a period of collapse, their perception of the situation from the inside is more powerful than it appears from others watching from the outside. Although addressing and changing your mindset for your own benefit is essential, be careful that you are not sculpting your mindset to what you perceive others want. Let your situational masker help you by telling you what things look like on the outside, but not so much that you change to match what others want. This will most likely give you a sounding board to show you the things to which you overreact more often than not.

Collapse That Made an Underachiever

In my own life, I have been in a collapse situation a few times, so this is the most embarrassing chapter to write. I wrote several versions of what you are reading, and this is a calmer version in which I have resolved to describe only what is appropriate to the topic.

The first time I was in collapse was when I was so young that no one of that age should have to experience such an event. I was most likely an undiagnosed autistic child with tendencies to see more of the logic and less of the emotional and social aspects in many situations. My childhood environment was very illogical, placing many situations outside of my comfort level. My memories include a sense of confusion when I was directly confronted with illogical situations, which caused me to disengage and to watch the sequence of events from a distance. This distance was not always physical, but often I simply regressed inside myself and detached some portion of my thought process from my conscious self. I have often wondered what this looked like from the outside, but from watching the behavior of my son, I believe I have seen glimpses of it.

This separation into two fragments was a large portion of my identity, as the local version was subjected to the illogical, superstition-filled surroundings in which I often found myself. As a part of their religious practices, the adults around me praised the practice of "accepting without proof." I was required to accompany members of such groups on sidewalk preaching events during which predictions of the end of the world were shouted into a sarcastic, ridiculing crowd of random onlookers. Given that I was a child who struggled to interpret social cues, my exposure to crowds of people who were displaying negative body language was confusing to me on all levels.

Though I attended public school, I was instructed and was expected to discount any thoughts or ideas the school taught if they were in any way opposed to the religion's unsubstantiated beliefs. These clashes between education and belief involved lectures of reprisal when books sent home from school were perceived to be opposed to religious views. Other times, technology was deemed a source of anti-religious influence, which required its removal from our home. In general, my home environment was full of superstitious practices and promoted illogical conclusions.

I was about eight years old when I made the first decision that defined my own personal path and that led me to the first instance of collapse in my life. I came to the clear decision that many of the superstitious, illogical conclusions I had encountered required me to explore alternative opinions. At some point after making this decision, when it had become a practice of mine to find any alternative explanation for each illogical explanation, I was told just to accept. The controlling structure, which mostly consisted of my father, seemed to have resolved that I should be bent back to the family's belief structure at any cost. The level of disparate resolve to regain control over the misguided child nearly led to them openly labeling me as the target of demonic possession. Several times, I would wake up to séance-type rituals involving oil, holy water, ashes, and other items. Other times I was paraded in front of live TV broadcasts during which ministers attempted to perform exorcist rituals while proclaiming they cast out the demons of teenage rebellion.

This dynamic, caused by the conflict between the real and the superstitious, began my pattern of avoiding and separating from control. The areas that were the most defined by this illogical to logical separation were also the largest. This was most widely defined by the way that the religious group contrasted with my public education, so I disengaged from both. My disengagement from these two institutions, interestingly enough, was punishable on both sides.
204

We were supposed to get good grades at school, but were not supposed to just accept what the school told us. In becoming an underachiever, I made it more of a goal to have the lowest grades possible than simply to give up trying. The underachiever status was easier to accept than the continued conflict and the whispers of teachers about how my disconnected behavior prevented me from focusing. If I openly showed that I did not care, they seemed to leave me alone.

This collapse resulted in my inability to function, which led to a state of self-miniaturization on all levels of my development and a general acceptance of my inadequacy. The continued pressure to conform, which the extreme and illogical rituals and behaviors helped to fuel, brought me to such a detached point that I did not care whether I lived or not. This feeling of indifference to life was all that actually resonated with my family's supernatural fixations. The extreme fixation of their beliefs emphasized the morbid side of Christ's crucifixion death in a way that idolized martyrdom. Finally, when I snapped, I had figured out my place within my family. If I died doing something that they could at least live with, if not be proud of, then they could use it to fit into their purpose in some way, even if only as a warning to others. I left every day with no thought of returning, looked for reckless activities that would place me on the edge, and freed my mind of the worries of death and destruction that gripped my family's belief structure.

When this snap occurred in me, I discovered that I felt alive for the first time in my life. I felt like I could accomplish anything. I felt immortal, and nothing held me back anymore. This process, though something that no child should have to live through, started me on the path to what I am today.

Navy Low Point Turned to Triumph

I experienced another collapse following some of the great success I had in the Navy that I discussed in earlier chapters. I was aboard my duty-station ship, the USS South Carolina, where I had been serving for some time as a nuclear engineer. This collapse occurred when an exam structure that we needed to pass to maintain qualification introduced an environment similar to what I endured as a child, one in which my logical nature chafed against anything illogical. At this time in my life, I had not yet determined that my conflict with anything illogical was the cause of my collapse. I entered another state of underachieving, and I began to just perform my tasks, finding ways to enjoy them and counting down the days until my tour was over.

In short, the progression of my process of enjoyment set in motion a series of events that gave me the opportunity to take on the monumental task of qualifying to be the supervisor for the entire nuclear plant. This would never have been the case if this entire process had not become known. At that time, I was at the rank of E-5, and we had several E-7 personnel aboard who were not able to qualify for this level of station. After a several month effort and board examination, I became the youngest and only E-5 to hold this qualification at that time (for Surface fleet) in the entire Navy.

Ultimate Collapse of Self

As I write this section, I feel like I am looking into a mirror more than ever. I am living proof of the fact that anyone can reach any possible emotional and cognitive state. Being able to link the various states in which I have personally been has enabled me to determine the hierarchy of thought length and the perception of self versus time lived, as explained in the chapter, "An Eternity Followed by Twelve Lifetimes." People make individual journeys through life, and how they progress and navigate the various times when they find themselves at a breaking point becomes the largest part of their character. Now I am going to tell you about my most severe collapse, the point at which I hit rock bottom, which has defined me ever since.

I had been married for five years, and my first and only son was on the way. I had resisted having children for this long in my marriage because of the sense of disconnectedness I had retained from my childhood and because of the feeling that something was not quite right in my marriage. My wife had finished school after five years of hard work, and now we were reversing roles. My wife took a job in her field, while I enrolled in a university to begin my college education. Since my wife was now the breadwinner, she wanted to make the decisions and wanted us to have a child. I decided to overcome my fear and agreed to enter this new phase of my life.

Since my work had required me to travel often, our relationship had mostly been limited to the weekends up to that point. It soon became apparent that this was really the first time we had lived together, other than the weekends when I had returned home from traveling. We had such different biorhythms that we were unable to keep any matching schedule whatsoever. By her sixth month of pregnancy, my wife was extremely uneasy. She had taken to staying in the other room of our small apartment, and she did not want to interact with me at all. She was being treated by doctors and counselors who assured me that it was just an extreme reaction from postpartum depression, which had begun prior to birth. The prognosis was that they were doing everything possible to help and that it would "soon pass."

When my son entered the world, he was a few weeks early and had jaundice that required him to be under a lamp for the first few weeks. During this time, my wife's family visited, and we were all so involved, everything seeming happy. Her symptoms of depression seemed to have passed. Right after her family's departure, like watching smoke clear from a gunfight and looking around to determine who was still standing, my wife snapped back to her pre-birth behavior. Once again, I was informed that her doctors said it would pass, but she kept me at arm's length from any involvement with her or the counseling sessions. I did not question her, and I gave her the space she needed. Even when I saw the medications that she was being prescribed, I did not ask for an explanation for them.

Staying home with my son, taking college courses, and training for the next season of the Colorado Strongman Competition put me in a very structured routine. I chose a gym that had day care, and we hired a responsible teenager to watch my son while I was at school. I gave my wife all the room she needed to get better, but the return of the person I had known never happened.

My son was eleven months old, and I realized that he would be raised in a broken home. My entire childhood experience came crashing down on me. I fell apart. I barely ate or drank any liquid for several months. Even though I was at the healthiest point in my life and had a 4.0 GPA after nearly two years of college, extreme triggers of this sort had reduced me to a state in which I did not think to take care of myself. During a two-month period, I worked so hard I injured my back, and I had neglected my dietary needs so severely that I got a bladder infection from the excessive amounts of performance supplements I was taking for my training while not drinking enough liquids to pass them.

The bladder infection was so severe that it turned into a kidney infection, which I left untreated other than to dehydrate further with alcohol. I ended up in the hospital with a case of septicemia. If you are not familiar with this condition, it is an infection carried through the bloodstream, which until the modern era was always fatal. It is the ultimate cause of death when a person dies from gangrene. I spent two weeks in the hospital, the first week entirely incoherent. When I regained my senses during the second week of recovery, I wondered why nobody had come to visit. As cell phones were not prevalent in everyday life back then, I was unable to get a hold of my wife and missed my son insanely. On the ride home, I asked my wife why she had not come to visit me or brought our son to visit, and her response was not fully digestible for years to come. She replied, "They told me not to expect you to live, and I realized I was free." We went home mostly in silence, and she left me on the couch with my son and went out the door.

It became obvious over the next few months that two things were going to define my existence from then on. The first was that I had a chronic fatigue condition from the septicemia, which had left me with nerve damage to the point that, if I stood up for more than a few minutes and did not sit back down, I would get lightheaded and pass out. At first, the doctors told me this condition would not last too long, but then after six months, I still could not stand for more than a few minutes. The second thing that would define my existence was that my wife had completely moved on in her mind, and the "freedom feeling" she had described seemed to be the notion that the person to whom she was previously married had died in the hospital. I was not that person. This meant she allowed herself to openly date other men while I stayed at home, incapable of even standing. Because I had been in the mindset that her postpartum depression would subside over time, I remained in a state of denial for a long time, thinking that even the open dating was something that would pass. I pretended that nothing was wrong and just waited. I focused all my energy on our son, whom I raised by lying on the floor at his level until I could stand up. Some time passed before I returned to school, and then both school and my son became my entire world.

Holding on to a state of denial put me back into the separation of real and unreal that I'd had when I was younger. This disbelief of reality and continued denial left me in a condition like that of a child believing in magic or mystical figures, with reality and fantasy no longer distinguishable. The disconnection of my childhood conflict with my father, which at that point in my life had never been addressed, heightened this confusion. Though I had moved on from the programming of superstition and religious beliefs that science had disproven, which was given to me during childhood, I had never tried to resolve them in my own mind.

Here was another situation in which the only influences I had in my life were inducing the same levels of confusion that I had so violently resisted, first when I was a child and then again in the military. In any case, the situation continued for some time, as my wife verbally reassured me that our family was intact and that everything was fine, all while continuing to openly date other men. This started a trend that I could not resolve for years to come. The only explanation I could fathom for the difference between what I was being told was happening and what I was seeing with my own eyes was that one of us had to be stone crazy. No one makes up what I was being told unless they are crazy—or unless I was crazy for so wrongly seeing what was in front of me.

The illusion that created this situation continued, as each time I questioned what I saw or brought up the contradictions, the pushback to keep up this surreal facade got stronger—to the point that my sanity was directly under attack. Since I was on a scholarship funded by the VA, I had an assigned counselor I could speak with, and the fact that I was in counseling became the reason that I was the one who was crazy. The more I questioned my wife's behavior, the more drastic the counterattacks on my sanity became. Worse, because my family was at such a remote distance and because my medical problems limited my movement, I did not have anyone else to turn to. The only companion I had in my life was the person I had married, and she was not making any sense and appeared not even to resemble the person I had once known.

210

Her meltdowns would switch from fits of tears, complete with admissions of how she could not control the stories she had fabricated about people around her, to fits of shaking fear, laden with explanations of how I had done something to hurt her or my son, all while he and I watched as she cowered in a corner or locked herself in a room. As I described earlier, my primary predetermined flaw is to always question myself, so this was difficult for me. I became unsure if I was able to address what I saw and even questioned my sanity. Confusion, isolation from others, and continued input from someone I thought I could trust put me in a state of such shortened thoughts that I was unable to think.

It started when my wife filed for divorce, and then under threat of divorce, I was informed of the conditions for reconciliation, which appeared to be an incriminating list of actions. These included admitting that I was entirely at fault for our problems and getting treatment for mental disorders that my best friend had determined I had. The treatment was outlined for me, as was reapplying to the VA for an increase in my disability compensation. I began working through each step of the treatment with the threat of divorce hanging over me if I were to step out of line in any way or disagree with her incriminating requirements.

The true nature of her intentions became apparent one day when I saw what happened just out of sight of our home. There was no plan for reconciliation. The sequence of events that was unleashed when I confronted the situation unveiled the true purpose of the incriminating requests. With calculated precision, I was thrown into the "strike first and hard" situation that ruthless divorce attorneys typically recommend to clients. The fact that I looked like a bodybuilding monster, even though I only had the physical capability to craw like a baby, made me seem like a fun target. Anyone would believe I was a threat by looking at me, but I could easily be overpowered because of my fatigued state. The next few months, many of which were spent not seeing my son at all, were the darkest of my life.

211

Recreating Myself

Since there was nothing left of the person I had been, I needed to recreate and rebuild the person I was going to be for the rest of my life. I have spent some time in recent years watching and helping others through these types of life collapses. The one thing that I have repeatedly watched with great interest and have tried to understand is the childlike regression and reduced emotional maturity that people experience in these circumstances, which is typically followed by exceptional growth in some areas afterwards. The most effective religious leaders in my memory had turned to religion in the course of similar life events, and they were exceptionally effective at communicating how these events had brought them to their religious convictions.

In my own experience, I had continued my college career during this time and became exceptionally effective in pursuing my studies. In learning of people with other talents, I found similar stories of rags to riches following such collapses. The similarities in how people had gained exceptional skills at these times led me to consider the skills that I had gained at these times in my life. When I had emerged slightly beyond the low point, I found myself ensnared in the dilemma of choosing between the labels of mental illness and government fraud. At the same time, I was laboring under diminished mental capacity, which allowed me to wonder which of these labels was accurate. I opted to try to understand my own inner workings because I wanted to understand how I had gotten into this condition.

During my period of rebuilding, I pursued my education in computer science and business, but I also continued to visit my VA counselor with more regularity, adding the third tier of self-awareness to my rebuilding skills. The latest person who had injected poison into the people aspect of my life cycle did so proclaiming religious motivations. When she determined on a religious basis that I could be dehumanized enough to justify removal from my own child's life, I was unable to offer a defense within the bounds of that same religious structure. Once again, this created such confusion in me about the purpose of religion that I avoided seeking solutions in a religious context.

I have spent some time comparing my explanation of self with the explanation of self that others have gained from similar collapses. While others often base their definition of self on religious conviction, mine derived from the logical influences to which I was exposed during this rebuilding phase. Some people, I observed, turned to a social network for comfort, and they ended up becoming a master at understanding and influencing people in a virtual space. Others turned to work in the business world, with great success in their fields. In each instance, the person's expertise correlated with what they immersed themselves in at times of suffering. When I looked at this pattern of suffering and emergence, I recognized that the correlation could be explained by the nature of the person's condition and by the psychological effect of what had happened to land them there. I will talk more about recreating oneself and recovery in the chapter, "Rebuilding After Low Points."

Low Point Changes Life Forever

At this point, you might think that I couldn't possibly have had more major ups or downs in my life, but I will now describe the next phase of my life, which changed my life forever.

After four years of health struggles following my collapse, I met, dated, and later married a beautiful woman with three children of her own. The joining of our families presented challenges because my son, who had been diagnosed with autism spectrum disorders, was very different in speed and biorhythm from my new wife's children, especially the one closest to his age. Over the next few years of integrating these children, I gained a lot of insight into both my son's condition and my own similar condition, with which I have struggled my entire life.

The fast-paced daily routine of our household caused my son to shut down repeatedly. I also overreacted to the stimulus emotionally, which did not help. Although my son only lived with us for the summer and most weekends, the situation was aggravated by a war that developed between my wife and my son's mother. A third woman in the scenario made it even worse: my wife's ex-husband had remarried, and his new wife and my son's mother had joined forces in an effort that still baffles me to this day. The dynamic with my son's mother reached the point that she had learned how to make me question myself and my role in nearly every situation involving my son, so my new wife took it upon herself to shield me from this by handling all communications regarding my son.

At some point, both the integration of our family and the continued struggle with my ex-wife caused a breakdown in which my son and my new wife were no longer able to live in the same house. A problem that I had tried to ignore and never resolved had come back to precipitate yet another life-altering change. As the second summer of the full family living together approached, my new wife and her mother, who had moved in with us, determined that they could not handle my son living with us for the coming summer. I felt trapped, mentally disabled, and thus unable to cope with the situation, so I decided that my son and I would move out of my new family's home.

As you might imagine, there was a final, climactic event with much leading up to it, that proceeded the event which I will tell you about now. At age thirty-seven, I learned that I possessed genetic traits that had led to several early deaths in recent generations of my family. I had just returned from a two-week vacation with my son across the western United States to close out the summer. The first morning back, as I prepared for work, the weight of everything I had put off for the summer came crashing down on me. What I assessed to be anxiety began to present, which prompted me to ask my supervisor if I could work from home that day. The discomfort persisted and then worsened as the day went on. By dinnertime, the problem was extreme, and a phone call with my brother prompted me to realize that I could not hold the phone to my ear with my left arm.

I checked myself in to a hospital, and after several hours of examining me for chest pain, the doctors decided to perform a more decisive nuclear test. To the dismay of everyone including the doctors, they found I was having a heart attack.

When the End Is Defined

After several cycles of reduced capacity followed by ever higher, more successful and triumphant rebounds, the overall effect of these cycles had taken their toll. My persistent nature had only served to keep me circling the wagons around a larger area with each lap. For the first time in my life, I had to reassess the excesses in my behavior. I needed to reset my life cycle to a manageable level. How to do this was somewhat of a new task for me.

Recall the idea of the last perspective lifetime that I discussed in the chapter "An Eternity Followed by Twelve Lifetimes." I define it as the time between when a person learns that the end is imminent and when they actually pass from this Earth. Few of us have the opportunity to experience the last perspective lifetime and then live beyond it. It is like being over the edge and back when doctors tell you that you are one of those people who simply drew the genetic short straw—that medications can minimize the risk of a catastrophic even reoccurring, but that they cannot guarantee the effectiveness of the medications—and then you then live on despite that.

Knowing that medical treatment was keeping me alive and that I would have to anticipate and accept this uncertainty for the rest of my life, I started to grow a new awareness. As one teeters between the eleventh and twelfth lifetimes, every event can change from, "This new situation could begin the end," to tipping you into the twelfth lifetime. Then you come back to, "OK, I have some more time," which lets you go back to the eleventh lifetime. For me, this has provided the gift of productivity and the desire to explore the reasons and driving forces in life.

Recovery and Life Reset

Recovery from my heart attack differed from my recovery from the septicemia nearly a decade before. Recovery from my heart attack came not only with the realization that I had certain physical limitations but also that those limitations could define the end. I was taking a number of different medications, each of which had side effects that limited my performance. I had to admit that I was no longer able to perform for endless hours or to be the most persistent, hardest worker. I needed to find a way to remake myself once again. It was back to the drawing board, but this time armed with the knowledge that I had accumulated in the course of an action-packed lifetime. With the combined knowledge that I had amassed from my university education, life experience, and the help I received from some great experts on how to market and position myself, I set out to change my life by engineering my life path.

Determining the Practice That Leads to Success

As I have emphasized when describing my most exceptional successes, some components of engineering the practice of success stand out. The first is determining your path. In this determination, I have found that, when I set goals and accomplished them, the act of accomplishing the goal actually caused more disruption than if I had not set a goal. The path is always there, and it does not have an ending point the way a goal-oriented approach does. This leads to the second practice that stands out and that determines success, which is to aim beyond where you are. When we define the next step beyond the current task, we provide urgency for and validate the current task. Lastly and equally important, we need to enjoy the process that continually returns us to the task.

Struggling for a Purpose

For a few years after my heart attack, my primary life path involved reconnecting with my son and releasing the feeling of failure that came with letting go of my second family. I sensed that serious damage had been done to my son—and to his relationship with adults in general. Every weekend, we would spend as much time as possible traveling through the mountains, snowboarding, riding motorcycles, boating, and many other activities. During this time, he was reaching the latter part of his sixth perspective lifetime, and I could see him building the lists of things that he liked and disliked and developing a desire to make his own decisions. At the same time that he wanted to make his own decisions, his ability to see the repercussions of those decisions beyond their immediate achievable results was very limited.

Hardest Decision of My Life

Something that has confused me to no end is that when some people end an intimate relationship, they find it necessary to do harm to their previous partner's new relationships. My relationships with both my first and second wives became wars, followed by truces, followed by what appeared to be friendships on some level. In each case, my subsequent relationships became targets of attack.

Conflict and stress were a large part of what had led to my heart attack. I knew that my physical limitations would not just go away and that I would have to live the rest of my life thinking about my health and safety. Therefore, I knew that I had to remove these negative influences from my life entirely. I took the approach of being brutally honest in telling the first ex-wife that I had spent, by that point, more than $80,000 on legal fees, which could have paid for our son's entire college education. Based on experience with my other children, I knew that one estranged parent could make decisions for their child that is hurtful to the other estranged parent, so I specifically asked that we not go down that road.

Somehow, my attempt to avoid that road contributed to a wrong turn onto that very road. Open communications led to direct requests followed by demands for exactly what I had asked not to happen. At the end of my son's fourth grade year, I moved a few miles away from the school he attended, since it allowed to be more involved in his day-to-day activities. In doing so, I triggered a violent attempt to eliminate my increased involvement in his life. Over the summer between
218

his fourth and fifth grade, my son decided that he needed to move to a special school where, in his view, they would not require him to do all the reading, writing, and math that he disliked at his current school. As his father, I resisted this decision. He felt so strongly about it, however, that he became convinced that I wanted to keep him from doing what he wanted. My resistance was, in fact, an attempt to reset his conditioning, an attempt that admittedly came several months late.

A court order had been in place for a few years that mandated that my son could not move to another school without an explicit order from the court or the agreement of both parents. At that point, I was at odds with the desires of a ten-year-old. It also appeared as if my ex-wife's goal was to make me spend as much money as possible—and as if she endeavored to influence my son to make any decision possible that would remove me from his life. Apparently, I had opened up Pandora's Box by explaining my concerns about our son reaching the age at which children become more influenceable. My desire that neither parent should use him to make decisions that would cut the other parent out only seemed to fuel the fire with ideas of what to do to cut me out further.

With a heavy heart and after much deliberation, I decided that it was time to let my son grow up, even though it was still a bit early. I was stuck between being the bad guy to my son and being the absent father, with increasingly no middle ground. To this day, I continue to debate whether I made the correct decision; however, knowing the consequences, I decided to let my son change schools. Allowing him to go to the new school sent ripples through every aspect of my life. The move limited my ability to have him for weekday evenings, which affected the number of overnight stays at each home. This turned me into a human slot machine, not to mention the effect on my son.

As this was going on, I began a new job in which I was assigned to create a team for my employer and develop a new market. For the first year of the job, I had to address eight motions in court related to my family difficulties. My employer's legal team became involved in the case, and I incurred $10,000 in debt above the legal fees, which I was able to cover out of pocket. I could not maintain the environment that I was in because of unforeseen outside influences, but resetting to a manageable level required a lot more than I originally expected. The company I worked for provided options for intercity transfers, and I decided to obtain one. I needed to reset the people poison in my life, so I chose the available city farthest from Denver, which was in Florida.

The transfer gave me the ability to start undoing the disastrous financial situation I had gotten into over the last two years, but something else inadvertently happened. I found that the life path that I had followed for a long time—the path that had set me toward achieving several college degrees, purchasing large homes, and moving up in the business world—was no longer relevant. I was in such a struggle to stay in my son's life that my focus became about that. Though I did not realize it at the time, I had inadvertently made preventing my son from being taken away the goal that I was working toward. Though it seemed like a path that would be there for the rest of my life, the change in my health, which I now saw would be fatal to me if uncorrected, made it become a goal I disregarded.

Lost Direction and Purpose

I had formulated the goal as achieving an eminence in my career that would prevent my son from being taken away from me. I had spent eleven years trying to get over someone's attempt to label me and destroy my value of self. I never achieved the goal, but due to the circumstances, I passed it by and rendered it invalid. On many levels, it felt like a failure because I had pulled away from something that I couldn't resolve. I knew that I had to reconcile myself with what I

220

had done in order to have any kind of life whatsoever. If my son was to have a father at all, I would need to be there when he's older, not kill myself with something that was poisoning me over time.

The main reason I tell people not to set goals is what happened to me next. With no path whatsoever, I sat all day and looked at my list of tasks and workload with no incentive to pick up the next thing on the pile. I had credentials, houses, and enough personal cash flow to rival a solid small business. I had great opportunities at work with prospects for advancement, but my self-directed work to move forward stopped. Granted, I could pick up the phone and have meetings to discuss the future. I could give advice based on a great accumulation of information. However, my mindset of having a hard work ethic and of making progress had entirely evaporated.

I came to the realization that, even though I had made great advances in my life to reach a higher level of income, I was actually bringing home less income than I was previously after a tax bracket increase, legal fees, and increased child support. My direction already gone, my monetary reward incentive was also gone. I was working twice as hard, seeing my loved ones much less, and the only benefit I saw in the entire situation went to someone bent on destroying me.

The second year of my new position was destabilized by the groundwork that had been laid during my first year. Defending against a legal onslaught, which required hundreds of after-work hours and several emergency trips to court, pushed me into mental overload. Looking back on the situation, I realize that I was a poor employee. I came to work for a company to build them a business, and my overwhelming personal situation made my work for them secondary at best. I did not come near any of my sales goals or personal performance quotas. Though other factors aligned poorly, and the market for my area of expertise was weak across the board, my personal effort was probably the worst of my life.

After two-years on the job, which my contract required me to fulfil, the company and I parted ways due to mutual dissatisfaction. I continued to be lost and debated the next path I should follow. Some might call this a midlife crisis, but whatever the case, I had a hard time at first understanding it myself. I had always been so successful at everything I had done. What was different about this time compared to other times in my life? The realization I came to has led to much of my work for this book and the topics of engineering your future. As I mentioned, my long-term path had been removed. I needed to have a new long-term path, but obviously working not to have my son taken away from me was not going to work, since I had voluntarily given him some space and distanced myself for a while.

While reviewing some of my older writings, which actually comprise the first few chapters of this book, I realized that the three process areas that drove me constituted my long-term path, while working past where I was at that point and finding a way to enjoy the process were what moved me along that path. If I was to positively engineer my path as I had done before, finding my path would be the first step. Since my son was born, I had been dedicated to building a secure future for him. I had to make a new path that still included working for his future, but this new path also had to take into account that he would not always be nearby.

Finding My New Path

Even though I had been in my skin for close to forty years, I felt the same way as many people in their early twenties do. At their age, I had gone directly from high school to a job and then had
222

rushed off to the military, with many things unfinished and with more work to do than time to do it. I had never really experienced feeling lost before. It was like a "Middle Earth" type of motivation. I felt like I had absolutely no reason to work on any of the tasks in front of me. I had list after list of tasks and could determine which tasks were more or less important, but why did I need to do them?

I was in this state for about ten months. I was able to work on some items and move myself forward. My mind never really slowed down, however. It was busy working, but my thoughts did not have conscious direction. I found myself thinking about many of the things I had spent my life working on as well as about situations I saw around me. During this time, I pondered what it was that I was missing. I thought about what I could do to regain motivation. When I finally realized what I was missing, it happened all at once, and I was able to commence a new path rather quickly. However, identifying the problem was more difficult than I would ever have imagined.

It is easy to tell others that they need to be motivated and that they should pursue achievement in their lives, but seeing a reason to do so is something that people can only do for themselves. I have talked to many young people who have expressed that they watched previous generations chase achievement and work so hard that they had no time for anything else. Many younger people actually have negative associations with achievement. They are content to have more time for themselves and desire fewer possessions that they associate with giving up their time. In the modern age, many have replaced possessions with virtual items, places, or surroundings that they can reach in the absence of monetary reward. However, I will not focus on this topic here.

In my situation, I realized that I had to have a new path. In many ways, I had identified with the younger generations that seek less achievement. Therefore, my path had to include not only my previous life's work and the skills that I had achieved, but also my new perspective lifetime and the cognitive abilities that I had developed over the last few years. I felt that I had outlived my value in the corporate structures in which I had previously been ingrained. I was highly compensated and educated, but now I needed to start to slow down my pursuit because of my body's inability to handle physical stress. At the same time, workforce trends had moved toward an around-the-clock, work-life environment, using handheld technology and social media on a continuous basis. My physical limitations were not going to support constant involvement with social media, which was becoming the norm for employees and thus expected by most employers.

When it finally clicked for me after ten months of the "Middle Earth" lost feeling, I had found my new path. From this point on, my life would be about two things: documenting all of my thoughts and building a future in which my son and I could work together when he became of age, so he could decide for himself.

Chapter X

Determining a Path

Don't set goals! I cannot stress this enough. When you set a goal, it puts horse blinders on you. The process that I will describe does not limit you to one thing. It does not require you to complete something that you started, even if the environment changes. So many people set a goal and bury themselves in its accomplishment, only to find out that the thing they worked toward would have not been the best use of their time. If they had changed one little piece halfway through, it would have been much more successful.

Software development projects are notorious for these types of blunders. A group may spend two years creating an inventory control system, and when it is nearly complete, someone will decide that the inventory could be insurance rates and that the system could be used to sell insurance. Then millions of lines of code designed for products, locations, and supply logistics are left in place, and only the front-end interface is changed. Now the system makes a thousand decisions to do nothing each time it processes a policy line item, and it does this a thousand times for each policy. No harm, no foul. Right? Then people wonder why it takes five minutes to give a quote while the competition does it in half a second. When does it really matter?

People do the same kinds of things with their lives, adding countless subroutines each hour, day, month, and year. These take up time, and time is all we have in life. The hardest-working people are often not the most successful. This is because they waste their time, much like the inventory software system. Lost time matters if the most valuable thing we have is time. Let's think about how we arrive at our direction in life and what drives us to the next thing at each step of our lives. Do we consciously think about it, or just fall into it? No matter your personality, knowing what you are heading toward will benefit and guide you, even if it is only subconsciously. We need to stop "pushing" toward the end by making goals and "pull" toward what lies in our desired direction.

There are times when goals have value, especially with a process that should lead to an endpoint or decision. For instance, a business meeting should have a goal. When the goal is reached, the purpose of the meeting has been achieved. For the most part, these will be times when multiple people work together to complete a task, the finality of which no longer requires them to join efforts. Whenever we want to plan a stop and to break indefinitely upon finalization, goals are great tools.

Determine the Path

Ponder with me for a minute. Do you know what the path is for your life? Where do you see yourself next year? In five years? Ten? If you have a path, how did you determine it? If not, how do you think someone would plan the path for his or her life? Would you try to eliminate failure? In an earlier chapter, I talked about how to fail. I chose to bring up the topic of failure first because many people have set up their current path based on "not failing." From an early age, our "logical thought stoppers" ingrain in us *not* to do things. *No* is the first word most of us learn as toddlers. We learn what we do not want. As we discussed in the chapter "Human Logic and Thought Patterns," we associate learning what to do with what *not* to do.

A common definition for diplomacy is the art or process of acquiring learned methods of protecting one's organization or oneself from future retribution, via the use of foresight and thought in the course of current and future actions. Entire countries and societies use the

226

negative approach. We react to situations to reduce our pain. Diplomacy, the practice of countries attempting to resolve international disputes, is about minimizing pain and retribution.

Fantasize with me for a minute. In the course of your life, there are many great moments. Picture yourself striving to be in those moments. Let's examine your future from a different point of view, not from the point of view of how to minimize pain, but from the point of view of how to seek euphoric moments. Look at ways to organize and use foresight as you act to achieve your desired situation instead of living merely to minimize retribution.

Knowing Yourself

Determining a path requires that you know some things about yourself and that you have a measure of honesty with yourself about your true desires, feelings, and comfort zone. In this chapter, we are going to look at many lists of things to consider, things that will not pertain to everyone but that will help you to think about the direction you desire for your path.

What do I need to know about myself? What topics should I explore that will give me insight into what my path should be? Here are some areas we will consider: Whom do I envy? How do I want people to see me? How do I want others to treat me? With whom do I want to surround myself? What environment do I want to be in? What situations make me feel alive?

Whom Do I Envy? I Would Like to Feel Like I Perceive This Person to Be

Whom do I envy? "In my life, I would like to feel the way I perceive this person to be." I have found that this is the best place to start when pursuing self-knowledge in order to determine one's path. What I mean by "whom do I envy" is, what kind of professional or high achiever has the kind of life that I would like to have? Many of us were very young when we first identified particular individuals or a kind of professional that we'd like to be like. You may have wanted to be a doctor, a firefighter, a police officer, a baseball player, a teacher, etc. Before I list a few categories, I will tell you whom I envied in this way and exactly where it started.

I was already a young man and had a professional job that I was proud of, but I viewed it merely as a way to make money to have fun with my friends. One day something changed, however, and I began to want to achieve a professional status that would differentiate me from someone who worked only to play.

I was working at a hospital overseeing a project to remove asbestos from ventilation systems. I was introduced to the building engineer, whom I will call Bob. He kept everything mechanical for the entire hospital running smoothly. Bob and I only spoke for five minutes or so, and I am sure that he would not remember our encounter at all. In the course of my work, I was all over the hospital. Everywhere I went, someone mentioned Bob. Each time, however, it was more like a whisper of reverence. Every reference to Bob was a display of reverence for the ghostlike, grandfatherly, all-knowing figure. He had kept the building in tiptop condition. Every engineering facet of the building system sparkled like new. Each department had relied on him for some critical action that had saved lives because of equipment he had repaired. Other accolades reflected the way he helped maintain certain comforts, such as by repairing the plumbing of a coffee pot.

In the time I was there, at least five people from different departments of the hospital had brought in some homemade baked goods or ribbons of recognition to present to Bob. For nearly two weeks, I did not run across Bob, but the nearly silent whispers of his appreciation rang in my

228

ears many times each day. When I finally had to make a trip to the basement engineering room for the inspection of a ventilation system that had undergone asbestos removal, I was shocked to see the boiler system for the entire building meticulously laid out in pieces, with each piece perfectly cleaned, inspected, ready for reassembly, and arranged in the exact order it was removed. It looked like an engineering drawing with each part disassembled on a page with all the connecting hardware and parts shown for reassembly. Off to one side, Bob had stooped down to look at an O-ring that sealed one of the covers. Without looking up or being distracted by me in any way, he ran his finders around it, said something to himself about how it needed to be replaced, then tagged it with something, turned to a list of part numbers in a manual, and added the information to a list.

After an initial moment of amazement at what seemed to be an assembly-line project fit for more than twenty people, I greeted him and introduced myself. I mentioned that I had heard his name often around the hospital. In response, he joked about how many things break in a hospital. We talked for a few minutes mostly about the boiler project. He answered a few of my questions about some of the precision measuring tools meticulously placed around the work area that were packed in foam cases like a hitman's sniper rifle in the movies. As we talked, we walked over to his bench area, which was packed full of hundreds of little accolades, such as the ribbons I had seen the woman upstairs bring to work to present to him. Our conversation ended with him solving an issue I'd had a few days prior, about which I had spoken only with someone in a different department of the hospital. To address the problem, he had actually prepared a document—without ever having met me—and had it ready at his workbench to hand me on this, our first, meeting. As a young man of nineteen, I was more than impressed. Bob seemed to know everything and was completely on top of everything in his domain. I wanted to be this person. I wanted people to look up to me the way they did to him. I wanted to have the flexibility of his position. I wanted to feel that I was able to resolve any situation that I encountered as he

appeared to feel. I wanted the confidence and the competence he portrayed. I wanted to have

the same well-maintained things around me. I wanted the same quiet serenity that filled his

environment.

Almost all of us can recall a similar encounter or exposure to an individual whom we admire. In

some cases, we may have felt starstruck when we interacted with someone who seemed far

more advanced than us or even untouchable—maybe someone who is the kind of high achiever

listed below.

> Famous movie star, singer
> Philosopher, thinker, distributor of knowledge
> Successful self-help provider
> Team coach, group organizer
> Successful engineer, innovator
> Business leader, chief executive
> Project manager, people manager
> Parent of child superstar, those who raise a healthy successful family
> Famous sports or action star
> Church minister, spiritual leader
> Community leader (PTA, mayor, chamber of commerce)
> Politicians, those who represent others, government leaders
> Established litigation lawyer (Judge)
> Psychologist, counselor, family support, child protection

I realize that this list is not all-inclusive, but it's a good start toward getting you to think about the

type of person you envy. The identification of this type of person can provide you with a path for

your personal development. Even though your perception of such a person when interacting with

them may not have affected them, your desire to model yourself after them, or after your

perception of them, can be the strongest factor in your life.

How Do I Want People to See Me?

After you have identified a person or type of person that you envy and have thought about your archetype for personal development, the next thing to think about is how you want others to feel towards you. This is important, as behaving with others in a way that builds you up internally is a big part of a person's stability. Some people feel good about themselves if others think they are fair and impartial. However, the same people may feel out of place if others think of them as wealthy or like to engage them in debate. Discovering such insights into oneself may not be easy. Thus, you should start to pay attention to yourself and be honest about what makes you feel comfortable, complete, or relaxed and about what makes you feel uneasy, overwhelmed, or unfulfilled.

Respect me as fair
See me as an expert
Are in awe of me
People generally like me
Let me be their confidant
Think I am rich or wealthy
Try to be like me
View me as unique and independent
They want to empathize with me
Want to be submissive to me
Want to follow my leadership
They fear me
Fearless, self-sufficient, Stoic
Wish to engage or debate with me
The opposite to any of these

Once again, this list is not all-inclusive, but it will give you an idea of what kinds of things to think about regarding the way people view you. As we look at ways to engineer the aspects of your life cycle that pertain to people and situations, you will see that each person actually has a lot of control over where they position themselves in regard to how others interact with them. For now, we just need to be aware of what makes us tick and how we want to shape our paths with the influences that make us the best version of ourselves.

How Do I Want Others to Treat Me?

Next, we need to discover how we like to be treated. The different ways that people interact can be either supportive or disruptive. This also varies among individuals, and it can be seen in both children and adults. I have found that this important factor affects my levels of stress and anxiety. I enjoy being around groups of close friends in a private setting, as I need both the downtime and the calming, determined resolve of people in one-on-one situations. However, I also work effectively in crowds and can seamlessly navigate large, completely random group environments, such as at a conference. Usually, though, I need some downtime away from the crowd afterwards.

I have worked with many people, however, who prefer to have all of their downtime amidst large, random groups and who thrive on the attention they receive in such environments. I know from attending conferences with such people that they are just warming up for the main event, namely, the party afterwards. Here is another list of characteristics and characteristic responses that should be suggestive about what kind of personality you have.

Set an appointment
Amiable, open door for anyone, anytime
Leave me a message
Don't talk to me; I will talk to you
Small, close group of friends
Large anonymous parties
Completely random crowds
One-on-one conversations
Revolving door for a community of friends
Communal sharing
Like-minded and supportive groups
(churches, clubs, professional groups)

With Whom Do I Want to Surround Myself?

Another important consideration in choosing your path is determining what type of people you want to surround yourself with. I personally omitted this consideration when I first chose my path because I wanted to emulate Bob, the hospital engineer, and I didn't think much about the people surrounding him. Though I was well aware that he interacted with people extensively, I concentrated solely on his achievements. When I later addressed the question of whom to surround myself with, I chose different personality types that I found supportive. The following list contains ideas of the types of people with whom you could potentially surround yourself.

Appreciative and enlightened by me
Strong and physically fit
Adventurous people
Relaxed, meditative, and calm
Amiable, content, warm, and loving
People that think I'm the bomb diggity
People who are loyal to the death
People who are surrounded with the helpless and destitute
Dissident, anarchist or self-sufficient
People who validate, verify, and support me
Successful and wealthy
People who think they are attractive
People who need to be corrected or enforced to behave
People who enjoy correcting or enforcing others

Often, the path you pick and the people you encounter on that path are at odds. An example is choosing a career path in which the people who surround you need to be corrected and controlled, such as in the judicial system. In the judicial system, you may be surrounded by people who have broken the law, have difficulty controlling themselves, have addictions, or are disruptive. Continuous interaction with such people can negatively impact the people portion of your life cycle. Like a game of numbers, if 90 percent of the people you are around all the time have broken the law, have little respect for social expectations, or have addictive personalities, your perception of the world can become such that everyone appears to be a criminal, and your tolerance of small infractions of the law may reach a higher level than someone who spends their time in a monastery or museum. Thus, a police officer, attorney, or judge, though tasked with upholding the law, may become prone to breaking the law themselves because of their association with the lawbreakers around them.

What Environment Do I Want to Be In?

The environment you want to be in can affect all three portions of your life cycle. It can surround you with people of a certain demographic and affect the majority of your interactions, but these can have a positive or negative effect depending on the other selections you make for your path. Here is a list of environments that people might enjoy and that they may desire their path to progress toward. When considering various environments, keep in mind that many of them involve the energy that is received or that is needed to maintain them.

> Urban – hustle of activity
> Rural – Slow pace, quiet
> Prestigious, respected, not necessarily famous or wealthy
> Interactive and supportive community
> Fashionable, updated, and trendy community
> Communal, cooperative, and egalitarian community
> Modest and content community
> Wealthy lavish
> Famous spotlight
> Peaceful tranquil – group or independent
> Defiant, live outside expected norms
> Self-sufficient survivalist

In many cases, the environment can make the rest of the life cycle fall into place. People can decide from the moment they embark on their chosen path to be in the geographical location that their path leads them to. For example, an aspiring singer may desire to move to Nashville even if it means living on the streets and having a minimum wage job. If their path centers on singing, the chances of becoming a singer while living in Fargo may not be the best, even if they make exceptionally good money working in an oil field. Moving to the right location may result in less success at first, but by moving where they will meet people in the music industry, they will have a better probability of progressing on their desired path.

What Efforts Do I Enjoy Being a Part Of?

In my own life, I have found it much easier to work on things when I care how the outcome will affect other people. What makes work interesting is the satisfaction that the effort yields. Some things that I have completed successfully have not made me feel good, while others, which may have less value to those around me, have satisfied me. When I was required to sell services for a large consulting company, I felt at odds with the overall approach because achieving the goal gave me a negative feeling. It is important to know which efforts make you feel good and to think of them when determining your path.

In nearly any industry, even within the same organization, you can find and choose from among different categories of effort depending on the kind of effort the tasks in that category will support. Here is a list of some outcomes to which people often relate, and which yield satisfaction in one or several of these areas.

Everyone can improve from what I do
Everyone is made equal by what I do
Everyone listens to what I do
Everyone is enforced to follow what I do
Everyone leaves me alone in what I do
Everyone knows me for what I do
Everyone engages in what I do
Everyone likes what do
Everyone is challenged by what I do
Everyone is jealous of what I do
Nobody knows what I do
Groups of people profit from my efforts
My organization is better because of what I do
My work benefits me alone

How you feel after completing something is often a function of your upbringing, your direction, and the events in your life. However, sometimes it is desirable to adapt to enjoy the results of a particular task. A work environment that fosters appreciation for the completion of tasks can often mold employees to enjoy the feeling of completion even in areas where they may not have before. A social group can praise or reward people for both negative and positive behavior by regularly praising the completion of tasks. These are more a factor of human behavior and personality. People can change this predisposed wiring just like any other part of themselves. For this chapter, however, we will look only at identifying and knowing these things in ourselves so that we can determine what best suits our path.

Which Situations Make Me Feel Alive

This is the area that I found in my personal life has to be explored, as it is very closely linked to the mindset portion of a person's life cycle. I have found that the situations that make me feel alive are those in which I am working hard, feeling accomplished, and solving a difficult problem, but I also like to make people laugh. Some of the others on this list are not important to me at all—to the point that I will walk away from situations in which people are trying to convince others about topics in which they hold strong beliefs. In addition, I enjoy sharing and thrill seeking, but not as the center of my core.

> Making people laugh
> Feeling of winning
> Taking risks or gambling
> Sharing with people
> Working hard, accomplishing
> Convincing someone of your strongly held beliefs
> Being popular, center of attention
> Finding the answer, solving a problem
> Making people jealous, seeking validation
> Excitement, thrill seeking
> Doing things you fear
> Large social interactions, parties, dancing etc.
> Spiritual awakening, renewal of convictions

In the chapters "Enjoying the Process" and "Setting up Success," we will talk about adding activities to your life that fulfill you as an individual in these areas. Fulfillment is something that we all need. Nevertheless, most of us do not take the time to understand what this does for us, or we deliberately prevent ourselves from understanding. In many situations, religion has convinced us that the denial of self is what our communities expect of us. To deny ourselves the situations that make us feel alive renders us imbalanced and volatile. I have been living proof of this, as my upbringing left me with the understanding that my needs were not as important as the needs of others. Moreover, living this lifestyle for prolonged periods gave me a level of resentment that showed through to those I treated more highly than I treated myself. I will not dwell on this now, but I know that I owe many apologies due to self-induced conflicts that I fostered for years while not addressing this aspect of my own life.

238

Areas to Engineer

Now that we have looked at the components of setting up your path, the process of constructing a path will come more easily, and for many it will all just suddenly appear. If you just circle one (or a few) of the items from each list and compile them into a common list, you can now try to see if the path you are currently on supports the selections you made. If you did not have a path before you went through this selection process, you now have the building blocks to start creating one. When doing this exercise myself, I have found that each time I look at my path after making some more refinements to any of these areas my path shifts a bit.

Along your path, you will need to add a few things that reinforce the overall direction. You can do the things that will help you reach the benchmarks of your path sooner, or you can do them later. Often, you will need to complete some of these at the proper times in order to chart the next bend in your path. In the chapter "Working Past Where You Are," we will focus on the definitions of each path's items, but for now, we will look at what these items consist of. Areas to engineer that have to be added into your path to support your direction include the skills you will need to support your path and the influences you will need on your path. We will also discuss some limiting factors that are a product of our own humanity.

You Don't Have to Have It All Right Away

Engineering your life gives you the building blocks of a reproducible process that generates success. However, like anything else in life, it will not come immediately, and it will feel uncomfortable at first. A clear understanding of the process and the confidence to be able to execute it will come with practice and following a routine. The oft-used expression "Fake it until you make it" is fitting here. I always tell people to find someone whom they feel handled a particular situation in an ideal way. When you are in a situation in which you are not yet comfortable, just act the way you saw your trendsetting person act. Remember that people around you view you by your actions and do not know whether you feel uncomfortable in the situation. If you act like someone you saw who appeared to be comfortable and confident in the situation, then you will be perceived as such by the people around you, no matter how you feel about it yourself.

When people evaluate others, they create a perception of that person often based on very little actual physical evidence or details. Think about someone whom you view as popular, successful, exceptionally talented, or intelligent. Now think about how much you really know about them. Do you know them personally? For example, have you heard of Albert Einstein's theory of relativity? Do you know what comprises the theory of relativity? Most people in the Western world have heard of Albert Einstein and have even heard the name of his work. However, very few actually know what it means, and only a very small percentage of people have ever read his work. We perceive his value through the lens of his fame among the average population as a "recognized scientist."

What can we take from this? Is it more important to be an exceptional scientist or to be recognized as an exceptional scientist? People spend less and less time actually investigating topics and more time blasting social media content to anyone who will spend the time to review it. Thus, getting people to spend the time to review material is actually more important than being exceptional or than having exceptional content that nobody will spend the time to examine. If we look at people whom we perceive as famous as if they are not just exceptional but
240

also able to create an exceptional image or following based on reproducible patterns, it changes the game. If they can create such a pattern, then anyone can follow the same pattern and do the same thing. Right?

More so in our digital age than ever, the things that are used to identify someone as exceptional are at everyone's disposal. People's perceptions are based on less and less actual physical knowledge year after year. The perception of someone's image is based on the amount of content, on the activity of others in response to the content, on the personality of the content provider, and to a lesser degree, on the content itself. The activity of others can be faked or enhanced in many ways in this modern digital age, but it also grows as the perception grows.

Building the Amount of Content

If any content provider wants to display to others an image of popularity or success, the first step is to appear to others as someone of that caliber. What amount of work would distinguish someone at a certain level? How much exposure, how many formal publications, how many collections of content, how much experience, how many credentials, or how large a portfolio would it take? These are the first influences you should work on to create the magnitude of content that matches your desire.

Engineering you future is not only the title of this book, but also is the process, direction, and steps to build the content you need to show that you are exceptional. These things do not happen by themselves, but they are the most easily reproduced and the most teachable to others. The next few chapters will be the most important, as they provide the building blocks and processes to accomplish this in your life.

Interaction with Others

When others engage with you along your path, it does a few things. Yes, as we have discussed in this section, you must enlist others to build an image of the popularity or success of your work in the eyes of your audience, but it also helps with your mindset. It helps you build a feeling of competence. Thus, you gain confidence. Interaction with others also provides reassuring feedback, which is necessary for you to feel accomplished. Reassuring feedback is something we will talk more about in the chapter "Enjoying the Process."

A great reference for both building the amount of content and influencing the activity of others can be found in the "High Performance Academy" program by author and personal development program speaker Brendon Burchard. Brendon has an interesting style for setting up a career path as an expert with reproducible elements and components. Many of these seem to revolve around the psychology of how a person perceives the credentials of an expert. His training shows how, in the new era of online visibility and marketing, creating a portfolio of such items is all that is necessary for someone to position themselves in their market (Burchard, 2014). My impression of his work is that it is a practical guide to "fake it 'til you make it." It is a great resource for anyone interested in establishing the perceptual items needed to achieve expert status. I definitely recommend taking one of his academies to enhance your path and mindset.

Personality of the Content Provider

Where and when do the people we see day after day in the media obtain their dynamic, likable status? Were they born with the talent to have everyone read their content, listen to them, watch their actions, and be entertained? No, they invested years doing what brought them celebrity without any reward until they became adept at it. They got to the point where they stopped caring about the people who did not enjoy what they were doing and only focused on those who did. Then the group of people who did enjoy their work slowly grew to the size it is today. Some of the early haters converted over to enjoyers, and others are still out there quietly fading into the minority. Build your confidence and resolve to focus on the people who enjoy what you have to offer.

For content providers to enhance their own personality, gaining confidence will be important. For this, the mindset portion of your life cycle needs to be addressed, and understanding the confidence-competence loop will benefit you. I recommend checking out the work done by Nadine Love, who divides the confidence-competence loop into unconscious incompetence, conscious incompetence, conscious competence, and unconscious competence. People start out not knowing that they do not know something, and as they gain awareness, they become conscious that they are incompetent in an area that they did not know about previously. Once conscious of the new area, they can build competence by exploring the parameters and boundaries of the new area. Then when their new competence becomes second nature, they reach a state of unconscious competence. This allows them to be able to do something without appearing nervous, which demonstrates confidence to others. (Love, 2014)

Progressing through the stages of the confidence-competence loop becomes much easier when looking at it as a logical pattern and identifying its components and progression. Expect that you will feel uncomfortable until you understand the parameters and boundaries of any new activity or event. Be at ease with knowing you are uncomfortable when you start a new process. While feeling uncomfortable, expect to do it enough times to become comfortable. People often say that it takes thirty days to form a habit. Similarly, it takes around the same amount of time to become comfortable and confident in any new process you initiate.

I have placed the value of the content itself last. Many people would put this on the top of their list and thus will always fail at engineering success in their lives. The value of your content is the thought process you add to the world. If you take two lists of common things that everyone knows and express to the world how you view the interrelations between these two lists, then you add value to the world. You are valuable even if you only say the thing that everyone else is thinking. This is because all people need to know that they are not alone in their thought processes. People contrast their own value and accurateness against the public explanations of others. The greatest value I gained from fourteen years of higher education was not the education, but the knowledge of how I compared to others. I now know what I know and what I do not know about many subjects in comparison to the rest of the world. If 97 percent of people do not have a master's degree, then just knowing that you do is a ranking of your value within your own mind, but you could not rank yourself without others' public content.

Why do people like to watch television shows that depict the worst sides of people or the lowest character in society? It's because they rank themselves according to what they see and hear. This content of low character or uneducated opinion lets them feel a step higher than what they are observing. Yes, they feel good about themselves. People feel better about themselves by trying to compare and contrast faults at the highest level they can cognitively manage. If you think about content in this light, it is beneficial to have a few errors and to be less than perfect. Becoming human makes the content have value, so striving for perfect content actually reduces the personality of the content provider and the activity of others, as well as the amount of content. Focusing on the content itself reduces all three aspects that portray you as exceptional.

What Skills Do I Need Along My Path?

Skills are actually the easiest to acquire because there is no time dependency involved with gaining them. As long as you have a path and don't set goals, you will not be disappointed with any achievement or lack of achievement in this area. Learning skills is often about repetition, which you can do by setting out to achieve a desired metric relative to the time it takes to complete a task. We will discuss the recurrence of tasks and metrics in the chapter "Enjoying the Process." These areas to engineer will only be effectively added to your path if you enjoy the process of gathering and gaining them. I will tell you from experience that the accomplishment of a desired metric and the gathering of skills will not help you follow your path if you force them on yourself and punish yourself to master them. Similar to a child in grade school forced to memorize by repetition, the part of your brain that memorized items enter when forced will bring back the emotion associated with forcing it when you try to recall them. I have found that I personally separate things learned under duress from those learned enjoyably. The chemistry in your brain is different when you are forced to learn under duress, and for me, these items, when learned in such a manner, always have that same emotion associated with them when I recall them later. I did not, actively and effectively, become able to retain learned information until I enjoyed the process of learning.

Though there are many more items that could fall under this category of skills than I could possibly list, I came up with this reference list to give some examples. In no way does this list include every possible type of skill that you might wish to acquire.

Education
Rehearsed skills, coordination, sensory, voice, instrumental
Dexterity skills
Confidence, poise
Public speaking
Athletic ability
Teamwork
Interpersonal skills
Management, leadership
Motivational, inspirational
Business rehearsed skills, marketing, communicating, sales, process, financial
Aggression, self-control, patience
Articulate, quick wit, debate skills
Memory, stamina, endurance

For each person's path, the necessary skills will be different. Military personnel may need aggression training, but a jazz musician would probably not add it to a list of top priority skills to be acquired. Some of these may also come into your path to fulfill a personal aspect of your life. For example, many office workers or engineers that spend a lot of time on the computer for work may want to take up a hobby that requires the use of their hands. In such cases, a person may purposely add the skill of woodworking as an outlet and distraction. I have known many people who chose an entirely unrelated hobby as a pastime to relieve the stress of their primary career. Often, their pastimes eventually became their full-time occupations. Because of the positive emotion they associate with their pastimes, these people enjoyed their pastimes much more than their initial careers, which made them extremely dedicated. Their effectiveness is what made their hobbies become their careers. In my own life, I reduce the stress of my computer-related occupation by exercising very aggressively, which also balances me.

What Influences Do I Need in My Path?

Everyone needs to plan for and add influences on their paths. This is something I have had the most difficulty with in my career. It has taken me many years to understand the value and stop fighting against it. Because I was raised in a rural setting surrounded by survivalists and farmers who would rather work themselves physically ill than ask for help, networking for business has been difficult for me to embrace. Until recently, I have not spent a lot of time in my professional career aligning myself with supportive influences. Even now, this remains difficult, as it has been so ingrained in me that hard work will speak for itself. I have to constantly remind myself with every business contact that I need to embrace the fact that we both want to move the relationship forward, and I have to tell myself not to act as if I have it all covered.

Now that I take on the role of mentor more and more often, I wish like crazy that I had embraced such a working relationship earlier in my career. If twenty years ago I had received the advice that I give now, I would be ahead of where I am in so many ways. The following list of things that will help and give support also outlines areas that need to be engineered into your path.

Alignments and mentors
Notoriety, recognition
Trust and loyalty
Financial backing
Emotional support
Distraction and self-fulfillment
Affection and romance
Direction and motivation
Space and deference
Security and safety
Feedback and guidance
Maintenance and coexistence
Affirmation and praise
Emotional triggering (anger is better than despair)

For now, I am taking the time to identify these areas, but we will talk about integrating them into

your life-engineering process in the chapters "Enjoying the Process" and "Living the Process."

Some of these areas are very interesting, as they are more along the lines of self-talk and actions

that motivate or enhance your performance than they are tasks, achievements, or milestones

that you can surpass.

Remove Toxic and Add Positive Influences

When evaluating the influences you need in your path, first identify external toxic influences.

Yes, many toxic influences reverberate within us, but we have been working on that all of our

lives. Let's take a different approach and start to address the influences we can see around us. If

we start to look at the things that we can influence, then often what we see in the mirror will

start to adjust as well.

Identifying toxicity starts with knowing yourself, so we can engineer our influences to be supportive to us instead of always trying to bend ourselves to everything. In earlier chapters, we talked about the building blocks of personality and beliefs, which should have helped with thinking about your own limitations. For each person, these will be different. Some people thrive on energy and lots of social interaction, while others may feel overwhelmed and shut down in environments with many external stimuli. Some may enjoy heated interpersonal conversations and debating strongly held beliefs, while others experience anxiety in these situations. As we go through these exercises, note any extremely toxic influences that conflict with the things you have learned about yourself.

When you first start looking at the process of engineering your life, you will usually find yourself more focused on removing negative influences than adding positive ones. That's ok—it's why you're reading this book. Over time, as you address the negative influences, you will spend less and less time removing negative influences and start to add new, positive ones. For now, the best approach is to attempt to convert negative influences into positive influences one at a time as you encounter them.

People

Identify the people in your life. Categorize and rank them by the degree of influence that each has in the components of your life cycle. Some may have more influence on your mindset than others do, while others may have more control over your situation, such as a boss in a work environment. Think about the interactions you dread the most and consider how and why they affect you. We do not want to focus on the negative, but it is essential to understand where you encounter toxic people and how they affect you. Remember that this does not mean that they are bad or evil people, just that they elicit something in you that may be detrimental to your life cycle or enjoyment. It will help to think about these people in terms of all the influences needed in your life. If they are disruptive to the influences that advance you on your path, you should consider them toxic influences. Any person who is disruptive to multiple influences that advance you on your path is exceptionally toxic. If someone is high on your list of influences and is disruptive to the influences that advance you on your path, that person will have a large negative impact on you. The following list can be used as a guide to evaluating the people who influence your life.

Least Changeable - Most Influential

Family
Friends
Neighbors
Co-workers
Authorities
Acquaintances
Organizational peers
Member peers
Conformity leaders (church)
Demographic peers
Inspirational peers
Motivational influences
Passersby
Virtual social network

Most Changeable - Least Influential

There is absolutely no reason to have people in your life who are extremely disruptive and who fall on the "Most changeable-least influential" end of your list. At the other end of the list, you will want to add people to your least changeable portions who are supportive to your life path. Though some of these will move up and down the list, I would challenge anyone who places community, organizational, or conformity items toward the least changeable end of the list.

250

Social organizations that aspire to climb up this list will often be detrimental to the individuals who comprise them. If you have such an organization on your list, you may want to evaluate its importance to you and your life.

Locations

Toxic locations will often have toxins from both the situation and people aspects of the life cycle, but they may possess toxins related only to the physical or mindset aspects. If you found yourself in an organization that had cult-like tendencies and that tried to move to the "most important-least changeable" end of the spectrum in its members' lives, it would definitely fall into this category. An example of someone whose personality makes a given location toxic would be an alcoholic working at a bar. Although the person might be able to make a good living at a bar, the bar would be a locational toxin. Another example, which may be less obvious, could be going to the mailbox at a high traffic time of day. Though a harmless task, it may draw you into recurring conversations or expose you to event planning, which takes time away from other productive activities. The locations that become a distraction or that add influences that repeatedly draw you away from your path have to be identified before they can be addressed.

Least Changeable - Most Distracting

Time spent at residence
Working location and hours
Educational or influence-building activity
Work-related tasks, timing, and selection
Instructional or skill-building event
Conformity event (religious, community)
Social gathering event
Pastime activity selection and timing
Resource gathering (shopping etc.)
Biological needs
Planned event and duration
Self-guided hobby or pastime
Time performing a particular task or activity

Most Changeable - Least Distracting

Once again, while many of you could certainly add to or rearrange this list, I thought it was a good place to start considering locations. We can determine our location to add positive influences and remove negative influences by our timing of different activities. By documenting the times when locations are more distracting and then ranking them as in the list above, let's start to first rearrange or change the ones that are toward the bottom. Slowly augment conscious decisions that are toxic by replacing them or by making small changes to your timing to make them nontoxic. We will continue this discussion of how to choose our situations and locations based on the optimum mindset in the chapter "Living the Process."

Situations

A situation is typically composed of one's current location and one's mindset when the combination leads to a series of events. Often we can identify the situations that become toxic when combined with some of our own personality traits. We all know these, and either through repeated experience or through extremely negative events, we can identify the trends of situational toxicity. For someone who has a problem with urges to shoplift, spending a day walking through shops may not be the best situation. Or if someone drives alone across town to a beer fest and will have to drive many miles to get home, it may not be a good situation for that person.

Most Toxic Situation - Least Controllable Situation

Drinking & mechanical operations (DUI)
Drugs & alcohol at permissive social group events
Dangerous & extreme physical events
Traversing dangerous locations
Ticketed sporting or concert events
Exercise, training, skill training
Club learning and team events
Non-substance-using community events
Loitering in secure physical locations
Activities outside the family or group home
Social or group activities in the home
Self-exploring or non-interactive activities

Least Toxic Situation - Most Controllable Situation

By making a list of situations, we can also see some categories under which various situations fall. Each situation you find yourself in fits somewhere on this list. Though some of us have a high tolerance for risk and may choose to participate in situations that are high on this list, it is entirely up to each of us. However, if you continuously find yourself in situations that fall into the categories above your comfort level, situations that you often regret later, then let's try to understand what triggers you to do so. Often we associate certain activities with mindsets; for example, if you have foul moods, you may find yourself reaching for the same things each time to comfort yourself. If you are in a good mood, you might choose to place yourself in another situation. This seems to be common sense, but many of us do not stop to associate what we do when we feel a certain way. Starting to take note of those situations and knowing ourselves are the first steps. Map out and write down the activities you lean toward in various mindsets or emotional states. This will be the first stage in positively influencing this aspect of your life.

Address Habits

We have bad habits for two reasons. One reason is that the stimuli that would compel us to avoid these habits were not present when we initially engaged in the activities that became our bad habits. The other reason we began to associate negative emotions with the response that would correct the bad habits. This occurs repeatedly, either when life punishes us for being unprepared to handle a situation or during our training and our interactions with other people. We often do not address bad habits because either we do not know when to intervene or we associate the negative pain or consequence with another person and not with the situation or ourselves.

When addressing habits, first locate the points at which the stimulus arises, and then identify when a response would be too late to affect the outcome. By following the three process areas, which I will outline in the second half of this book, you will naturally set up effective habits that do exactly that. Many books have explored the topic of which good and bad habits one should

have and which habits the most effective people possess. The book *The 7 Habits of Highly*

Effective People is a great example. Here, however, we will not so much look at habits specifically

as we will examine how to set up your overall path through life in order to implement that which

makes exceptional habits effective.

Remove the Bad

The bad habits you address in your life may not be the same as the list of habits that others

might determine that you need to address. Do not rely on others to determine what a bad or

good personal habit is. However, you should take input from multiple people who experience the

same habitual issues that you possess in order to determine your own list of habits that you may

feel are not good for you. I will give you an example. In my life, I have personally determined to

address habits such as the following: region-specific speech patterns that I developed while

growing up or traveling, the bad tendency to make assumptions and stereotype people I meet,

some poorly adapted interpersonal interactions that made my partners feel negatively, some

physical and nonverbal communication patterns I had in social situations, some time

management and procrastination tendencies, and a lack of grace when being confronted with

criticism.

Many outsiders would probably not notice my interpersonal habits, my assumptions and

stereotyping, or even much of my speech pattern, but nearly everyone I have known would add

to this list that I have a bad habit of over-analyzing every situation. This bad habit was not on my

list because I see it as my greatest strength, and attempting to remove its negative aspects would diminish the inextricably linked, positive aspects of the same skill set. Be careful to note what drives you and what things that others may consider bad that would reduce your primary strength or dominant personality trait should you try to fix them. In my case, I was convinced at times in my life to suppress this strength in an effort to conform, and doing so removed my effectiveness in every other aspect of my life.

Build the Positive

To build good habits, you first need to understand what traits will be beneficial to you and will promote your success. Once again, these will become apparent as you address the process areas that I will continue to define in the remainder of this book. Implementing the processes that promote a successful life will address each of these habits. I will show you how to do so by meeting your human needs and following the lifestyle steps that lead us to productive results.

Punctuality
Expressiveness
Acceptance of others
Effectiveness of actions
Time management
Motivation and drive
Physical and interactive socializing
Communication

You will read many times in this book that, if you focus on the things that drive you to be successful, the rest will fall into place. Large life changes are never beneficial. People who make large changes may gain some good practices but will also lose many of the beneficial aspects of their pre-change selves. The process of life engineering is in the adding of successful elements and practices and in letting our life flow in the same positive direction.

What Human Limitations Need to Be Addressed

Human limitations are what eventually stop everyone. Unfortunately, none of us will live forever, and the varying degrees of our ability define and separate us more than anything I will talk about in this book. Recognizing where your limits are and being able to separate a limiting feature from something that is just outside of your comfort zone is challenging. Professional athletes continuously push their bodies beyond their comfort zones and test their physical limitations continuously. If they did not, they would not be at the top of their games, but they have learned this balancing act as part of their life processes—to push hard enough to have pushed beyond the rest, but not past their own physical limitations, which could end their careers with a crushing injury.

How many people who started out as athletes would still be athletes if not for the one time they pushed past a limit and suffered a career-ending injury? What percentage of people find the balance of pushing performance to the limit, but not over it, for long enough to make a career as a professional athlete? Are these people inherently better athletes than others are because they can sustain this balance? I do not think so. They have learned a process, and many of them have been taught that process since they were young. This is why successful athletes often have successful children. The children of successful athletes observe their parents' traits and absorb them into all aspects of their lives before they even develop the understanding to be aware of it.

I believe that people are never terrible or exceptional at any activity by nature. When people seem to be exceptional (or the opposite) at an activity, you will find every time that they love (or hate) doing that activity. The interest they have to keep doing the same activity repeatedly makes them exceptional at it. This is something we will talk about in depth in the chapter "Enjoying the Process" where we will look at how to create this effect within ourselves. In this chapter, we are looking at the balancing act of pushing ourselves to do something repeatedly, to stretch our ability, but without exceeding our physical limitations.

With athletes, it is obvious what the limits are. The medical and sports medicine industries have analyzed the human body for years. The products created to enhance one's physical ability and to protect against injury are orders of magnitude better than they were just a few years ago, but consider the following questions. What physical limitations constrain us in other areas of life? How far can we push our brains to learn? To what extent can the human body withstand sleep deprivation? What level of consumption of foods, chemicals, or environmental byproducts is too much? What degree of mental and social duress can an individual endure? In general, what amount of environmental factors becomes overwhelming to a human on a physical, emotional, or psychological level?

Our bodies have limits to how much short- and long-term stress they can handle. The high-performance, physical needs of our ancestors caused those who anticipated hardships, danger, natural disasters, or environmental trends to reach reproductive ages more often and to pass along both genetic and learned knowledge to their offspring. Anxiety provided people with the means to rapidly address and thereby survive in those quickly changing, adverse physical conditions. Though they may not have exceptional value today, they are still within us, and we need to understand and reduce the adversity that triggers them.

Our bodies are natural wonders full of chemical releases that trigger operational balances. One bodily function may trigger another, which in turn triggers a third. We often hear of medical treatment that changes a patient's internal balance, causing something unexpected to happen. We call this a side effect. Take medicine for the sinuses, and end up with dry mouth or constipation. Then we take a second medication to combat the side effects of the first—and often a third to combat the effects of the second. Like an engineering system, one change migrates to the next until the entire system regains balance at a different level. Our bodies need things that we often do not consciously identify or, worse yet, that we consciously do not want or avoid at all costs.

Human social codes and the expectations of others place many of our own needs at odds with each other. We are supposed to conceal many of our needs for interaction or attention if we are not in a certain sanctioned relationship. We are not supposed to make our reproductive needs apparent, so much so that we feel shame or embarrassment about functions that are as natural as eating or sleeping. The use or denial of these systems in our lives send our bodies into as much shock from change as starting a new medication that triggers side effects.

When I was a teenager, I developed one of my earliest self-help solutions. I approached peers who had extreme cases of acne and pointed out to them that the last few people I'd helped had nearly eliminated their acne. One at a time, this treatment—though unconventional and something parents do not want to hear—worked. You could watch the trend and identify which teens had become sexually active by how much their complexions cleared up. I am not sure whether the medical profession has any research on this or whether it has no interest in pursuing the topic because it might not conform to social norms. I am sure that most parents would prefer to find any other option. Nevertheless, if you view this trend as if it were an engineering system, then it is apparent that teenagers' systems tilt out of balance when their sexual organs begin to function at puberty. They are not aware of what their bodies need to restore balance because their cognitive reasoning does not allow them to explore this possibility. This is like taking one medication that causes the side effect of a strong desire for food, which in turn causes a second side effect, namely, acne, which we treat with a third chemical to reduce the effects of the first and second chemicals. But restoring balance to the system may be all that is required to reduce each of these negative side effects.

Realizing Our Needs

First, admit your human needs. The most repressed human needs are the most difficult to meet—the things we consider our dark side or possibly deem taboo. Though I am not going to expound on how to explore or understand yourself in these areas, I will note that they will place you more at odds with yourself than anything else will.

As humans, we have the exceptional capability to override our own needs for what we consider a higher purpose. We can decide to eat something we dislike because we think it will make us become healthier. This, however, places our decision in opposition to our bodily desires or potentially our actual biological needs. When a strong need is ignored, the mind tries to overpower the body's requirement, which creates a surreal feeling that leads to an inner conflict. The more people decide to ignore their own bodies' needs, the more unbalanced they become. As someone in this state of denial tilts even more out of balance, they increasingly blur reality with unreality. If they were already feeling this confusion between what is real and what is not, it would make them susceptible to believing things that are obviously unreal, which they wouldn't believe if they were in a fulfilled mindset.

Identifying and fulfilling human needs makes a person more able to see when things outside of themselves are real or unreal. The military, organizations that use brainwashing, and cults implement the techniques of denying the fulfillment of human needs over long periods followed by convincing people to continue the activity that denies those needs. This makes them susceptible to suggestion, and at the right level in this process, people can be influenced to do things that would in no way be acceptable to them—that would even repulse them—if they were not in this mindset.

By meeting your most basic bodily needs, you can reverse your surreal feelings, and your cognitive ability will start to shine above its previous levels. Let's look at a few things to consider when evaluating your mental, physical, emotional, and social needs.

Exploring Our Needs

Exploring your needs is about knowing yourself. As with maintaining a swimming pool, we cannot expect that it will be fine if we just throw some chemicals into it. We need to know that when it rains or when leaves collect on top, the added content changes the balance, and it will grow algae if we don't remove the leaves and put extra chemicals in it. When many people swim in the pool on a particular day, we will need different chemicals, but also we need to know that adding too much of any of the chemicals changes it in yet another undesirable manner. The entire idea is to maintain it the optimum pH balance to ensure the clarity of the water.

Our bodies work the same way. We have optimum operational ranges for intake, excretion, rest, environmental stimuli, mental interaction, etc. Understanding our limitations is a process of exploring the optimal ranges for each of these items and determining where our body reaches balance. You should identify your own deficiencies and strengths as well as which areas you have influence over and which you may not. Some people, for example, cannot shift their sleep patterns without detrimental effects.

Once you gain an understanding of your own needs, how well you act on what you know about yourself is what I consider emotional maturity. Many of us understand all the things that make ourselves tick and understand which ranges are optimum, but we allow ourselves to be directed by the random flow of life and surrounding events or stimuli. Wisdom has a few parts, some of which I take from the famous serenity prayer, but I have added life-engineering principles as well.

1) The ability to identify the patterns of my own behavior
2) Know my own limitations
3) How to take positive actions on the things I can change.
4) The grace to accept or offset the things I cannot change
5) The ability to tell the difference
6) Ability to continuously increase the percentage of the time I accurately take effective positive actions

I have found that I need to apply this approach of self-exploration to several areas of my life and that my body has rhythmic patterns, which I refer to as biorhythms. My memory, cognitive ability, physical needs, social interaction, and emotional maturity all need to be in balance with one another and require adjustment after changes to each of the others. My weaknesses have been relatively consistent, but they have been triggered by changes in the balance of any of the other systematic trends. I have determined that the trigger levels for each biorhythmic factor have been relatively similar each time that they occurred, so that they could be predicted with some practice.

If I arrange the aspects of my life that affect my personal balance and maintain them in the ranges that have kept me the most stable, these triggers all but disappear. For the most part, the uncomfortable triggers are a product of my unfulfilled needs. I have found that these seem to fit into the categories of internal or external needs for fulfillment.

External needs for fulfillment affect all three portions of your life cycle, but they derive from things that are outside of yourself. We have to create ways to interact with our external environment in a manner that fulfills these external needs. Some examples of ways to fulfill these needs include acquiring items, procuring services, or attending events.

> Social interaction
> Intellectual stimulus
> Down time
> Self-indulgence
> Praise and acceptance

Internal needs for fulfillment mostly affect the mindset portion of your life cycle. For the most part, balancing the aspects of your human needs that adjust your mental and physical attributes fulfills these internal needs. The focus of fulfilling internal needs is on reducing the triggers that cause unwanted actions or results. Many internal needs are items that directly nurture the human body, which I refer to as biophysical.

> Anxiety
> Social inclusion
> Spiritual
> Biophysical

Time and Interaction

All human needs for fulfillment have a recurrent aspect to them. Much like your need to consume food several times a day, each of these has some time-dependent element, and most require interaction with other humans. Many people will admit that they need a vacation when they get stressed-out at work and start to become ineffective, but such downtime fulfills your needs better if you plan for it. We all have an optimum balance of productivity and downtime, just as we require a certain number of hours of sleep per day or week. We become more productive when our minds are balanced with the optimal ratio of downtime to working time.

As it is much more difficult to restore the chemistry in a swimming pool after neglecting it for long periods, neglecting the balance of human needs for long periods also influences our effectiveness. Be honest with yourself. Evaluate each of these internal and external human needs for fulfillment and determine what is optimal for you. Knowledge is the first step when adding these to your path. We will continue talking about this topic in later chapters.

Physical Alignment

When you steer your life in a positive direction, a large portion of maintaining the optimal balance requires looking at the physical things that you need to control. These physical aspects of your life are often things that we let guide us. For years of their lives, many people will resist taking control of these aspects. In my case, a strong rebellious streak aligned my thinking with some preconceived notion that controlling the physical aspects of my own life was allowing me to be controlled. In reality, everything around me was controlling me. I let myself be controlled as if a randomly blowing wind set my own personal physical attributes to whatever influence was in my life at the time. By not taking control of these aspects, you allow them to control you.

Schedule

An important aspect of your life to engineer is your schedule. I advise that you don't fear a routine. Don't let others set and determine a routine for you, but don't fear your own. Accounting for your time and being honest with yourself about your abilities in this area will be the keys to your life engineering. Knowing the timing for activities based on your body's requirements (biorhythms) will be the difference between setting successful expectations and setting unreasonable ones. You will not allow yourself to succeed if you expect yourself to accomplish something that your body does not biologically support.

Schedule around your limitations and know your weaknesses. If you work effectively for three hours and then become unfocused and just stare at your work, determining to force yourself to work eight hours straight does nothing but set you up to fail. Honestly assessing your limits will start you down a path toward affecting the outcome of your own efforts. If you lose effectiveness after continued focus for three straight hours of work, then plan for breaks that renew your focus. Often, people in the work environment head straight for the coffee pot to address focus issues. Most of us determine that the easiest way is to use drugs to push performance past personal limits. I am not advocating for what is better or worse for each individual. Nevertheless, in my life I have used this easy way out to refocus myself, but since I have been more focused on engineering my life in recent years, I have come to rely more heavily on other ways to push past my limitations, such as by scheduling around my needs instead of forcing through them.

As we design a schedule for a more effective life, the primary focus should still be to reinforce our life path. We need to plan to support the three areas we addressed in the first chapter that make us personally fulfilled. Let's revisit each of these three areas:

- Enable you to maintain your environment
- Have you working toward achievable project completion
- Progress toward long-term direction

Maintaining Your Environment

First, we need to schedule to have satisfaction with our current environment. Maintaining the things around us relaxes our minds on a biological level that supports the comfort on which we base everything else. Though some people may vary when it comes to the degree of order they need, humans across the board need to have control in their environments, which is most important to people when their control over their environments also makes them biologically comfortable. So let's start to base our schedule around some simple concepts.

1) The next successful event starts at the end of the last
2) Everyone needs to add a few indulgences
3) Every item should support my biorhythms
4) Outsource, outsource, outsource

We have talked about most of these already; however, they may require some explanation. Above all, my first priority for maintenance is to think about the next similar event after the one currently being performed. As children, we do not know this concept. We put the empty box of food back in the pantry or use the last towel, paper product, or consumable food item without thinking. Children have not yet grasped that some tasks have to be performed between the last time given items were used and the next time they want to use the same sorts of items. If we think of maintenance as the foresight to look ahead to the next successful event beyond the present one, we begin a pattern of removing from our lives the stress of an environment in disarray.

Whether we plan for them or not, we will engage in a few indulgences. Let's explore some behavior that we have all seen. A woman, for example, who is accustomed to indulging in deserts decides that she is going to eliminate deserts altogether, so she throws them all out and begins to eat healthy foods. Soon, she is at a Dairy Queen in the middle of the night with uncontrollable urges. Imagine if instead, this hypothetical woman were to begin gradually moving toward a more desirable outcome, such as by purchasing smaller deserts. Imagine if she then were to resolve to reward herself with one of those deserts only *after* she has walked around the block. At the same time, let's say that she finds ways to make walking around the block more enjoyable, such as by attempting to engage people in her neighborhood in conversation to keep abreast of their goings on. A process such as this might result in eliminating the urges, or it may cause her to forget about them as she interacts with other people.

Supporting your biorhythms is also important to successful maintenance. Determining that you will do something when you are most intensely primed to do the opposite will set you up for failure. If you decide to read and study every day when you are the most stimulated toward physical activity, reading will become something you feel you do poorly. If you decide to workout

267

at a time when you are the most motivated and interactive at work, you may often skip your workout time. If you schedule sales calls at your low point in the day, you will not show the excitement that would be beneficial to make your sales. If you decide to clean your house on Fridays, but Fridays are the days you feel most social and easily distracted by talking to others, you will probably become frustrated with cleaning and give up.

As you focus more on engineering your life, you will start to see success in everything you do, which will demand more of your time for productive tasks. Remember that it's ok to let go as long as you have another way to maintain. These rudimentary tasks associated with maintenance are the most easily outsourced. Being comfortable with that will allow you to move up to higher levels of thought, which will ultimately make you more successful at progressing down your path. My recommendation is to allow yourself to outsource these types of tasks as quickly as you are able.

Completing Achievable Projects

Scheduling achievable projects to fulfill the human need to feel accomplished is the next thing you will want to think about when setting up day-to-day tasks. Maintenance activities will be scheduled as part of your daily routine, but projects that are fulfilling will be a bit longer in duration. Thus, you should break them down into things you can do in a block of time or a single work session. When the scope of your projects gets larger, they can evolve into weeks and months, but they should always be broken into achievable pieces. Turning the page on each is very important. A job that does not allow you to turn the page and finish achievable, fulfilling projects in a manner that makes you feel accomplished will not make you feel complete as a person.

In addition to the tasks that fulfill projects for work, you should also include some fulfilling tasks that make the process enjoyable. Many people overlook this need. They often do not feel they have time to schedule enjoyable activities into their routines. For many years, positive and fulfilling feedback for my work was rare and unpredictable. One day after feeling excited to work on something because someone had expressed appreciation for my work, I realized that every time I had positive feedback like this, which had really driven me to a higher motivational level, it was something I had initiated myself. What a revelation! People have to start the process themselves of encouraging feedback that motivates them. We will talk more about this in the later chapter, "Living the Process." However, keep in mind that these things need to be planned and added to your schedule.

- Things to make you feel alive - Resets the clock on your motivation
- Efforts that return positive feedback down the road - makes others give you support that you are progressing
- Do some things that people you admire do - makes you feel like you are the person you want to be

The things done for your own future motivation can be thought of and separated into a few categories. As you can see in the list above, these things are scheduled into your routine. These things, though often intangible or not quantifiable, are the most important you can add.

Long-Term Direction

Scheduling activities into your routine to fulfill your human need for moving forward is as important to you as scheduling any other kinds of activities. These activities are what we defined in the skill and influences list—the activities that make you feel like you matter in life, but that often do not give you much on a personal level when you are doing them. The routines you add to your calendar to fulfil your need to move forward must require a degree of determination on your part. We will talk about this extensively in the chapter "Enjoying the Process," and as it is appropriately named, these activities must be enjoyable.

- Insert some types of skills you need to have
- Insert activities that promote your long-term direction
- Identify and define the next phase of your path

It should be obvious to anyone defining a path that the first two items in the list above add influences and skills that will be necessary parts of the routine and schedule. However, the last item is something that we have not talked about much up to this point. It is the key component of the later chapter, "Working Past Where You Are." By the time you are working on tasks and scheduling activities in the current stage of your path, you should not still be defining the current stage of your path. The reason we have a path and not goals is so that we do not become shortsighted and too focused on the result. We want to be able to let our paths adapt.

As your current or future needs subtly change, you should be able to adapt your path without an entire change of direction. How will you know which branches to take and which branches may just be whims that seem good at the time? By continuously defining the steps you will take after you complete each task, you will naturally identify these branches. The step-by-step completion of a task and the identification and documentation of the next task should go hand in hand.

The process should be 1) work a task, 2) identify the next task, and 3) add it to the list of tasks to be accomplished. You never want to start working the next task right away because that will prompt you to follow whims. However, when the next tasks that you defined start to point in a new direction, this branch is validated by many needs. The tasks that you identify should be for more than just the next stage of your path. It is best to identify tasks at least two stages out. For example, a freshman should be defining his or her junior-year tasks. By following this process, you will identify and reassess the best path in the future as part of a continuous effort that will become subconscious.

Positive Direction and Your Schedule

Most of us barely affect the timing and direction of our life events. In fact, I learned this very slowly in my life, mostly with age. In fact, I used to sabotage myself with respect to the timing and direction of my life events. I usually only succeeded in accomplishing things that were beneficial to me after trying every other possibility. In other words, even though the benefits of taking positive control of one's schedule seem obvious, it is often not so easy to put into practice.

Let's look more closely at how to think about scheduling and direction. In my experience, people's day-to-day schedules are mostly driven by escaping discomfort in all three areas of the life cycle: situations, people, and especially mindset. This largely means the alleviation of undesirable thoughts. If we are thinking about reducing discomfort, we become very reactive and often are not proactive at all. We spend years of our lives merely reacting to life cycle stimuli around us. Since the majority of us do this, we subconsciously spend the majority of our energy reacting to the reactions of others. We may be reacting to a reaction that we initially started during a previous interaction with the same or another person—a dizzying cycle.

Many people act in a reactive mode to patterns that the natural order randomly causes. We know these as expected norms. Most people adopt collective, universally accepted schedules that we are all expected to adhere to—or at least to be aware that most people do. These include daily, weekly, monthly, and yearly norms. We know that a workday should begin in the morning and persist roughly through dinnertime. Most of us seem to follow some kind of 5-6 day workweek, followed by a day of relaxation to complete the seven-day calendar week. We relate months or calendar quarters to schedules, often for quota- or status-related items. For example, we may think the police will issue more speeding citations to make their quota by the end of the month. Yearly, we often make judgments and determinations about long-term directions or paths, such as corporate earnings or seasonal playoffs for sports.

Any pattern can be beneficial if it is well known. The patterns mentioned above are very well known, so making the best use of them should be relatively common sense. Nevertheless, we first need to adjust the philosophy of how we think about schedule to be more proactive than merely escaping discomfort. How can we take each of these collective, universally accepted patterns and define our lives to work around them to make ourselves as effective as possible. Furthermore, to be effective, we must also distinguish our own unique biorhythms and styles of thinking and interacting to produce the best proactive approach that works for each of us.

Biology and Schedule

I have frequently addressed biorhythms and the natural tendency of people to perform more effectively during certain conditions, emotional states, or physical stages. My own biorhythms may resonate with others or may be entirely different from those of others. I have found a few types of biorhythms that enable me to tune my performance abilities. They are the following:

1) The body's production of energy
  - Ability to produce heat
  - Cognitive, physical peaks and dips
2) Timing of sleep cycles
  - Awake time since sleep
  - Length of sleep cycle
3) Amount of ambient stimuli
  - Daylight
  - Energy level (motion)
  - Audible sound
  - Other sensory stimulation
4) Diet

Let's look at the way that your individual biorhythms can be combined with the collective, universally accepted patterns to make an effective schedule. Once again, your biorhythms probably will not match mine exactly, as they are typically different for each person. However, seeing how mine relate to my situation should help you produce your own effective schedules and routines.

Daily

On any given day, energy levels, ambient stimuli, anxiety levels, and nutrition all significantly affect a person's ability to perform. I have found that my body reaches its highest production of energy, including its ability to produce heat, later in the day. Thus, the number of hours since I have been awake greatly affects my ability to be productive. Moreover, you have likely often heard that each person requires a certain amount of sleep each day to be effective. Realistically, it is impossible to get exactly eight hours of sleep each day. In my case, however, I have found that I do not need the same amount of sleep each day. In fact, my own biorhythms for sleep would be better described as needing 7-8 hours of sleep for every 28-32 hours of time, but as you can see, this sleep schedule conflicts with the normal expectations of the length of each day, based on our planet's rotation.

Each day's nutrition likewise has an impact on the effectiveness of the body's overall capabilities. I have found that the typical American breakfast of starches and grains hinders my body's ability to be productive earlier in the day. I am more effective when I consume high-protein foods in the morning and more starchy foods later in the day. However, adding a sugary portion to my morning meal seems to enable my thinking process directly. This is something that I have heard relates to the brain's need for simple sugar for optimal cognitive operations.

Ambient stimuli—things going on around me—also greatly affect my ability to perform. When I enter a setting with abundant stimuli, and it is my intention to engage, the stimuli tend to trigger my shutting down, but if the same level of stimuli gradually builds around me when I am in the same environment, I can effectively engage. In order to optimize my ability to perform, therefore, I have to manage the timing and scheduling of my involvement. I am much more effective when I arrive somewhere prior to the stimuli building up than I am when I show up after all the activity is in full swing. Some people have told me just the opposite. They are energized by stimuli, and they are most effective if they arrive at the peak of activity.

Whether it is due to ambient stimuli or a biological limitation, anxiety is something I struggle with on a daily basis. The twenty-first century contains a much higher level of stimuli than any other time in human history, and it continues to build. The traits that people have developed to cope with their environments over the entire scope of human history are not the same as those that are required for this new environment. Anxiety, which is a biological reaction to protect someone from danger, is now being triggered by nonstop environmental stimuli. Since the stimuli that

274

cause anxiety are nonstop, dealing with their effects has to be incorporated into each day's routine. A large portion of my schedule, mostly on a daily and weekly basis, is based on this requirement. When I make reducing anxiety the main goal of my routine, my ability to relax, focus, and be productive seems to fall into place.

Setting up a Routine

As you can see, building a daily schedule around your individual needs integrates factors that add to your ability to perform. I structure my day around several aspects of anxiety control. First, I am most effective when I awaken before daylight in the morning, when stimuli are the scarcest. Light, energy, and sound stimuli then build in my consciousness, and I am not overwhelmed by awakening when they are in full swing. I do best to arrive at my work location prior to everyone else, slowly allowing myself to adjust to the environment as the stimuli build. This factor controls my anxiety level, which reacts more to the shock of abrupt changes in stimuli than to the overall level of stimuli that exist in the environment.

Similarly, at other times of the day, anxiety control is required to set an internal pace. In the evening, I start to work on controlling anxiety patterns to prepare myself to be relaxed and capable of going to sleep at bedtime. This may be easy for some people, but in my case, my biorhythms cause my energy to build toward the evening hours. My body produces more heat in the evening and will peak right when most people would be tired if they were to effectively maintain a twenty-four-hour-a-day sleep-wake cycle. Literally, I have to spend the four or so hours prior to bedtime designing the three factors of my life cycle to slowly reduce my anxiety levels. The people I choose to be around in the evening need to have personalities that exhibit calm behavior at that time of the day. I need to make sure I place myself in a situation that slowly reduces input stimuli over this period. Finally, calming my mindset is the largest part of controlling the direction of anxiety overall.

When I evaluate the anxiety controls and the schedule that I have integrated into my evening in particular, it is apparent why I resisted this type of schedule as a younger person. Controlling for all three of the life cycle components was much more difficult when I lived in a shared culture with a revolving door of friends and when I was in situations in which I was not able to control how the numerous people contributed to my mindset. This is why I advocate so strongly for the three-day focus. I have tight control over evenings for my anxiety needs, but only for three nights a week. That way I can allow myself to have a culture of many friends and dynamic situations for most of the week, while still having times to be productive.

My evening routine for the three evenings of focus (Sunday-Tuesday) ends with an hour or so of very relaxed stimulation. This is very important, as I ultimately need to control my mindset in order to be able to fall asleep. Activities that lengthen my thought process while focusing it on a single line of thought are the most effective. This is why people will often be able to fall asleep while reading a book, but the wrong book—or social media—can incite thoughts and shorten thought lengths, which end up stimulating a person's mind. I have found that material with a historical theme works well because events in history already happened and because there is only one line of thought to follow. Reading about a government conspiracy or watching something on TV that incites many possible outcomes—and thus lines of thought—will send my mind into a spin cycle. My absolute favorite, final, calming activity is to watch a calmly narrated historical story or documentary on TV. However, shows that contain commercials with fast, flashing visual stimuli or loud, percussive auditory stimuli are not recommended. If you are watching TV, it is best to have a pre-recorded show that allows you to skip the commercials or, better yet, an uninterrupted movie. The longer and slower the plot unfolds, the better the final calming effect will be.

Adjusting body temperature to what is optimal for sleep is also effective during this evening calming time. For me, removing heat from my body makes me tired. I enjoy a cool environment at this time of day. Once again, however, this will be different for everyone, so find out what works best for you. Some people eat something light, which makes them tired, whereas for others, any food will make them alert in the evening. Avoiding stimulants is one aspect, however, that is effective for almost anyone. I would not recommend any stimulants (coffee, cola, etc.) after the mid-afternoon low point, which for me is around 3:00 p.m. I will plan to have a mild stimulant at that time but nothing afterward, at least during the three days that I must have a good night's rest.

Since my body's biorhythms peak in the evening, the opposite situation occurs in the morning, when I am less able to produce energy—and body heat. I have found that raising my body temperature by using external sources helps me to achieve a productive state faster than allowing energy to build naturally throughout the day. In my younger years, I had difficulty waking up and getting motivated for my day due to this fact. A sauna or bathroom that converts into a hot room for the mornings has changed my life entirely. It has become a daily routine to wake up, turn on the heater, and take as hot a shower as I can handle. Once my body reaches a certain level of temperature, energy production seems to kick in. Using this technique, I am able to reach energy levels that would otherwise take me closer to lunchtime to reach.

Many dietitians, nutritional experts, and even many ancient religious patterns advocate consuming less in the evenings and more in the mornings. Buddhist monks are not permitted to eat anything after midday. Following my own biorhythms and adjusting to eating less late in the day whenever possible has also been a hugely effective practice for me. The adjustment of nutritional content at various times of day is also common. For example, starches or sugars known to cause immediate energy should be avoided at times when we are trying to calm ourselves. As you can see, starting to think about many of the things that make you effective on a daily basis is just common sense, but it can make a great difference in your productivity, especially when combined with the need for weekly routines.

Weekly

As I mentioned above, my body is optimized on a 28-32 hour wakeful period to 7-8 hour sleep period. To account for the non-twenty-four-hour optimal pattern, shifting my amount of sleep time per day as well as tracking the accumulated sleep time over the entire week makes me more effective. In learning this about myself, I found that various durations of sleep are more effective than others are. For instance, I am effective occasionally on as little as two hours of sleep, as long as it does not persist for multiple days in a row. However, if I get more than two hours but less than five, then I seem to wake up in the middle of a sleep cycle, which makes me ineffective and prone to errors that on several occasions have been dangerous. The next increment that seems to work for me personally is 7-8 hours of sleep. While each person may vary when it comes to the amount of continuous sleep required to be most effective, it is important to know yourself and to know when you are most and least effective.

Designing the week's schedule has been the most important for me personally. A structured weekly pattern most effectively enables me to merge my individual biorhythms with society's collective, universally accepted patterns. In order to do so, I recommend looking at scheduling from a different vantage point than most people usually do. Most people live for the days off and the weekend when they generally have less discomfort from which to escape, but if we take the approach of minimizing discomfort during the times when we can be most effective and productive, we can carry over less discomfort from those days into the weekend, producing an overall positive result.

As I mentioned earlier, for many years I resisted proactively scheduling for myself. This was because it seemed like too much work and, in part, because I associated freedom with living in the moment. In any case, not doing anything proactive came naturally and required less effort. I can assure you that I was not making my life easier by not being proactive. I created chaos in my life and spent more time combating the results of my unpreparedness than anything else. Once I got over myself and became proactive, I realized that the freedom I sought was in the preparation and foresight to reduce chaos and mishaps.

So let's start to think about how we can fool our minds, so to speak, into making the construction of a productive schedule less taxing. Weekends and days off require less higher-level thinking (longer thought lengths), so your mind spends more time in the state of brevity and fun thoughts (shorter thought lengths). For these days when focus is not as important to make you effective in your career, you can less proactively prepare for a full night's sleep. On weekend days, I do not even think about a schedule or plan for anything other than living in the moment. This also allows me to be less restricted and to act carefree. Thus, I give myself a pass and gain the ability not to feel bound to my self-restrictions for much of the week.

When I reduced the week to the days when proactively planning sleep patterns was absolutely needed to be effective, it was really just Sunday night through Tuesday night—three nights. If I focused on proactively scheduling a full night's sleep for three days a week, the rest of the week seemed to just fall into place. The times when I was in the state of brevity and fun thoughts on the weekend just took care of themselves. The ability to limp through Thursday and Friday with limited sleep fit within my body's need for the 28-32 hours of wakeful time for every 7-8 hours of sleep time. Adding one more night to include Wednesday night was optimal though not required for maintaining a tight, effective, productive schedule. Three days a week to focus and restrict my schedule was not that much but made for a significant difference in my productivity.

When I began to make it a habit to prepare each week to have a good night's rest on the three nights starting with Sunday, it changed many things that I did not even expect. First, I did not begin work on Mondays with a weekend hangover anymore. When you start anything with a negative foggy feeling, it is difficult to enjoy anything about it, and that is what I had done with my work for years. I would come in each Monday dreading the beginning of a new week because the feeling of exhaustion and inability to focus was always associated with Monday—and thus work in general. Secondly, I was then able to be productive early in the day, and I often arrived at the office earlier than most people did. This in itself laid the groundwork for many more things that were direct consequences of my alert productivity early in the week.

Over time, everyone I worked with gained the perspective that my emails were the first in their inbox each morning. In the minds of co-workers, this ranked on par with management-level activities. There is something different about the first emails in the morning versus even those sent the evening before. Due to the magnitude of responses I got to early emails, I was now able to show more productivity, which included eliciting the cooperation of others in the first few hours of work, than most people could accomplish all day. As many of us have found, the secret to productivity in the modern digital age is the ability to influence others. Having early or the first communication from someone in the morning establishes them as a priority during that day. This is even more effective when it also includes the first few days in the week.

When you combine both of these strategies, you will feel more alert and better about your own abilities, and the responses from others will become more productive and interactive. This combination will change how you think about your work, your job, and your life. In my case, the high productivity for the first few days of the week enabled me to shoulder a heavier workload on those days and to feel less stress in the last two days of the workweek, greatly improving my work-life balance. Three of the seven effective habits outlined in the book *The 7 Habits of Highly Effective People*—being proactive, putting first things first, and synergy with others (Crovey, 1989) —are greatly affected by this one life approach. This focus on sleeping well for three days a week enabled me to adopt all of these habits without really trying. I cannot understand how and why I lived my life in total opposition to this principle for so many years.

Monthly

As far as a monthly schedule is concerned, I have not identified many groundbreaking revelations that necessitate a monthly cycle to enhance effectiveness. As the primary human categorization of time, the month of the year seems to me to have been more relevant in earlier civilizations of farmers and hunter-gatherers than it is today. A productivity-based society seems to only require the monthly categorization of time for social interactions. There are many more ways to enhance effectiveness in a yearly cycle, which I will discuss in the next section, but unless you are in a sales-driven organization, monthly cycles do not have nearly as much impact as a weekly routine that focuses on merging your biorhythms with socially accepted norms.

Yearly

The largest thing to be gained from a yearly schedule or routine is the ability to recharge. In my own experience, since I focus my life on always working harder than those around me do, I did not take full advantage of the ways that yearly cycles could optimize my productivity until later in life. Some people seem to have this one down from the beginning. As I discussed in the "Absorption of Surroundings" subsection of the chapter "Building Blocks of a Person's Core," people who were born in a season of festive activities seem to have a propensity for cutting loose around the holiday seasons. I, on the other hand, typically looked to use those times to pick up the slack and catch up a bit on my backlog. While others pulled away from work for the festivities, sometimes I was even picking up the pace.

I learned later in life that I need my time to recharge. I may still use some time to catch up when others pull away, but I will also engineer some downtime of my own. However, I will often do this on a schedule somewhat different from everyone else's. Here are a few pointers. For a yearly schedule, I recommend examining the trends of when people are more or less interactive and exploiting those opportunities by arranging those times to focus, be productive, and recharge. For example, people will anticipate upcoming holiday seasons and will have explosions of interactive time, followed by periods of reduced interactivity. I will actually mark blocks of time on my calendar before and after major holidays and will schedule them according to what others will be unconsciously preparing for or inadvertently overreacting to.

People inadvertently overreact to things when they feel ashamed because they have not done enough. You can expect this to occur after an event or festive season, so having something in the works that can help people feel caught up will benefit both you and them. They will overextend to cover for this but will also be deceitful more easily, as they will be spending more time

282

bordering on the thought-length state of staying out of trouble. Expect to expend a bit more energy on maintaining your focus at these times, but keeping some previously undisclosed work available for release will be a game changer. These times will often follow people's return from longer leisure times, but not immediately after. They will occur long enough after the return that the interaction will have allowed everyone to compare and set priorities.

Unconsciously preparing happens to everyone, but it happens to some more so than others. I know that I myself prefer to front-load my tasks and work, so I will often be guilty of this. I want to slip away the last day of the week, when people are stressing at the last minute over what they have not completed, or to take my vacation the week before everyone else starts the holiday season. This has been effective for me, as I do not seem to miss productive times but still get my needed dose of downtime. Planning to return a bit early from socially accepted leisure times and to have something already in the queue for potential moments of inadvertent overreaction has served me well.

Closing

As I wrote this section, the words of some other people came to the front of my mind several times. I am not sure of where best to address this particular personality trait, so I decided to do so in the closing of this section. Some people I have encountered have expressed to me that scheduling anything and planning their day cripples their human spirit and creativity. If you possess this personality trait, you probably shook your head while reading the last section. To people with this mindset, I say, "If your approach works for you, please accept my congratulations." I personally do not know anyone successful in life that can live by such an approach. Yes, you will find several wealthy individuals who are successful and creative and who do so effectively with day-to-day, unstructured, unguided efforts. From what I have seen, however, each one of them will have someone else—or a team of such individuals—performing these structured tasks for them. If this is what you desire or what works best for your personality, it will be important for you to outsource the structuring and planning of your life's direction as soon as you are able to afford such services. To you I say find a talent agent or a personal assistant to support you and pass this book along to them, as I don't think I will be of much help to you.

Living Environment

When we look at the environment in which we live, it contains person-to-person interaction, random events, and external stimulating influences. These will mostly fall into the life cycle categories of people and situations. The living environment undoubtedly and ultimately will affect the mindset portion, and thus the entire life cycle. Situations and people are the portions of the life cycle that individuals often believe are, for them, unchangeable and that social pressure deters individuals from changing. The focus of motivational speakers and community organizations is often on the mindset portion of the life cycle, and you will often hear that your mindset is the only thing you have the ability to change. This is because the people who make these recommendations and who tell you that you can only control or change your mindset are themselves a part of the people aspect of your life cycle. They want to remain in that aspect, as it most likely gives them some measure of control over you.

A minister at a local community church is a part of the social control that oversees the family structures and the activities or situations of the community. The minister's interest is not to change the people portions of the group members' life cycles but rather to shift their mindsets towards the people and situation portions. Unfortunately, most of the social organizations people turn to for support with their living environments are a part of those very same environments. Your living environment often defines your self-talk, your feedback, and your activities. Toxic environments that control many or all portions of the situations and people in your life are the hardest to change. People who remain in the worst living situations imaginable all believe that they cannot even consider changing the people or situation portions of their life cycle.

Making Hard Decisions

When my niece was about eight, she and her entire family came to visit me. She was so excited on this visit because her father   my brother   had said she could ride along with her uncle and younger cousin instead of being stuck in the family car. This was the most I had ever heard her talk in my life. She chattered about everything. Repeatedly, at each stoplight, she commented about how we had the weirdest stoplights she had ever seen. After about five such comments, I asked what she meant by "weird," to which she responded, "they are up and down." It actually took me a few minutes to grasp what she meant, but then I remembered that the four or five stoplights in her little town in New Mexico were arranged horizontally with the lights across a metal pole that extended from the street corners.

Her fascination with these lights was interesting to me because it showed how much environment influences perception. This was one of her first times away from her town, and she had made a very deep-seated association between stoplights and horizontal fixtures, so much so that she viewed it as a universal reality because it was all she knew. Anyone that travels will probably have similar experiences. The first time something is out of place, it seems "weird," as she put it, but then as this newly discovered difference continues to appear in opposition to your perception of reality, your sense of reality eventually changes. One's environment, which includes situations and people, is the same way. Unfortunately, children are the most susceptible to this because of their limited ability to control what they are exposed to. By the time that we reach adulthood, when we have the ability to address these portions of our lives, we often don't know that anything else exists.

Much like the people who live in slums, if all you know is what you have seen for your entire life, you accept it as absolute immutable reality. I have visited someone who lived in Queens, NY on several occasions. On my first visit, I noticed that fifteen feet from the front of this person's home some garbage had been dropped in a small plastic bag, and my initial instinct was to pick it up and throw it away. When I went to do so, the owner of the home stopped me, said I was a guest, and told me not to worry because they would get it later. Upon my return over a year later, the same garbage was still in the same place, flattened from foot traffic, and the later additions of smaller items had contributed to the tattoo-like appearance of the fossilized remains. Hundreds of people, all of whom walked the same street, tolerated life in this environment, over which they had each apparently determined they had no control.

Cleanliness

As far as the aspects of one's physical living environment that relate to productivity and success, the most obvious is cleanliness. With few exceptions, the cleanliness of the environment directly correlates to a person's success. As we talked about in the chapter "The Process of Life Engineering," balancing your life is all about adjusting your life cycle in a maintainable manner. On the Life balance diagram, shown again here, the entire portion of the life cycle diagram that represents a person's stability is enclosed within the larger circle that represents the ability to maintain.

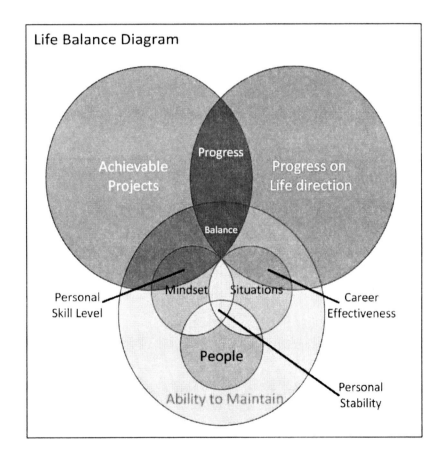

The largest part of maintenance is how you feel in your personal space. In my experience, how that space is kept defines whether you move on to the next level of balance or stay dormant without progressing in your life's direction. The saying "messy house, messy mind" carries a lot of truth, as a dirty and cluttered environment will subconsciously summon the feeling of uncompleted tasks. When you elect not to complete these physically unresolved tasks, you retreat to accepting unresolved tasks on all levels of your mindset. With such a mindset, you will also be entirely immersed in a situation of clutter and disorder. Only others who feel comfortable in cluttered and disordered environments will continue to maintain a long-term presence in your life. At that point, you will have aligned all three aspects of your life cycle with stimuli that hinders progress and success. Your mindset will accept uncompleted tasks as the norm, while your situation will become less than desirable for sustaining successful productivity, and you will be in a state of reduced self-esteem with an unbalanced life cycle.

Turning all three elements of your life cycle in a negative progression can occur simply by ignoring this single aspect of your own life cycle. If this continues over time, it will lead to periods of your life that will produce an overall feeling of negativity. When many people group together in these situations and with these negative feelings, it gradually becomes infectious. We all know these sorts of environments: we refer to them as slums.

Changes to Surroundings

I cannot begin to tell you how hard it is to change the surroundings in your life and especially the people aspect of your life. To begin to do so often takes exposure to an exceptionally toxic situation and a strong desire to break free. Engineering this aspect of your life sometimes needs to be done abruptly, but other times it requires a more gradual process of changing or of guiding situations so that you connect yourself with the types of people who can help move you along your path. In the process approach, the progression of choices you make serve to place you in contact with people who support your path, steadily increasing the percentage of time spent

288

with them and decreasing the amount spent with people who do not support your life path. Whether someone chooses to abruptly make changes to the people aspect or to change through a slower process is a personal decision, and only the person in the environment can decide which is best and which may or may not be possible.

In the environment I was raised in, aspects of life that modern science had proven wrong functioned as a central control structure. The only way to perpetuate such controls was to program into children a strong belief structure, to the point that not questioning the controlling structure itself becomes the most deep-seated belief. As discussed in the chapter "Human Logic and Thought Patterns," beliefs are a logical thought process stopper. To maintain easily disprovable beliefs for the sake of control requires establishing a belief that stops any logical thought process that could be perceived as questioning the control. Maintaining a controllable level of isolation is the only way to sustain this environment with the new generation of offspring. In this control structure, a belief had to be instilled to the effect that breaking the isolation could not be a notion that was logically analyzed. Thus, don't even think about it.

My assessment of the situation as a younger person, without fully understanding why I felt trapped in the environment, was that making a change from such a control system required an abrupt break. Could there have been another way? Knowing what I know now, I am sure I could have made those changes more gracefully. With my emotional maturity at the time, though, I could not see past myself. I just knew I needed something different. From speaking with a few other people who were caught in either the same environment or a similar environment in which others tightly controlled their life cycles, I have found a few approaches that I recommend.

The requirements for a progressive change to surroundings, which include the people aspect of someone's life, seem to follow a few patterns that can also be reproduced. I can group these into several areas that seem to fit into most of the experiences and stories I have heard.

1) Follow a trailblazer
2) Have a situational distraction
3) Have someone to take the journey with
4) Have a trusted mentor

First, find or follow a trailblazer. Having someone who broke the mold ahead of you is a great benefit. My younger brother was able to follow a path that led him in a direction similar to mine, while maintaining some semblance of belonging to the original control structure. Since one person had already entirely broken from the control structure, there was a fear of more controllees being lost. The central control leaders were more motivated to bend the controlling structure to prevent the loss of additional controllees. This is an important theory for those who want to make such changes. The trendsetter does not need to match your desired path exactly, but it should be someone comparable in the minds of the controlling structure's leaders.

The second thing is best described as a distraction. Think of this like a magician's misdirection. What can I make the focus so that I am not the primary concern or target of the control structure? This can be someone who is more misguided and thus requires more attention, or it can be someone who just saps the energy and occupies the time of the controlling structure's leaders to make them too busy to focus on the activities through which they exert their control. Once again, to return to the example of my brother, he was able to slowly migrate away from the controlling structure of my family, in part because another brother had returned to live with our parents after some difficulties in his life. The return of his entire family—him, his wife, and his two children (with more on the way)—into our parents sphere enabled my younger brother to remain under their radar and to gradually migrate to his own path.

Have someone to take the journey along with you. Find like-minded people who are traveling the same kind of path. This is when a significant other who is committed to the same progressive situational changes is a great resource. The feeling of not doing it alone will help anyone. Here is a word of warning about this area, however. If whomever you select to join you on your path toward changing your environment decides to abandon the path midway, it can really affect your progress. In my own case, I chose a significant other with whom I shared a common focus on improving both of our paths by shifting our surroundings away from each of the strict control structures of our pasts. However, at a life-defining point, the mate I had chosen shifted her perspective of the past controlling structure when she seemed to decide that our efforts to break away from our control structures were actually just a ploy to gain control *within* those structures. Such a change often arises when the status of the actions to break free of the controlling structure positions those who attempt escape as leaders of the remaining controllees in the structure.

What happened in my case is that my significant other began to be viewed by her original control structure—her family—as a leader of the family. Breaking away with me made her become a leader, and thus she became a part of the controlling structure. When she was effectively offered a leadership role in that controlling structure, it changed her outlook on the structure entirely. I watched her new role influence her to entirely embrace the old control structure now that she was in charge. The old saying that power corrupts played a large part, and it became a hindrance to her growth. She entirely adopted every trait that she had determined had held her back in life in exchange for the one thing she needed: more power.

The final thing that will support you in your efforts to make a progressive change involves your internal mindset. A slow migration is, in my opinion, more difficult than a clean break because you are continuously in a situation in which the controlling structure is present in your life. It requires resolve on a daily basis to push forward along your own life path when the existing controlling structure continuously provides easily taken opposing options. Seek guidance from a person, such as the trailblazer, and use them as a sounding board for your decisions and direction. This could be anyone that you respect and trust who is outside of your current controlling structure. Have this person be a mentor for you. Other options for a mentor could include a person that you look up to for career guidance or someone you are modeling your life path after.

In any case, I do not envy anyone who is in a situation in which others tightly control the environment of their life cycle. As I write this down, I have to add that, if you find yourself in a situation like this, please reach out to me, and I will attempt to support you in any way that I can.

Diet

Controlling your diet is essential, and though I will not spend too much time in this book on the ways that you can eat healthy foods, control yourself, or incorporate health and fitness into your life path, I will note that self-awareness is crucial in this area. Your body knows what your needs are on a biological level, yet most of us ignore the signals that our body gives us. We as a species have gained the ability to use our intellect to overcome our bodily needs, which greatly helps us achieve our objectives and surpass all other species on the planet. On the other hand, it largely impedes our ability to meet our dietary needs.

292

To provide an example of what I mean, I will share a story from my life that I wrote a few years prior to most of this book.

One morning, I was at a restaurant that specialized in breakfast and noticed a man speaking loudly. He was with someone who appeared to be his wife, and he seemed the sort who speaks loudly by nature. He had his back against the window, through which the morning sun shined, casting an angelic light around him. I did not pay much attention to his conversation, only to his behavior. He was a larger man whose girth betrayed his apparent tendency to overeat. The restaurant we were in was a local diner that, to my eyes, was accustomed to serving portions of food that were entirely too large.

While watching him, I noticed that bursts of spittle flew from his mouth—as if from a spray bottle—as he talked. This would not have been nearly as noticeable if his back were not to the sunlight, which illuminated these eruptions of aerosolized saliva along with all the dust particles in the air.

Of particular interest to me were the patterns in which these discharges of spittle occurred, which I related to his body's natural demand for food. He continuously spoke loudly as his server walked to the table with food. When he saw that she was coming toward his table, he would salivate more, increasing the bursts of spit as if someone were pumping a spray bottle as he pronounced each syllable. The first trip was a false alarm. The food was for another table. As the same things happened several times before his table's food actually arrived, I felt like I was watching one of Ivan Pavlov's experiments. After his food arrived, he continued to speak loudly, and I continued to observe the pattern of his explosive salivation throughout his meal.

This pattern interested me in a scientific way, as I was relating it to the way my own body reacted to my desire for food. I watched out of the corner of my eye with almost a morbid fascination as he proceeded through his meal. In the meantime, my meal arrived and I myself began to eat. I did not think about how this spectacle ruined my appetite until I wrote this section because at the time I was intently curious about what I was seeing.

His pattern of salivating was constant until about three-quarters of the way through his meal when it almost stopped entirely. This fascinated me, and I wondered if at that point his body was telling him that he was full by stopping its natural reaction to produce saliva. I watched to the point of almost staring and observed him begin to take small drinks in between bites to compensate for the lack of saliva. At the same time, my thoughts turned toward my own body's signals as I watched myself go through the same thing. The exact moment I quit salivating, I evaluated how my body was feeling.

I realized that I had reached the point where I knew I was full exactly when my body naturally halted saliva production. I had instinctively stopped eating, and I found myself just sitting there with half a plate of food and watching out of the corner of my eye as the man made progress on his plate. At that point, watching him and anticipating his bursts of spittle, which had gradually begun to include particles of food, was turning my stomach. Once I felt full, my body modified my ability to curiously watch this event, abruptly triggering my sense of disgust.

However much this scene bothered me, I nevertheless continued to watch as my curiosity overruled my disgust. I watched him power through his meal and consume every bite, every morsel of food. The moment he finished, he threw his utensils down on his plate with a large clank and sighed to signal his great accomplishment. Then he and his wife, who had also completed a similar mission, gathered the check, paid with exact change for the breakfast with no tip, and walked out.

I reflected on the incident and realized that this experience was very beneficial to me. I had often realized that I was full long before I completed the meal and then many times took a few more bites, trying to finish the bounty, as I was taught to do when growing up. The one thing that was missing from my experience growing up, however, was the initial portion control of only taking what you need. The restaurant, as many American food places do, overloaded the servings in an attempt to give customers a sense of value in their dining experience. Watching this man eat made clear to me when I should listen to my body's signals and how I should respond to them, and it sharpened my awareness of the amount of food that I actually need.

Watching the man, who was powering past his internal triggers on a mission to complete the task, showed me the method and sequence of events that probably occurred for him on a daily basis, or even at each meal. How do individuals become aware of these triggers and only take in the calories that they require? I wonder if this happens when someone is young, if one can learn this from watching others, or if it is possible that one simply never learns how. I have lived almost forty years of my life, and until I sat in this situation, I had not considered in quite this manner the act of eating. Though I have learned to recognize when I need to stop eating and though I usually listen to my body's needs, I had not previously observed that my thirst when eating and my need to wash down my food was my body signaling that I was full.

I could go on and on about how the American way of life causes this, as I hear others claim all the time. People want a way to blame someone else for the behavioral patterns that they have acquired over time. They want to believe that the community is to blame for their health and their habits. From my perspective, people's own bodies signal what they need, but people do not follow those signals—often because people do not possess the self-control to listen to those signals.

Intellectual Control Over Instinctual Triggers

Recently, someone explained to me that I should never eat a particular food item that I have eaten my entire life. This person told me that there is an entire movement to get this product outlawed, even though people have been partaking of it for thousands of years. We as a culture have started to identify all kinds of foods that are not good for us because some study came out saying that a particular item causes cancer or digestive problems (or any number of other maladies). Often we quit eating them altogether only to find out that removing the particular food or preparing it differently eliminates some important nutritional content, which causes us to have deficiencies in other nutritional areas. To replace many of the things we have removed from our diets, some nutritionists even advocate using certain nutritional supplements that are used for livestock.

Now that we have come full circle, we convince ourselves to narrow our diet all the time, which changes the balance of nutrition in our bodies. When our systems are out of balance and we become sickly, we determine that we should consume concentrated versions of the same raw materials that we have been removing from our diets one at a time, which will throw our systems out of balance in yet another way. Meanwhile, we have lost track of the fact that, once upon a time, humans had urges to consume the nutrients in the proportions that their bodies needed.

Without advocating for whether a particular dietary item is necessary or not, let's look at the process by which people are able to entirely separate from their instinctual triggers. With

296

livestock, it is effective to place a salt lick out for them, as they have the instinctual triggers to consume salt. Cows will not stand at a salt lick and completely consume it. They will only ingest as much as their body desires. On the other hand, we humans have developed a higher level of thought that allows us to circumvent instinctual triggers.

When my son was a toddler, he liked to suck on an older, rusty toy. Instead of confiscating it as I watched him lick the rusted metal, I decided to try the same thing myself to see what appeal the taste had to him. Though not something I enjoyed, when I tasted its strong metallic flavor, I decided to pick up some vitamins that advertised iron content. Although most parents would remove such toys, maybe we should take a closer look. The research of Shonkoff and Phillips (2000) has shown that "the most common form of malnutrition in the United States, iron deficiency, can affect the growing brain and result in cognitive and motor delays, anxiety, depression, social problems, and attention problems" (qtd. in Child Welfare Information Gateway, 2009).

We can conclude from this that we do still have biological triggers associated with taste for the things our body needs. Pregnant women proclaim this all the time when they suddenly crave foods whose taste they may never have even liked before. Being more aware of our own bodies and our own needs may reveal that we have more capabilities within ourselves than we previously thought.

References

Burchard, B. (2014) High performance academy, author, and personal development program

speaker

Child Welfare Information Gateway, (2009), "Understanding the Effects of Maltreatment on

Brain Development," www.childwelfare.gov

Crovey, S (1989) The 7 Habits of Highly Effective People: Powerful Lessons in Personal Change,
Free Press

Love, N., (2014) *Hot Confidence: Conscious Pathways to Take You from Mini-Me to Magnificent*

Chapter XI

Working Past Where You Are

After I had been practicing life engineering for many years, I became aware of a third main type of life engineering process, namely, "working past where you are," which I had been practicing subconsciously all along. Year after year, I had felt frustrated with others who do not engage in such a process. Showing my frustration ended many relationships and probably made me unbearable to many people. I would become frustrated because I myself focus on this learned skill in every aspect of my life. However, most people do not think this way, let alone engage in such a practice. What made me unbearable is that I had expected others to engage in such a practice, and when it would become obvious that they had not, I did not exhibit much tolerance. Instead, I would become annoyed with them for not directing their own lives proactively.

My intolerance toward such people is something that I have only realized during the writing of this book. I have always enjoyed children and loved their spontaneity. They demonstrate that becoming bigger or older is a step-by-step process that makes actions become available to them that they were not permitted to do or were incapable of doing previously. They anticipate the next year, their next birthday, or the next phase of their development, such as middle school or high school. They look forward to the next phase's contents, benchmarks, and rites of passage. They define each of these for the next phase while they are in the current phase. Children do this instinctively because they want the next phase. What happens to us as adults? Do we reach a point at which the next phase is undesirable?

I have known several people who stop working past where they are. They reach a decision not to define the next step. They decide to live where they are without a plan for the next step, and so they die inside.

In my relationships with such people now, I disengage. It has so sickened me that my impulse is to remove them, either slowly or drastically, from my life—even with children when they are old enough to engage in such practices and make choices of a certain level of maturity. Some view working past where they are as necessary only for children; these people think that it is no longer necessary for themselves because they have learned all they think they need to learn. Others realize that this behavior is a lifelong practice that will define either their success or their lack thereof. As parents, instilling a sense of a lifelong need for such a practice is the most profound gift we can give to our children, and most of us give it to them without thinking about it via our own actions. Or rather, we show our children either that we do or do not, and our children follow suit.

This is why the parents' phase of life affects children during their developmental years. I have seen families with several children in which one child has decided that the practice of working past where they are is not required in their adult years, while another child in the same family has turned the practice into a lifelong pursuit. In some cases, this is traceable to the parents going through a low point in their lives during their child's formative years, during which time their children gain an entirely different perspective on this aspect of life than they would have normally. Even though the low point was a temporary speed bump in the parents' lives, the children gained a life-changing perspective.

Parents, don't beat yourselves up just yet. Notice that I did not say which child had which perspective. Remember that the programming of motivation and beliefs in each person is also a

300

combination of things that individuals do for themselves (nature versus nurture). Some people will form a positive, life-changing belief out of an entirely negative situation. In some situations, the low point or life-changing event that the parents experienced may be the impetus for their children to build successful lives by continuously working past where they are. The children may subconsciously decide to follow what they see, or they may make a conscious decision to rectify a deficiency that they perceive in their environment. Whatever the case, people can control only their own lives. Thus, being the best version of yourself and thereby setting the most positive example is the best that you can do.

Goals Kill Working Past Where You Are

In the last chapter, I started out by saying that you shouldn't set goals. I said that because I have found that extremely goal-oriented people have the most problems with this practice area. A goal is like watching the finish line as you run a race: the closer you get, the shorter your focus becomes. You keep looking at the finish line, pushing yourself to exert all your energy and give all you have. You don't reserve any energy, but instead expend every bit by rationing your energy to exert the last remaining bit as you approach the finish line. The result is that you have exerted all your energy and done your absolute best, but you have not budgeted for anything beyond the finish line. After the completion of this goal, you have to stop completely, recover, reevaluate what is next, determine your new surroundings, and then plan where to go next.

Life is a continuously changing stream. If you focus on a single finishing point, you will lose focus on the rest of the changes around you. If you are swimming in a stream toward something that is upstream, when you take your focus off the stream and make the object (goal) your focus, you lose sight of the bigger picture of the stream. What happens when the stream changes so that you and your goal have changed positions and you are now moving with the current, against progress, swimming in entirely the wrong direction? Setting goals encourages this kind of monomaniacal focus. To be successful and to direct your work continuously in a positive direction, you must constantly evaluate your path by setting your focus a step ahead of each progressive step you make.

"The Greatest Project Manager" is a story I like to tell because it is about one of my first experiences with management, when I had the opportunity to work alongside a few of the best managers that I could have ever had access to. I was working at the United States Air force Academy at the time and was in the middle of a bit of a work dispute between two parties with different understandings of the definition of my job. This was between the contractor I worked for and the USAF leadership, each of which had different expectations—to say the least— concerning my assignment. The Air force had included my position in the contract after removing a lieutenant colonel position, but the contracted company had shifted me to this same position as a junior project manager. Since that is more of a side note, I will not dwell on it too much other than to note that it resulted in my having daily interactions with very high-ranking officers in the Air Force while I was still relatively inexperienced in my career.

This job gave me the opportunity to work on a major construction project with a management team that was part of the Army Corp of Engineers. The majority of my duties involved working on the same project directly with two project managers, whom I will contrast here. One of them was a very seasoned, soft-spoken man, and the other, in his late forties, was very dynamic and outspoken. Both were exceptionally organized, and both maintained a highly efficient project to which hundreds of contractors and sometimes thousands of workers contributed. However, there was a large difference between the two. The more seasoned manager spent a bit less time

302

expressing himself during our discussions of each of the project's phases. Instead, he turned to something else that he was doing all the time, and this preoccupation, while obviously important to him, was not apparent to me at first.

At the conclusion of a project, it is inevitable that conversations among project participants turn away from the project's business, which is usually complete before the participants disperse. At this point, conversations move toward less meaningful subjects. The manager that I viewed as less outspoken had the quality of working past where he was; instead of engaging in the less meaningful conversations, he would begin to look at future projects and phases. He had learned to default to working past where he was. He was not anti-social or short with anyone, but he just never seemed to be involved in conversations when they reached the point at which everyone else realized that they had gone too far, wasted time, or moved on to inappropriate topics.

Watching this dynamic unfold over time, I realized that the seasoned project manager was very excited for the next phase of each project when the initial meetings for them came around. The second manger was quite comfortable on the current phase of the project or the current project, but he became very nervous when it came time to start the next phase of the project or a new project. The seasoned manager actually wanted and anticipated the next phase because he was working past where he was.

This became especially apparent at the end of the project. The seasoned manager was constantly busy even when there did not seem to be anything left to do on the project. We were wrapping it up. So what was he so intent on doing?

The outspoken project manager was on the spot with wrapping up the project. He took care of each project signoff item and became increasingly meticulous as the project drew closer to its end. In fact, because there were fewer outstanding items left to do, he became more and more particular and focused on getting the tasks done correctly. This occupied progressively more of my time as well. We had a goal of finishing this project, and by God, we were both going to do the best job ever. We worked long hours late into the night, and on several occasions, the outspoken manager made comments about the other manger not pulling his weight and not working as long of hours as we were. His references insinuated that his counterpart may not have been as skilled or dedicated as we were. They were often directed in jest at the more seasoned manager's lofty reputation. The outspoken manager and I, admittedly, both agreed that the more seasoned manager's stellar reputation did not seem to be deserved.

Our work schedule grew intense, and at the same time, our vision of the project became shorter. We knew that the project was ending and did not want to miss any details. In retrospect, the seasoned manager did not slow down at all. He kept the same pace throughout the entire project. Unlike us, however, this project was not all he was working on. He continued to work past where he was, just as he had the entire time. One day, both the outspoken manager and I received an email announcing a meeting about a new project on the horizon. The seasoned manager was organizing this meeting and had exceptionally detailed plans for the new project.

As the meeting unfolded, the seasoned manager passed out blueprints and a detailed list of tasks for a new project that displayed hundreds, if not thousands, of hours of planning work. The blueprints were designs for a multi-year project, which the seasoned manager had no intention to complete because the project would extend into his retirement years. As I was still early in my career, I was starstruck and inspired by the learning experience. However, the outspoken project manager struck a very defensive posture as if he felt trivialized. He was upset that he had not been included, but when the details unfolded, he realized that he had been included the entire time. He had been working right alongside us during the preparation, though he had not recognized that this preparation was anything more than random, passing conversation.

As the meeting went on, it became apparent that we all had been in the middle of every stage of what had been planned and that neither the outspoken manager nor I had been looking far enough into the future to know what was in front of us. As the current project neared completion, we had both shortened our views repeatedly until we both only saw the remaining project items. Since a limited number of items remained on the current project, we inserted tasks to keep ourselves busy so we could feel as if we were still accomplishing as much as before. In retrospect, those tasks only served to increase the anxiety of everyone involved, and in many cases, they appeared to be some kind of power trip to several of the project's contributors.

Had the seasoned project manager not been there to bridge the work seamlessly from the current to the future project, there would have been a complete lack of direction at the end of the first project. We had no plans beyond the completion and finalization of the current project. Moreover, all the information and knowledge were transferred from the current project to the plans for the future project. Much of that work would have been lost without this meticulous documentation of each lesson learned and process performed, all of which contributed to the next project's design plan, and an entire committee would have been necessary just to initiate the plans for the next project.

Feeding Into Enjoying the Process

Think back to a time when you were approaching the end of a phase of your life, such as completing high school. You focused only on the end of this phase when the time was dragging on and when each day was long because, like watching a clock, each minute seemed longer with anticipation. When you first made the decision to do whatever you were going to do after high school, such as attending a particular college or joining the military, your perspective toward your current phase instantly changed. It suddenly became less relevant, but at the same time, it also became much easier. You started to enjoy the last bit of time in the current phase because it had become merely a stepping-stone toward the next phase. The next phase had many unknowns, so in comparison, the current stage seemed familiar and, therefore, easy and relaxing.

Recall the example of a goal being like running a race and watching the finish line. In the race, you exert all your energy and give all you have, without reserving any energy, while expending everything by rationing your remaining energy until the end. Which seems easier to handle, the relaxing, "this stage is easy compared to the next" or the stressful, "exertion until the last"? Here are a few things that happen in your mindset when you practice working past where you are and that change the "you" portion of your life cycle (your mindset):

1) You minimize the collapse and physiological loss of direction after the completion of a goal.

2) You start to enjoy the process of your current task relative to the unknowns of the next.

3) You are less overwhelmed because you are more prepared for the next phase as the tasks overlap.

4) You are more effective because you adjust your current effort when defining the next.

5) You increase your confidence by becoming more prepared for the future stages of your life.

6) You are more effective because you identify changes to your path before opportunities slip away.

Working past where you are feeds into your mindset, and it affects the other two life-engineering process areas, which are discussed in the chapters, "Determining a Path" and "Enjoying the Process." Time after time, I have felt the pressure lift while working on a task by exploring and defining what the next phase of the task will be. Knowing how you will apply the current phase makes it relevant and necessary in your mind. The feeling of relief springs from the reduced uncertainty about the validity or accurateness of what you are working on. Enjoying the process, which we will discuss in the next chapter, is often about adjusting your emotional state to what you are doing "right now." When I experience this sigh of relief, its completion and, later, the memory of that phase take on an entirely different meaning to me. Positive energy is about how you feel and how you remember feeling.

When some people play chess, they approach the game by looking at the entire board and reacting to it at each turn, making the least costly move. Then they wait for the other player to move before they reevaluate the board and respond to their opponent's move. Anxiety and concern will cloud their minds as they wait for the next move. If you were to approach the same game from the perspective of people who are working past where they are, you would play your turn and plan the next few moves all at once. You know why you made that move on that turn, but most importantly, you await your next, preplanned move with the anticipation and excitement that it will be successful. Your mindset with regard to the entire game changes to excitement as opposed to concern. The difference is that over time your brain associates an overall memory of one of these two emotions, whichever is felt the most.

The Strongest Biological Trigger

This section is a bit of a spoiler for future content that I have been compiling, which will most likely be the subject of a future book, but I feel that this particular concept is so relevant to this chapter that I must include it here anyway. We as people are attracted to certain traits in other people, sometimes so strongly that we seem to lack the ability to control our attraction. I will save the reason for this for future material, but the particular trait that in my experience is the strongest involuntary biological trigger directly relates to working past where we are. This biological trigger causes people to be attracted to other people whether there is also a sexual attraction or not. People in general are drawn to this particular trait more than they are to any other.

Physical Example

Many of us are familiar with the concepts of acceleration, deceleration, and steady state. We instinctively know how these concepts apply in the physical world. When we drive down a multilane highway, we subconsciously take note of the cars traveling in a steady state around us. These vehicles keep pace with our own vehicle. We pay attention to where they are positioned

308

and know that, if they are in a steady state (neither accelerating nor decelerating relative to us), we can briefly divert our gaze from them, and they will be in the same relative position when we gaze at them again. We keep such steady-state entities in our minds, but we don't particularly think of them as individuals, only as a group or as part of the background environment.

When one of the steady-state vehicles around us starts to decelerate, it immediately vanishes from our perception of it as part of the background environment, as if it had never existed. The same is true of a decelerating or slower-moving vehicle that we approach. We pay it no more mind than we do a passing roadside object. Why do we totally disregard the details of decelerating entities or of objects that we view only as things we quickly pass by? And why do we group the nearby steady-state entities in our minds and memories?

In contrast, if a vehicle accelerates behind us or approaches from behind, our focus shifts to that vehicle. We start to pay it attention and follow it, retaining memory of its movement distinct from the environment of all the other vehicles around us. We comment on these vehicles, take note of them, and know details about them, having paid no attention to the vehicles in a steady state or decelerating. The faster a vehicle is accelerating, the more it attracts our attention and stands out in our memory. After a long trip, we recall the motorcycle or the red car that rapidly passed, while having no lasting memory of the thousands of other vehicles around them. Why are we instinctively drawn to the accelerating vehicles?

This is our strongest innate biological trigger for attraction. We cannot help being attracted to accelerating entities around us. This attraction transfers to entities that are improving or to people who are perceived, by others or by themselves, to be gaining in their lives. Yes, like the accelerating vehicle, we seek out the people around us who are flourishing, who are becoming more relevant, who are popular, who are capable, or who are growing measurable resources in any way. Human culture development proves that those who are attracted to the growth and acceleration of the people around them are the most successful at passing along their own genetic makeups—including the attraction to acceleration—to the next generation. Why is this? It is because the people who are attracted to the most effective leaders have gained in value along with those leaders, and their cultures have expanded effectively and remain on this planet to this day. An attraction to people who are accelerating leads to success. You will have a greater capacity for success if you align with someone who is succeeding.

Working Past Equals Acceleration

Working past where you are is equivalent to accelerating in your life. The difference between someone who is accelerating and someone who is not is the effective application of the knowledge of what lies ahead. The knowledge of what lies ahead springs from defining the next step, stage, or path. The further you define items ahead of you, the more effective you will be at transitioning into the next phase. Effective transitioning into the next phase leaves unfinished action items in the current phase, which you can delegate to other people. Thus, working past obstacles causes acceleration and opens up success for others to share.

When I talk to young people about dating and attracting the opposite sex, I tell them to focus on working past where they are because the attraction of everyone around them will follow. If you want the attention of a young woman, you will be better able to include her in a future activity if you know what you will be doing in the future. When you have activities planned anyway, you do not have to plan a special activity for you and your date. If you have a list of things that you do every week, which can grow and expand to multiple things next month and to hundreds of things next year, then people will just start to join you. In fact, even though a less-attractive person who follows this pattern may not get a date on the first, second, or even third try, when they have a

310

plan for the future that continuously unfolds, they will eventually get the attention they seek from the person they desire. People cannot ignore this biological trigger.

Effects on the Accelerator

As the one accelerating, you will want to be prepared for certain aspects of the dynamic created by this biological trigger. People are attracted to growth because of an uncontrollable urge to participate in this growth; however, participation means different things to different people. In general, people want to ride along with someone who succeeds, accelerates, and grows in order to share in the benefits. However, those who ride along will slow the growth of the one who is accelerating. The intent is to ride along, but the outcome is often to hold back the person who is growing.

In my experience, I have encountered a few notable mindsets of others in relation to someone who is accelerating. The first, as I described in the paragraph above, involves the people who want to ride along. They are interested in using the benefits of accelerating growth to benefit themselves. Often, this is helpful because when you are working past where you are, you want to move on to the next phase before the current phase is complete, and having people ready to step in to complete the remaining tasks is beneficial. However, you cannot control where such people attempt to engage or place their efforts. In fact, often they will attempt to compete at the same level rather than take over where the accelerating individual left off. Quite similarly to the secondary competitors that arise with any successful product, these people will use the ride along to gain an idea, which they individualize, and they create an offshoot that becomes an alternative trajectory to the initial growth.

People with certain personalities want to align with those who are accelerating. These people often become fans and desire to be associated with the growing person for many personal, individual reasons. These people are usually very respectful and provide positive feedback, which is something we will discuss much more in the chapter "Enjoying the Process." Using these people to set up recurring affirmation of your success and your progress will greatly support you as the accelerating person.

The third variety of mindset belongs to those who have become the most troublesome for me personally and who have often become detrimental to my growth. These people want to use someone who is accelerating to compare against their own growth. In some cases, this can fuel friendly competition—as long as it is not continuously engaging to the point that it takes up too much of your time and you cannot maintain your acceleration. The detrimental cases are those in which the comparing person was interested in proving their own worth by reducing the worth of others. This personality type will be detrimental to the accelerating person almost every time. Historically, these have often caused violent conflict when certain factions of resistance to effective leaders had to be removed from their distractingly influential positions.

In my own life, people have contacted me hoping to gain a friendly position with me. One took quite a bit of time identifying and reviewing my work. They showed interest in almost every aspect of what I was doing until a certain point when they switched their focus. At that point, they decided they were much more advanced than I was. They seemed to change their position and adopted the opinion that I did not deserve the initial respect that they had given me. In one such case, someone spent several months seemingly to become a friend, with interest in becoming a business colleague, and then the person proceeded to explain how my entire life's work was just an overly intellectual attempt to wastefully reclassify things. Following their evaluation, they proceeded to start teaching me the benefits of methods that were alternatives

312

to mine. I politely listened to them and then responded with inquiries about how I could shift my entire path toward the correct direction they were describing. The resulting conversation was similar to that of a person who had converted a non-believer to their religion. This individual's disregard for my entire life's work reached such an epic level that I wondered why they had ever bothered to contact me in the first place.

After the knock to my ego subsided and I had picked myself up off the floor, so to speak, I figured I should look over that person's works and efforts. In the modern age, a Google search tells all you need to know. After I realized that a search for the person's name produced no results, my anxiety subsided somewhat. This person had the mentality of people who are attracted to the biological trigger of acceleration with the prospect of tearing it apart in order to advance their own self-worth. This personality type is the most damaging, and the only way I have found to deal with people like that is to identify them and separate from them as quickly as possible.

What Makes Self-Actualization

Once you have followed the life-engineering process and have practiced it for several years, you become accustomed to not setting—or even having—goals. Instead, you end up being productive by enjoying the process of the work. Not having a goal for many years changes your outlook. You will find yourself working on things with an endgame that does not appear to be achievable at all. If you recall the chapter "Human Logic and Thought Patterns," we talked about the thing that makes people different from every other species on the planet. The logical thought stopper (belief) is what makes people do illogical things repeatedly when the direct outcome of the effort does not serve any immediate need. Working past where you are and experiencing the excitement of each phase puts you into a mindset of continuous work with no expectation of completion.

I can see how many of the greatest achievers in history reached such a point in their lives. The theory of needs, described by Maslow's hierarchy of needs, labeled the behaviors of those who do not seek rewards as self-actualizing. I see this as the level that people achieve when they are no longer working toward anything that other people recognize or that provides any satisfaction to their achievement. To self-actualize is to gain from within oneself everything one needs to support one's own efforts. In my experience, all people can engineer into themselves this self-trained and achievable trait.

Linking "Working Past" to Path

In the chapter, "Determining a Path," we talked about the influences you will need in your path. Adding your required influences into the process of working past where you are gives you the opportunity to plan ahead to improve yourself. By adding a course each semester at a local university, you can add both self-improvement and social interaction. You can practice public speaking at a Toastmasters club event or build your networking at a project manager's monthly meeting. Attending a lecture or helping at a local charity event may also be on a list of beneficial influences. Whatever influences appear on the list for your path, planning some at regular intervals will be essential for both your feeling of accomplishment and your personal growth.

Setting up Recurring Affirmations

Part of working past where you are is setting up future activities that will bring positive energy into each aspect of your life cycle. People need praise, but often they don't realize that they have control over praise. Recurring affirmation happens when the things you have done return to benefit you in the future by making you feel positive. Though you may think that I hate social media based on much of my writing, this is not the case. Social media is the best tool for recurring affirmation that I have ever seen. People have learned to do this very well, but often they do not do it to support their own productivity. In fact, most social media interaction reduces productivity. Once again, the next chapter will talk about this more.

You can also set up recurring affirmations in many other ways, such as with traditional, offline activities. Many religious organizations provide this to people on a regular basis. We all have a basic human need to interact with others, even if we are not actively engaging. At the most primitive level of our cognitive selves, we learned the practice of associating our thought lengths with our surroundings. As we talked about in the chapter "Thought-Length Hierarchy," this happens in the very early stages of our development. In my opinion, these needs are so hardwired because, later in life, we do not have the ability to reprogram or even to think at such a short thought length on a conscious level.

Performing or engaging with groups of uncritical people in religious settings fulfills these basic needs. Though I have often been at odds with these settings where individuals in a religion's control structure are socially pressured to adhere to actions that are unhealthy, I also see great value in these organizations when it comes to recurring affirmation. The feeling of acceptance and the praise received for participation are in my opinion the strongest and most effective tools that organized religion has for maintaining and building participation. Regularly attending a community outreach or religious organization definitely is one way to add recurring affirmation to your life.

Since religious and community organizations are designed to be accepting of everyone, it will also be helpful to add recurring affirmation from sources that require skillful accomplishment. Professional organizations, business chambers of commerce, university lecturers, or even performing arts groups are some great examples. The praise received from others because of a competence-based display or performance will be far more fulfilling and will affirm your feelings of accomplishment. I recommend maintaining at least one professional organization membership and finding a competence-based means of public, recurring affirmation.

Exhaustion and Shortsightedness

In an earlier section, I used going on a hike as an example for working past where you are. When hikers look to the next section of the trail in front of them, they define what is ahead in an attempt to make the current section less taxing and more enjoyable. After a long period of hiking you may also know the feeling of physically exhaustion over time. Because hikers start to feel fatigue, they begin to lose their focus on what lies ahead. They shorten their focus as they would in a race, looking only at the finish line, not because they are focused on the goal, but because of exhaustion. Often they do not realize that they have done this until they have shortened their focus so much that they trip over a root or a stone that they shortsightedly did not step high enough to avoid.

The wakeup call that rouses us from our shortsightedness often comes in the form of an accident, the repercussions of which we must then address. Many of us do not recognize the need to reset

316

this shortsightedness. Our bodies give us signs that we ignore. A good friend of mine was so determined to be successful in her life that she pushed herself far beyond anyone I had ever known. However, a considerable amount of her effort was devoted to combating the results of her shortsightedness, which was caused by the exhausted state in which she lived almost constantly. Because I often try to save those around me, I tried to pull her away from her primary focus for some downtime, which was always a struggle because of how driven she was.

I watched her sit at a computer for over twelve hours a day as she forced herself to complete a task that drove her to exhaustion. Because her work often involved editing images repetitively, her level of productivity was quite easily measurable based on the number of files she had completed. Often, I observed as she entered the state of mental exhaustion and shortsightedness midway through the day. She would sometimes sit on the same image for extended periods, allowing Facebook, texting, or her surroundings to distract and preoccupy her. When offered the suggestion to take a break, this self-driven woman would disregard the offer and respond that she had not yet worked enough hours. Her drive made her want to be more productive than her body was capable of.

We all have these times when we enter short thought lengths and become shortsighted due to exhaustion. I have known people who have multiple jobs whose evening job consists of manual and repetitive labor, and this befits them because of their shortsightedness. They could not continue their day job, which requires more insight and forethought, but they were successful at an evening job stacking boxes. In this area, knowing yourself is once again the key. You have to know how long working past where you are will be effective—not just each day, but also over time. Months and months of sustained focus on a project can also cause shortsightedness. Know when to take a break, and schedule breaks on your path.

Focus on the End

I am going to talk about something that is not instinctual for most people. We do not naturally think this way. It requires a conscious effort, but it is more difficult than creating a habit because the end of events or tasks does not recur periodically. Events and tasks are different lengths and end at different times. Some only take a few minutes, while others last weeks or months.

Since my son lives in a post-divorce situation with separated parents, and since both of his parents are extremely different in this respect, it is an area of constant discord. When he first arrives at my home for a visit, he dreads the most trivial tasks related to organizing or cleaning the house. After several weeks at my home, it becomes a nonissue as he becomes accustomed to my rules. When I discussed this with him last year, he explained why this was the case. He asked me why it seemed so much easier to do the dishes right after using them. He summed up the next issue in that one question.

This issue is what I call "focusing on the end," and I define it in one formula: "The next successful (fill in the blank) begins at the end of the current (fill in the blank)." This means that, no matter what you do, if you plan for the next objective at the end of the current one, you will be more successful. In fact, this habit is one of the most productivity-enhancing, success-creating gifts I have given myself. My son's question reflected his feelings toward housework, specifically about doing the dishes. He extremely disliked even thinking about doing the dishes—so much so that he exhibited a visible stress reaction at the mere thought of it. I asked him why it was such a problem for him. He replied that all of the dishes were dirty most of the time at his other home. The thought of cleaning dishes equated to the contemplation of a task that would result in hours of work for multiple people. He did not want to think about it because he had a stimulus-response reaction to it, which caused stress just by thinking about it.

We derive our feelings about many topics from our reaction to thinking about them. If you think about ice cream, chances are you do not have any negative feelings about that thought. You dislike some things because thinking about them immediately produces a stress reaction as you associate them with past experiences. In my son's case, he lost his stress reaction to doing dishes gradually by completing the small task of doing just one set of dishes, not an entire kitchen of dirty dishes. This changed his reaction to the task. He no longer had anxiety about the situation surrounding the beginning of the task because of his presence in my environment, in which I maintained a disciplined focus on completing the meal and promptly returning the kitchen to its original state. This is the most important gift I give myself, as I feel excited to begin the next task because no discomfort mars its inception.

Every effective, successful person I have met in my life has practiced this approach. Many relate it more to a desire to be organized than to an attempt to enjoy the processes around a certain task, but that is, nevertheless, what is accomplished. Here is a word of warning, however: while this has been what makes me the most successful, it has also caused the most discord when living in close quarters with other people. There are always different levels of tolerance among multiple people when it comes to practicing this approach. The individual who least tolerates strictly focusing on the end will end up causing the others stress. I had to find a balance between trying to focus on the end and not causing stress to others around me at the end of each task or project. In any case, I have found it more productive as an individual to push the stress to the end of a task than to be reluctant to start the same task because of stress felt at the beginning.

Practicing Working Past Where You Are

When you reach the point of working on achievable projects and scheduling portions of day-to-day tasks for the current stage of your path, you should not still be thinking about adding new tasks at the current level. Even if you are changing to a different branch on your path, you should already have defined the branch's change of direction at a level or so beyond the level at which you are beginning to work.

For example, if you had to plan meals for large groups of people, you would plan several days' worth of meals so that you could determine all the ingredients. Ordering products for consumption has to take into account product freshness and should account for leftovers and for items prepared via the same method that can be used over a span of several meals. Your planning may include making bread every night for the entire next day or making extra rice during the lunch preparation for later use in rice pudding, which the night baker will cook for the next day. You would want to have decided what to make for dinner well before lunch ends. In fact, you would not want to change a meal without a longer notice of at least several days. Changes of or insertions to a meal at the last minute would cause almost indefinitely cascading issues for future meals or ingredients.

Though changing your path will be required several times over your life, if you do not have at least the next two levels of your path defined, you should resist changing paths. Many people will start to define what they perceive to be the next level of their path, but then they determine that the current level should be abandoned and that a new branch should become their next level. Others will have obvious branches presented to them and will jump entirely over to the new branch, defining the tasks as they go. Immediately, many of us may relate these behaviors to the personalities of people we know or even to our own personalities. Although far from my personality type, the more impulsive variety of opportunistic people may benefit from leaping to the occasional new branch, but they will most likely find themselves in a pattern of not completing any of the branches they start. When the undefined tasks become roadblocks, the individual will be forced to stop altogether or to return to previously unfinished, now delayed, or irrelevant past levels.

The practice of "working past where you are" should include a task-to-task correlation between your current task and the next level (or two) of that task in the future. As I am writing this section, I know my next two levels involve writing a second book that examines the social implications of each topic and creating presentations or podcasts to help people better understand the concepts covered in this book. I practice my own ideas by continuously defining these next two levels when what I write triggers ideas that are relevant to each. I am not looking to work on either of these, but I have a working outline of each that tracks and captures my ideas. As you can see from the outline in the image, the last entry relates to this practice area and to how it fits into my thoughts for a second book. This is by no means official or formal, but rather a way to brainstorm the possibilities. In other words, one should not expect to find that comparing the outline below with my future book would yield a line-by-line match.

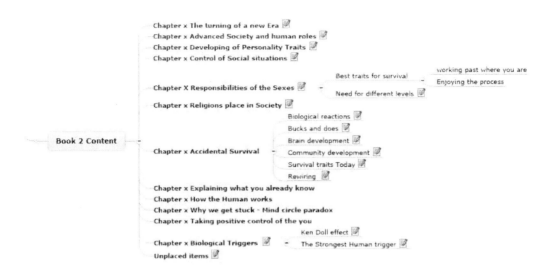

Recall my example of the greatest project manager. This is what the seasoned project manager was doing each time he seemed to be preoccupied while the rest of us were filling our time with unstructured chat. He was adding one future task at a time when they crossed his mind as they related to the current task. The outspoken project manager only realized later that he had been included in each step of the new projects, after first getting upset when he thought he had been blindsided. When the seasoned manager laid out the details at the next project meeting, the junior manager realized he had been included in the conversations, consulted about organizational decisions, and even given credit for his contribution, but all of this work and effort would have been lost if not for the process of the seasoned manager "working past where he was," not only with his words but also his documentation of the ongoing progress.

Implementing this process area is only done with conscious effort. It will not happen without taking some initial steps to set up the process. Finding a way to document the ongoing work is paramount to successful implementation. My tool of choice, which suits my needs for organization and documentation and which has been essential to my application of "working past where I am," is mind-mapping software. You can find many readily available mind-mapping software products, but you may also find that other tools, such as spreadsheets or task organizers, work better for you.

Remember, though, that finding an organizational tool only enhances your ability to document. The discipline to continuously use the tool whenever you have an idea or while you work on current tasks is entirely your individual responsibility. I have often heard people say that it only takes thirty days to form a habit. For me, this has been true—I can form a habit in thirty days. One trick I employ is to set my timer to vibrate every ten minutes during my workday to remind me to use my documentation tool. This is yet another time when being self-aware will also benefit you. Look for the times when your mind wanders from your current task and use that break to open your documentation tool. Often, my thoughts wander because I am thinking of something outside of my current task, which will often relate to things I want to capture anyway.

Documenting the Present

Documenting what you see around you and collecting what you know is the first step of "working past where you are." In order to start to assess the next step beyond the current one, you have to write down what actually happens in the present. When people ask me where to start, I tell them to write down what they do whenever they do it for a month—or however long it takes them to form a habit. Once you get in this habit, then the next step is to add additional components to the process of documentation.

Each time you write down what you have done, think about one or more things you could or should do to make that effort more worthwhile. If you have finished cleaning the floor, then another way you could add value is by stripping and waxing the floor and, after that, by sanding and refinishing it. You can relate both of these things to the next two generations of making the floor better.

Let's take the example of the following list of household improvements and show how documentation of the present leads to future success.

- Clean the floor

- Wash the walls

- Clean the windows

- Tighten the deck screws

- Dust the furniture

- Wash the dishes

- Fix the sink

- Vacuum the floors

- Sweep the deck

- Change light bulbs

- Make the bed

- Scrub the bathroom

- Water the plants

As we are performing these tasks and then writing down what we did, we may also note the following things:

- **Clean the floor**
  - The floor has water damage around the refrigerator, and the plant holders near the door need to have their leaks fixed.

- **Wash the walls**
  - The paint is chipping and fading around the west wall; accent blue on the wall would bring out the décor in the room.

- **Clean the windows**
  - The windowpanes are faded, and in the sunroom they have water damage.

- **Tighten the deck screws**
  - The wood on the west side looks weak, and upon further inspection, it appears termites have infested it.

- **Dust the furniture**
  - The carpet around the couch is much thicker, and paths indented in the carpet show that it needs to be replaced within three years.

- **Wash the dishes**
  - The sink is leaking, and the faucet needs tightening.

- **Vacuum the floors**
  - The electrical outlet in the family room is not working.

- **Sweep the deck**

- Leaves are dying on the tree to the left; overgrown bushes restrict the view of the play area.

- **Change light bulbs**

  - The cord on the ceiling fan is blackened, and the fan switch is broken. The shoe rack in the closet blocks clothing and light in the rest of the closet.

- **Make the bed**

  - Under the bed would be good storage for something less often needed.

- **Scrub the bathroom**

  - The tile is full of mildew, and some tiles are loose around the toilet. Bar soap makes cleaning the soap trays quite difficult, so switch to liquid soap.

- **Water the plants**

  - The old, rusty screws that attach the swing to the porch roof need to be replaced.

Although it may not be practical to document each item of housework, it does make for a familiar example—one that demonstrates the progression of how we identify the next levels of our life path while we are still completing the current level. You can see that each task led to another, specific future task, which you become aware of during the current level. If you resolved to commit each of these to memory, what percentage of these do you think you would remember to complete later? If you were to use the things that you noticed to make a three-level list of the next home improvement tasks you should undertake, then it may look like this:

Level One (Newly Identified Achievable Tasks)

- Get a water catcher for the plant holder near the door

- Turn off the water to the ice maker in the refrigerator

- Scrape the paint on the west wall

- Clean the gutters around the sunroom

- Move the heavy furniture away from the west side of the deck

- Tighten the plumbing connections on the sink faucet

- Check the breaker box

    - Is there a tripped breaker to the outlet in the family room?

    - Shut off the ceiling fan breaker

        - Are these two related?

- Trim the hedges by the play area

- Clean the bathroom tiles to remove mildew

- Take down the porch swing before someone gets hurt

- Tighten the loose tiles in the bathroom

- Schedule a shopping trip

Level Two (Tasks for When Funding Is Available)

- Call a refrigerator repair man to fix the leaks

- Purchase blue paint

- Purchase stain for the windowpanes

- Apply termite killer to the deck

- Schedule a professional carpet washing

- Plant a new tree near the dying tree to the left of the deck

- Call an electrician to repair the ceiling fan and the outlet in the family room

- Find and purchase an under-the-bed shoe rack

- Purchase tile sealant

- Purchase new mounts and chains for the porch swing

Level Three (Fulfilling Projects)

- Replace the carpet in the living room (three years)

- Paint the west wall blue (two months)

- Finish and seal the windowpanes in the sunroom (before winter)

- Replace the deck wood (next summer)

  o Include a new porch swing

  o Utilize the space where the tree is dying

  o Combine with repairs to the leaks in the sunroom

- Move the shoe rack from the closet to under the bed

- Replace the tile in the bathroom

  o Match the bathroom tile to the carpet and accent walls

  o Combine the plumber with the refrigerator repair

Wow! It's amazing what we can do when we add the small feature of documentation to our present list of tasks. We have made a valuable list of achievable next tasks that we can rank, organize, and prioritize. We have made a list of things on which we need to spend money to accomplish the next level of tasks. Finally, we have identified our motivation for each of the two lower levels by making a third planning level in which we combine those tasks and work on them

328

collectively. We can schedule the next level of tasks when we have the time, but only insofar as they are compatible with our future direction and our path toward higher levels. This gives us the ability to adjust our paths as we set our priorities.

We can bring in more people because we don't have it all in our heads and because we don't require ourselves to be involved in each next level step. These lists can now be turned over to another person entirely. You can see how performing this one exercise, which you can do while you work on your current level, can enable you to add more people. Continuing to grow your path and to produce multiple additional levels with each task fuels the acceleration discussed earlier in this chapter. When you have the ability to include others, you elicit the excitement of others and invite natural, human, biologically triggered attraction.

Chapter XII

Enjoying the Process

This chapter is dedicated to "enjoying the process" because of its fundamental importance to achieving success. The subject of the chapter is how to establish enjoyable processes that will lead you to success. As you might expect, "enjoying the process" has two conceptual components: enjoyment, or pleasure, and process.

Pleasure is one of the strongest human motivations. It is often stronger than other strong motivations. Sensual pleasure provides obvious examples of this, sometimes at our peril. For example, some people face great health risks if they do not lose weight, yet they gain weight because of the pleasure of eating. Or, couples sometimes conceive children "by accident" because they give in to temptation. They are driven by pleasure, which is to say, profound human instincts. But pleasure can also be a powerful motivation in achieving success. People who succeed enjoy their paths to success.

The idea of "process" relates to several themes we have been discussing. In the 1916 book *The Master Key System*, Charles Haanel says that when you master yourself, "you will find as much pleasure in the execution as in the satisfaction of attainment and achievement." First published as a correspondence course in 1912, *The Master Key System* teaches methods of thinking designed to help people master their own thoughts and minds. A famous quote of the Buddha is, "It is better to travel well than to arrive." Many wise people throughout history have realized that accomplishment is not the key to unlocking success. I believe that we are all capable of finding enjoyment in whatever we decide to do. Each of us can enjoy the process of achieving as

330

much as the result. We must first enjoy the process, and then we will have great accomplishments. The greater the achievement, the less relevant the accomplishment will be compared to how much we enjoyed getting there.

In the movie *Forrest Gump*, the main character is a man with very limited cognitive abilities. In fact, one of the more famous lines from the movie is when he admits, "I am not a very smart man." Despite Forrest Gump's lack of intelligence, we can all still learn much from him about how to enjoy the process. His limited intellect enables him to excel at very trivial tasks that most people would not enjoy performing repeatedly. Each stage of his life revolves around this feature of his personality. He performs trivial activities repeatedly until he gains an amazing mastery over them. For example, his love of running propels him to become a football star, a war hero, and finally a media icon. His enjoyment of Ping-Pong launches him as an international hero and celebrity, although he is unaware of it and it ultimately confuses him.

Forrest Gump's defining trait is persistence, and each stage of his life is defined by his persistence in performing tasks repeatedly. However, while some of us aspire to great feats, we struggle to achieve our aspirations. Why is this? A good friend of mine was so determined to be successful that she pushed herself far beyond anyone else I had ever known. She would sit in front of a computer screen working on a long list of tasks. She had great advice from coaches about what should be on her list, and they even had a formula for determining the number of tasks she needed to complete in order to consider herself more successful. Her job required meeting sales quotas. She knew that she had to pursue a hundred leads per week to garner ten follow-up conversations, which would on average result in three successful transactions. Thus, she would set out to acquire her hundred leads each week, but the struggle caused her internal turmoil that left a sour, determined look on her face. She had resolved that work consisted of punishment, meeting quotas, hours of production, and forcing herself to perform.

It was difficult to endure watching her both struggle to perform and fight the ill feelings her work gave her. Her long hours of feeling bad each day defined her memories of each task, each day, and the work in general. Living with a negative mindset gradually made her associate negativity with work, which led to her becoming exhausted. Much of her effort was spent battling her own shortsightedness caused by her almost constant exhaustion. This self-defeating condition stemmed from her belief that she was not supposed to enjoy the process of work.

Mindset of Enjoyment

Let's take a lesson from Forrest Gump. How can we enjoy the tasks that advance us on our paths? Often, it is simply a matter of how we feel about what we are doing. In the chapter, "Working Past Where You Are," I used the example of a chess game to describe how to transform concern and anxiety into anticipation and excitement by planning a few moves ahead, making the future less unknown and, therefore, less worrisome. Shifting from reacting to each move by the opponent to following a plan changes one's experience of the game from negative to positive. You can change your emotional perception of a task from negative to positive by changing your thoughts about the task in several ways. This, in turn, makes your emotional memory positive, which finally creates a positive overall memory and point of view of the task.

In some situations, I have made games out of repetitive tasks. This can involve friendly competition with someone else, or one can compete against oneself to complete a task more effectively, frequently, or thoroughly. In a very difficult naval training program, I used this in two different ways. First, since our study time was tracked, I resolved to log more hours than anyone else did. Next, since more study time meant less time for other aspects of my life, I decided to combine study with other activities; for example, I did my workouts during our hourly, ten-minute-long study breaks. I raced to each study break and tried to perform more crunches,

332

pushups, and other exercises than I had during the previous break. The anticipation of looking forward to the breaks and the ambition to study more than all of the other students put me in a positive mindset.

In many work situations, I used the same method of creating games to set up self-driven performance metrics. This made my metrics more stringent than the organization required, increasing both my value to the company and my sense of self-worth. It also gave me something to anticipate pleasantly each day. In many of my corporate jobs, turning my work into a game involved completing tasks or communicating with coworkers. I often made a game of sending emails to as many people's inboxes as possible before they arrived at the office in the morning. This simple transformation of work into a game, even though it was not conscious or deliberate, frequently gave people the impression that I was one of their bosses. When you think about it, it's human nature to rank thoughts in a hierarchy subconsciously based on hierarchies among people.

Enjoying activities apart from work or advancement helps us find enjoyment in work or advancement. In the example of my friend who believed that it was normal for work to be unenjoyable, she worked long hours becoming less productive the longer she worked. Sometimes, after she had accomplished forty-five minutes' worth of work in an 8-12-hour work session, I and other friends would drag her away from her work to have fun for a couple hours. That allowed her to work productively upon her return, accomplishing two hours' worth of work in the next two hours. When that happened, her stellar productivity gave her a sense of pride and accomplishment. Some people are naturally good at planning for enjoyable, restorative diversions, such as spa days, special dinners, sporting events, or relaxing trips. Others are not.

Many religious or modest upbringings promote humility, self-denial, and individual sacrifice. This is often why people feel they don't deserve enjoyment. As we will explore later in this chapter, examining our established beliefs is a part of creating a mindset of enjoyment. If you purposely deny your needs, you will constantly feel unfulfilled. You gradually superimpose the mindset of self-denial over everything you do and expect that you should not enjoy what you do. Similar beliefs determine which activities people *do* feel they are allowed to enjoy. They may believe that it's okay to enjoy working for a non-profit organization helping children, but not as a stockbroker working for commissions. This, in turn, determines how rewarding or lucrative their lives become.

I myself have struggled with addressing my needs. My own modest upbringing programmed me with many self-denying attitudes. I have always avoided physical enjoyment—to the point that I have derived pleasure from physical punishment. I actually feel accomplished when I deny myself and cause myself physical discomfort. Of course, many of us enjoy our daily workouts, which are a form of self-punishment. We have learned that we develop strength through self-denial and self-punishing habits. Our enjoyment stems from valuing the outcome of these habits more than we would value avoiding the discomfort.

The feeling of accomplishment is one of the most significant ways that we enjoy the processes in our lives. From our earliest ages, we learn that the most successful, popular, and memorable people are the most accomplished. It brings us enjoyment to feel that we have accomplished something or made progress. Thus, the outcome affects the mindset of enjoying the process, so continued performance causes us to enjoy the process. I would characterize the feeling of talent as such: people feel that they have talent when they are skilled at performing. Many of us might describe talent as something we have or something we do not have, like a gift bestowed upon one person, but not another.

In my life, I have become an expert at several things in which I felt I had no ability whatsoever when I started. Because of this, I do not endorse the notion that each of us possesses talents for particular activities. The appearance of talent springs from spending time on activities that we enjoy. We have interest or disinterest based on what we enjoy. Interest translates into talent as we spend time doing what we enjoy. The more time we spend developing a skill, the more successful we are at it; and the more successful we are, the more we enjoy it. Thus we build momentum. As we build momentum, we take our skill into new areas of achievement. Forrest Gump becomes a football star because he enjoys the process of running, which does not require skill at football. In fact, he does not even understand the rules of the game.

I once knew a child who seemed naturally talented at every sport he attempted during his grade school years. Had I had known him only at that stage of his life, I would have thought that he was a natural athlete. But I had known him when he was younger, when it was apparent that he had a mild case of ADHD and that his enjoyment in chasing things began when he was a toddler. Like a retriever puppy, he could not sit still, and he enjoyed chasing and retrieving. Thus, his interests in new activities flowed from existing strengths, from one activity to the next.

As people build skill sets and transfer them to new activities, the activities they focus on correlate with the opportunities for reward. We can use this facet of mindset to affect our own enjoyment of a particular activity. If we reward ourselves, we promote desire and thus enjoyment. This principal has to be applied thoughtfully, however, because it can be misapplied. A common business problem that has caused countless organizational failures is called, "Wanting A, but rewarding B." When organizations have this problem, they head in the wrong direction. An example would be a company that wants to have a high-quality product but pays employees by the number of units they produce per hour. Unfortunately, both external forces and our own personality flaws can create similar scenarios in our lives. We want to eat healthy food, but the healthier the food, the more expensive it is. The pricing of food rewards us for eating unhealthy food. We want to be treated well by others, but we overlook positive treatment and respond to perceived slights, effectively rewarding negative treatment with our attention.

Being thoughtful about what warrants our attention, whether in relation to ourselves or to others, greatly affects how much we enjoy what we do in our lives. A way to enjoy the process is to focus on how the task at hand will benefit your loved ones. Most parents understand this because even difficult tasks are pleasurable when done for one's children. In my case, my life has revolved around my son since his birth, and I recognize that this is instinctive. Consider how this relates to the development of humans over time. Dedication to offspring became a common trait because it led to the survival of more offspring.

Countless songs have been written about love and emotional pain. Without consciously thinking about it, we know that music relates to enjoyment of the processes in life, at least in part because songs explicitly refer to it. I believe this is why music is integral to our lives. A song can instantly transport us back to a remembered emotional situation because we relate the processes in life to—and associate songs with—our emotional states. Controlling positive energy is a matter of using logical thought to resolve our feelings, and when people cannot make this connection between logic and emotion, they feel uneasy.

Though the melody, harmony, rhythm, and tone of music serves other purposes, the messages of songs satisfy our need for connection with others, such as the songwriter who wrote the song or the people who have experienced the feeling expressed in the song. This connection creates the universal feeling of shared experience, which eases our sense of isolation and may prompt us to think, "I am not alone because some other person out there had the same feeling." I have listened to many songs while thinking about which processes in life the song relates to. Although

336

I am sure you can think of other categories, it has been helpful to me to group the music I have listened to into the following categories, which relate to enjoying the processes in life.

- I enjoy this (I am singing about something I enjoy)

- Why can't I enjoy (I am singing about my inability to enjoy something)

- I want to enjoy (I am singing about my desire to enjoy something, someone, or some situation)

- I changed for the sake of enjoyment (I am singing about changes I made for someone else's or for my own enjoyment)

- I am searching for enjoyment (I am singing about the process of searching for enjoyment)

- I am not enjoying (I am singing about something, someone, or some situation that I do not enjoy)

- I am reducing the pain of my lack of enjoyment (I am singing about reducing the pain that something or some situation causes me)

- I am preventing my enjoyment (I am singing about choices I made that interfered with my enjoyment)

We find ourselves interested in a certain category of songs at various points in our lives, but our interest changes to another category of songs. Why is this? In my case, I associate the music that attracts me at each particular point in my life with each of these eight categories. If I can't find a

337

way to enjoy the processes in my life, I will be attracted to songs that fit into the "Why can't I enjoy" category. If I were having a great time in my life, I would migrate toward the "I enjoy this" category of music.

At the end of this chapter, I have listed many different kinds of songs by very different artists, separated into these eight categories. I have come to realize that I derive positive energy from my logical understanding of my own emotional state. When I analyzed the songs that interested me according to how they related to my enjoyment or lack thereof during specific stages of my life, I had an epiphany. I discovered I had been focusing on music that matched the exact category of how I was enjoying my life processes. It had become like a map into who I was and my current category of enjoyment. Once I knew this about myself, I could begin to resolve how I felt and positively direct myself to migrate to a stage at which I enjoyed the processes of my life.

The concept of positive and negative energy is something that many people may define differently or even regard as irrelevant. I have often revisited the impetuses that drive me in a positive or negative direction. I classify them according to how they either trigger or relieve my anxiety. In general, how do they affect my anticipation of the processes that I expect according to my logical assessment? The aspects of life that create positive energy follow a logical progression, and my anticipation of them does not trigger my disappointment with the outcome. The causes of negative energy are unpredictable. The longer they occur, the more anxiety builds. Although many people believe they must focus on reducing anxiety and stress, they are, in actuality, attempting to create positive energy and striving to relate their logical progression to the outcome of situations. By shifting our focus to that which we can do, instead of reducing that which seems to build in ourselves, we can reduce our stress and anxiety in life.

Affecting Situations to Influence Enjoyment

If we accept the premise that anticipation causes stress and anxiety, then reducing anticipation should produce less stress and leave us feeling calmer. If this is the case, we can generate a more positive feeling by finding activities and situations that reduce the anticipation in our lives. Engaging in activities that give us relief starts us down the path toward enjoying the process of our lives. Individuals differ in which activities bring relief and enjoyment, but there are activities for every taste. One of the most significant for me is sharing my thoughts with others. I have been plagued by obsessive thought, analyzing every situation I'm in. Often my own thought processes have overwhelmed me when I was thinking about too many things, and this locked me into the process of gathering thoughts to contemplate. Combined with the subconscious worry that I will lose a particular concept if I do not periodically revisit it, this has caused my mind to swim in circles in a sea of thoughts—often around the same subjects.

For much of my life, I tried to keep all of this information in my conscious mind, organizing it all for some future access to each piece of content. Once I changed my focus to sharing this information, I found that writing down my discursive thoughts to distribute to other people relieved my need to constantly reanalyze various topics. This reduced my anxiety as if I had reached the glory of the open highway after hours in stressful, gridlocked traffic. Publishing my thoughts on a topic allowed me to stop thinking about it and to move on to the next topic. This new process gave me a sense of relief that I hadn't experienced before.

Along with relieving the need to reanalyze constantly, the unloading and the sharing added another dimension that contributed to my enjoyment. Humans are social creatures who take pleasure in the involvement and praise of others. When I worked in the corporate world, the most effective managers and the best places to work were those that provided constant feedback about my job performance. Whether negative or positive, this feedback gave people a checkpoint at which they could adjust their performance. The more regularly feedback was delivered, the more people adjusted their performance in order to elicit positive feedback. This relates to the driving force in people that I call "recurring affirmation."

Although a strong driving force, recurring affirmation—or regular praise for one's accomplishments—does not often occur on its own. Yes, you can join an organization that is better at this than others are. For the most part, though, you can effectively accomplish this yourself. Small, simple tasks done for a "thank you" from others can elicit recurring affirmation.

The enjoyment of tasks or processes in life makes us remember the experience favorably. If we add these enjoyable things intentionally, we can affect our own desire to return to the activity. Working out in the morning may make us feel good about ourselves that day. One thing that makes me feel ready for my day is to arrive in a situation before the energy therein peaks. Something about the energy building around me is more comforting than showing up in the middle of a high-energy situation. These are only suggestions, as everyone is different when it comes to which activities make them feel more comfortable.

Most of us would agree that the beginning of a task is usually more difficult than the middle of that same task. Thus, I have successfully used a physically enjoyable element to begin an activity in order to motivate myself. Knowing your own biorhythms will help with this. I have found it difficult to get up in the morning because my body generates less heat in the morning, which means I am always cold then. Knowing this about myself, I tried using a heater at the beginning of the next phase of my morning routine and planned to enjoy warming up in the morning. This provided incentive to leave my bed so I could enjoy warming up, which in turn woke me up when I became too warm. Each phase in the morning was designed to move from discomfort at the

340

end of one phase to relaxation at the beginning of the next. Another thing that I allow myself in terms of physical enjoyment is having a favorite treat, but only when I am primed for the next task. Thus, the enjoyable item marks the beginning of the next task.

In the chapter "Working Past Where You Are," we talked about using knowledge of the future to reduce the reluctance to begin each new task or stage. This, along with adding something enjoyable at the beginning of each phase, combines the practice of focusing on the end with that of enjoying the process of the next phase. Enjoyment is a combination of how you remember feeling about performing the task before and how you reward yourself for beginning the next phase. Each process and each task in life will be performed again later. If you plan for this, then the end of each will prepare you to start the next. When you know you have prepared for the beginning of the task that you are about to perform, your reluctance to begin it greatly diminishes. This one feature, in practice, can change your entire outlook on the way negative energy relates to starting new tasks.

The People Aspect of Enjoyment

To complete the theme of how we can positively affect outcomes in our lives, let us consider our interactions with other people. It is important to remember that no matter what we would like to believe, the only part of our interactions that we have control over is the part inside ourselves. Some people expend endless effort to change how others treat them. These people only succeed in driving others away.

We can do several things to improve our interactions with others. First and most importantly, we can give our attention to those who treat us the way we want to be treated. We often engage others when they are insulting or disrespectful because we want to prove ourselves, defend ourselves, or validate our actions. However, people who are insulting or disrespectful can be complimentary and respectful at other times. People learn to seek attention by being difficult. I use the term "interactional gratification" to refer to the way we encourage people to act toward us by rewarding positive or negative behavior with our attention. We need to engineer the interactional gratification in our lives to encourage people to treat us the way we want to be treated. Conditioning the people we interact with in this way is much like training a puppy; it requires that we respond consistently and appropriately to the various ways in which others treat us. Since we encounter some people only on occasion, we may only be able to carry this out within a closer circle of friends. However, with the rise of social media, others may also be able to observe the provocations to which you respond and pay attention. Some of you may actually be unintentional experts at making these assessments. I have noticed that many frequenters of social media can assess a personality by reviewing a person's past trends and comments.

Rewarding people for treating us well is a reactive approach. We can also initiate positive interactions. I recommend saying something positive to someone else each day, and social media is great for this. Back in my days working in corporate environments, I found that a monthly twenty-five dollar investment in a candy drawer at my office was invaluable for positively engaging people on a regular basis. Not only did having a treat for everyone positively affect the overall mood and the responses to cooperative efforts, but it also kept me well apprised of everything happening within the organization.

My son once reluctantly admitted to me that he believed that none of his teachers liked him. We decided that a good start to addressing the problem and helping him enjoy his classes would be to come up with a way for him to influence others to appreciate him more. Here are a few things to consider in this regard:

342

1. Would the other people in the situation want you to remain there more than they would want another, random person in your place? Think about this to determine if you add value more than an unfamiliar person would. A random person, such as a guest at a restaurant, does not cause any disruption, but that person also can be replaced with any other random person.

2. Do the other people in the situation want to have you there more than they would want some specific person? This second test mainly determines whether you add a unique personality to the situation. Making a unique contribution can be a challenge in a large organization.

3. Would it benefit the people in the situation to have you there instead of no one? The need to add value to a situation rather than drain resources or energy is the next level of becoming comfortable with one's surroundings. In the case of a restaurant, a guest not being there may actually be more desirable to others than actually having the spot filled. However, in an office environment, adding value is the key to being appreciated.

Find what you can contribute to the situation, such as your personality, your warm smile, your intent listening skills, your humor in conversations, your quality as a friend, your collaboration with co-workers, or your attentiveness as a student. Having a strategy to improve the experience for others in the situation will ultimately improve your enjoyment of the situation. Recall my example of the candy drawer. This one small effort, which cost no more than taking someone to dinner each month, made the office more pleasant for many people, but mostly for me.

Other people in the environment may have relationships with each other that affect your comfort but that you may not be able to control. These relationships exist mostly because of the nature of the individuals and the tasks that they perform together. This involves how people communicate their thoughts to each other. As we first discussed in the chapter "Thought-Length Hierarchy," this transference has a synchronization effect as one person's thoughts are absorbed by those around them. It's important to take into account what function someone is responsible for performing when considering what is appropriate to communicate to that person. For example, someone who works in a call center is not a good person to engage in solving a deep problem. For that person, an attempt to engage them in a deep problem is a distraction from their duties.

Modifying your environment by directing the thought lengths that will work best for that environment will support your enjoyment as well. This can potentially be overlooked for a while, as one can push through it as one would through any distraction. Over time, however, an environment in which you are trying to achieve tasks that are unsuited to the ambient thought length of others in the vicinity will cause frustration or discomfort, which may not necessarily cause you to dislike the situation. However, you will gain more enjoyment from a situation in which you do not encounter constant distractions.

Minimizing Adverse Triggers

Though we all can see the positive things we should be doing with our lives, we often have difficulty doing them. Even though we know the right things to do, why do we still seem to be the worst version of ourselves in the moments that we want to affect the most? It's because of our programming to react without thinking in situations in which our involuntary logical thought stoppers are activated. Remember that we talked about these thought stoppers in the chapter

"Human Logic and Thought Patterns," in which we associated these with beliefs. All of us have unwanted involuntary reactions of which we are consciously aware, but we have difficulty controlling them. At the end of the chapter on human logic, we started to explore how to rewire this involuntary programming. Because the triggering of these reactions in our minds affects our overall emotional state, enjoying the processes of our lives directly depends on exploring these involuntary reactions.

I have found that when one of my logical thought stoppers (beliefs) is triggered, the resulting emotional state and biological changes in my body are detrimental to my thought process, even if they might have been valuable in the kinds of situations our instincts are geared for. The more that adverse triggers occurred in my mind over a certain period, the less enjoyable that period became. Triggering these thought stoppers sends us into an illogical progression, miring us in emotional responses that are counterproductive. When these adverse triggers are a large part of our daily experience, we will remember them more strongly than other stimuli. Unless we have a career as a UFC fighter or some other job in which these reactions benefit us, the result of the continued triggering of these responses will be counter to our enjoyment of the process in which they occurred.

In the chapter "Human Logic and Thought Patterns," we found that the logical thought stopper phenomenon was neurologically hardwired into the brain. In essence, we have brain damage to stop thinking, which discontinues the logic. Reconstructing the logical patterns is something that I have spent a lot of time practicing in myself, and it appears as if I am able to drastically reverse the trend, though not completely, when I understand what to look for in my own behavior. Thus, this practice largely depends on being able to identify your own beliefs and patterns of response.

As I started to identify my own problematic beliefs, I discovered that the more unrecognizable the shutdown or the more violent the reaction to each belief, the more negative or the more often repeated the influence had to be to achieve that shutdown or reaction. As I searched my memory, I usually knew exactly how and when I acquired these beliefs. I was able to identify the people or the situation that contributed to them. I also found that, since these involuntary reactions are not rooted in logic, the accurateness of these beliefs was inversely proportional to the strength of the reaction I had to the belief. After realizing this, I also started to notice that the more violently or persistently a person clung to their beliefs, the less logically sound those same beliefs would be. In the process of exploring my beliefs, speaking with the people who had been most influential in enforcing or forming those beliefs in me was very helpful. My evaluation of their responses to my challenges to those beliefs gave me a good assessment of exactly how illogical their influences were.

The process of exploring my own logical thought stoppers has led me to experience many reactions from others regarding beliefs that I would not have encountered before. When I explored my own personality, I realized that it was mostly defined by conflict avoidance, but discussing beliefs with others does not align with avoiding conflict. This led me to discover that my avoidance of conflict was in fact a logical thought stopper that I had developed. When conversations reached the point where people started to discuss topics from which belief triggers would arise, my avoidance was actually in response to their belief trigger. In other words, one person's reaction then triggered a reaction in another—in this case, me—to stop conversing as soon as the first exhibited strong beliefs. Thus, the pattern was such that whoever had the strongest belief structure controlled my life.

Although I eventually learned to disengage from someone with a stronger established belief, others may be inclined to overcome the situation. The common element is that the adverse

346

triggers change one's enjoyment of the situation. Admittedly, some people may feel "high" from such interactions and may actually enjoy being placed in those situations. Either way, the adjustment of how often and how many of these we experience comprises a very large part of what we take pleasure from and thus of how we enjoy the processes of the tasks we pursue in life.

Though I admit that I do not have any expert knowledge of the biochemical reactions related to the things I refer to as adverse triggers, I believe that their influence is exceptional and that a large part of each of our driving forces is based on enjoyment. When it comes to people and situations, these cause us discomfort. However, I am aware that other factors of personal interaction—such as thought length, tone, body language, and many other forms of nonverbal communications—also add to this discomfort.

Feeling Inadequate

One of the most significant obstacles we face is the overall effect of adverse triggers, which drive us not only to feel negatively in a situation but also to feel we are inadequate. Human nature causes us to accumulate negative feelings over time and then to determine that we have performed badly and that we ourselves are incapable of doing better. Exploring yourself and understanding how shame and guilt affect you is something I would recommend for anyone dealing with feelings of inadequacy. I have enjoyed the work of Brené Brown in this area. Her work on what she calls "wholehearted living" has been very helpful to me in my personal life (Brown, 2010).

As we talked about earlier in the book, our memories of our emotional states do not have nearly the same durations as other memories. When we have felt inadequate for a time, we start to think we will never do better and will not be able to pull ourselves out of it because our short emotional memory can only remember this feeling, so we simply accept that this is who we are. Wholehearted living is the acceptance and embrace of flaws that we all have and that society in general tells us to hide deep down inside, away from everyone (Brown, 2010). Accepting our self-defining flaws and embracing the nature of how we live with them—instead of ignoring them—will make all the difference. In the chapter "The Building Blocks of a Person's Core," I described my self-defining flaws, which have driven each part of my life and personality. Until I accepted them and became open about them, I was unable to combat my feelings of inadequacy.

Minimizing my adverse triggers has been a combination of adopting a wholehearted life style and creating incentives that help me enjoy the nature of the process on which I am working. You can start down the path of designing your own enjoyment by reducing the logical thought stoppers in your mind and by creating an environment in which the people and the situation slowly allow you to shift toward enjoyable processes.

Engineering Enjoyment

We started out the first chapter of the book by talking about what makes up a good, bad, so-so, or exceptional year. When we think about how to engineer our lives to enjoy the process, the first thing I recommend is to break down the intervals of enjoyment into achievable slices of time. What does that mean? Let's look at a day and determine what makes a good day. Then we'll look at a week and determine which things lead to a good week. It will require some self-exploration to know exactly what things make your days and weeks better. Each person will have a different list of things that make a day or week better, but most of us can remember a time when we had something happen that made us feel good. Was it a chance occurrence? Was it an accomplishment? Was it the occurrence of a special event? Was it a peaceful period of relaxation or a learning event? Though I am sure that each of you could add to the list of things that make a day or week good, one thing I want you to notice is that each of them can be deliberately incorporated into your schedule. Most of us could make a list of things that made us have a good day or week, but few of us ever actually try to schedule them. We wait for life to create the moments in our days and weeks that make us feel good.

The second part of this exercise is to look at the things that made for a bad day or week. Let's explore what kinds of things we do not enjoy and start to remove those things from our lives. Often, these will have related qualities that we can group together. Frequently, the periods of negative emotions begin with similar triggers, even though they feel different. The principal things to look for are these negative triggers. They could be the way someone addresses you or responds to you. They could be due to self-reproach for how you performed or responded to a situation. They could be a series of events that exceeded the threshold of your tolerance. Most of you could add to this list. In any case, I want you to recognize that the knowledge of your negative triggers is what will enable you to start reducing the bad days and weeks.

Map out the things that comprise good and bad days and weeks and write them down. Make a list of them and keep expanding it. Put it on your wall. The foremost thing you will notice is that this list will begin to repeat itself. I was surprised at how few things actually triggered my bad days. For me, the most disturbing part of the evaluation of negative triggers was how many of them were entirely my own creation. Many of these were based on my own biorhythms. I found that my most prevalent negative trigger is when I am physically tired. The same external stimulus causes me to react entirely differently when I am tired. Before I understood this, I blamed the external stimulus, but now I see that the only things I can control are inside of me.

Once I learned the triggers that made me have a good day or week, I started to design how most effectively to repeat those experiences while also minimizing the negative triggers. Keeping an extremely rigid schedule is not the best way to sustain happiness, but success requires you to align yourself with other successful people. If you work the night shift each day, but if the people with whom you need to interact in order to further your success are on a 9-to-5 schedule, then working the night shift will not improve your overall effectiveness. A minimal alignment with others is necessary for success, and minimizing the rigidity of a strict schedule may be better for sustaining happiness. I take the same approach for setting my schedule that I would for engineering any system. In other words, I meet the minimum requirements for a rigid schedule, and then I allow the rest of the time to flow with less structure.

Situations that Make Us Feel Alive

When we previously discussed determining the path for our lives, we explored the things that make us feel alive. Until now, we have not spent much time thinking about them, but I did mention that they have to be scheduled into your activities. Enjoyment of the processes in life requires enjoying life in general, and the things that make us feel alive serve that purpose. While often short, these experiences produce such emotional responses that we retain significant memories of them.

As children, we instinctively choose to engage in activities that make us feel alive. We simply call it playtime. For some reason, as we grow up, we are continuously driven away from playtime. Each level of growing up teaches us to gradually remove playtime from our lives. For many of us, removing playtime with each stage becomes something we consider the definition of growing up. I often see young people who strike out on their own, living away from their parents for the first time, who determine that since they are now adults, all playtime should be eliminated. They

350

become completely serious adults and begin this phase of their lives without any fun because they believe that this is what it means to be an adult.

The amount of fun we have should not gradually dwindle to zero as we progress from childhood to adulthood. Yes, we teach our children to focus and to become more successful in each aspect of their lives, but teaching them to retain a certain amount of fun is also essential. Activities that make us feel alive should be included in our routines on a regular basis.

These activities should include short periods daily, longer periods weekly, weekend-long periods monthly or quarterly, and some weeklong events yearly. Many of us take vacations yearly and schedule the task of seeing all of the sights or doing all of the activities related to some mission that we have set out to accomplish. Activities that make us feel alive should be breaks from our responsibilities, and they should be different from the things we do in our task- and focus-driven time. They should serve to give us positive feelings, address social needs, experiment with new things, and avoid our dislikes.

Weekly Patterns

Let us consider how we should schedule activities on a weekly basis because this affects some of the changes necessary for the most effective daily schedules. When engineering my week, I elect to use a seven-day week with five working days plus one working weekend day per month, since much of the world follows that pattern. From there, I determine which days require a strict schedule and which do not. Since I am an anxiety-driven person, the things that require too much focus often cause me to feel anxious, but disorganization also causes me anxiety. The most effective pattern I have found is only to follow a strict, organized schedule for three days a week.

351

If I gear my entire week toward getting a good night's sleep from Sunday night through Tuesday night, and if I strictly focus my scheduling on Monday, Tuesday, and Wednesday, then this successfully aligns my schedule with the most effective people while minimizing my anxiety and reducing my hyperfocus to the most minimal time necessary.

This three-day focus also works for me because I have found that the most effective people engage in their aggressive interactions early in the week. People who are more social come alive later in the week and increase their interactions toward a pinnacle late in the week. Thus, shifting from the hyper-organized first three days toward a looser, more social last two or three days aligns with both of these types of people. The keys here are to acknowledge that we are social beings and to balance ourselves between rigid focus and loose social behavior. Adjusting my focus to match the times when the two types of people are more effective enables me to adapt well to the need for progress, and it allows me some flexibility and social interaction. A third focus in this mix relates directly to the tasks that I intend to complete, as opposed to aligning with other people. I try to start my tasks late in the week during the period of social alignment and maintain until early in the following week when the pattern begins again. I actually relax my activity levels, with the exception of workouts, from Tuesday through Thursday. The figure "Weekly Focus Patterns" may help to illustrate these patterns.

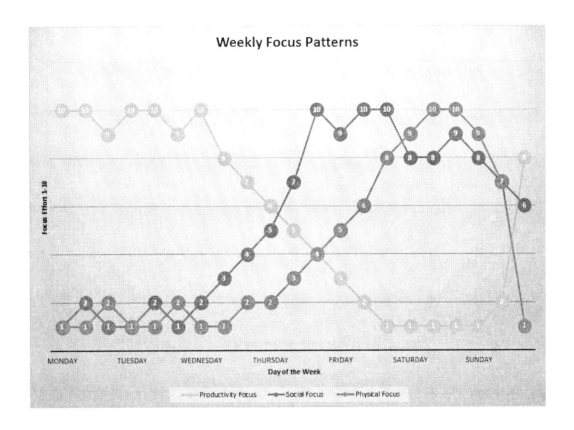

Weekly Focus Patterns

Focus Effort 1-10

Day of the Week

MONDAY   TUESDAY   WEDNESDAY   THURSDAY   FRIDAY   SATURDAY   SUNDAY

Productivity Focus   Social Focus   Physical Focus

On the graph, you should concentrate most on the line that represents productivity focus. For people whose job primarily requires performing physical activities, the productivity focus line and the physical focus line merge. In the Western world, many of us routinely have a day of rest before returning to work each week. I myself have done this for years. Often after vigorous weeks, I have slept or relaxed all day Sunday only to find myself unable to sleep Sunday evening. After years of dreading Mondays, we have conditioned ourselves to stay up as late as we can on Sunday evening for one thing after another, lengthening the weekend by clinging to it as long as possible. This renders us unprepared and exhausted when the time to be productive and focused arrives. Many of us will end up following the social focus pattern, not coming alive until later in the week, and missing the alignment with the most productive members of society.

The graph shows a productive life focus with the minimum time of three nights of good sleep for the concentrated focus on productivity, followed by three days of diligence. If that is all you do each week, and if you then totally relax the rest of the week, then in my experience the rest of the week will work itself out. Your natural biorhythms will grow to the high productivity levels, and the natural relief of that focus will continue to resolve loose ends for the rest of the week, gradually unwinding your focus. At the same time, the first three days of focus should delay the scheduling of most social events until Wednesday for early-resolution items. To increase the focus into Thursday and Friday, the focus of the social interactions should naturally feed into the scheduling of physical events for Thursday evening and through the weekend. The key transition point on the graph is the Sunday shift from energy to productivity. Everyone I have known who was extremely successful has added into their lives and successfully maintained this beginning-of-the-week shift in focus.

The second part of this focus, which will be equally important, is to focus on downtime and on time when you plan not to exert yourself mentally. The social-interactive aspects and the physical aspects are both a part of this focus, and planning for each of these aspects will be equally pivotal to your success. You can see on the graph that I recommend this downtime and that I shift away from filling half of each week with the days of heightened focus. Shortening our downtime, as many of us progressively do each week, is as detrimental as shortening our productive time. In fact, if you ignore your need for downtime for months or years at a time, you will find yourself, as I have at times, becoming less productive. I have lost productivity for entire weeks and months at a time, essentially because of this fact. For me, the period of continued focus without downtime caused me to become overwhelmed, which led to a collapse. Many of the times covered in the chapter, "Thriving at the Low Points of Our Lives," are the products of ignoring this balance for prolonged periods.

354

My daily patterns are mostly defined by the fact that my biorhythms do not operate best on an increment of sleep that fits well within a twenty-four-hour period. My body operates more optimally on eight hours of sleep over a thirty-hour period than it does over a twenty-four-hour period. Thus, less sleep for a stretch of a few days, followed by the need for more sleep to catch up, seems to plague any attempts I make to have a fixed bedtime and wake-up time each day. However, for this biorhythm, as mentioned in the discussion of the weekly focus patterns, it works best to plan a bit less sleep on the later days of the week. Since social events suit more interactive mindsets, this pattern develops naturally, so embracing it should also come naturally. In order to ensure a good mental focus when most needed, part of one's daily pattern should address how to minimize and recover from periods of less sleep or, later in the week, from periods of more physical exertion.

Focusing on time off and downtime is just as important, if not more important, to one's daily schedule as it is to one's weekly schedule. For me, this has more to do with basic human needs, such as minimizing anxiety, than it does any external forces. To strive for three productive days that align with the beginning of the week, which the majority of the world follows, is not as easy as simply wanting to do so. Humans have to be rested to perform, and in order to rest, they must have great control over their own mindsets to get themselves into a relaxed state. The downtime and reduced mental strain become the most important for controlling the human aspect. The preparation for an evening of rest, which entails introducing stimuli that lead up to the time for resting, is the primary focus of my daily routines.

Two mindset items are most pivotal. The first is embracing the fact that taking a break from one day to the next does not equate to failing on the first day's tasks, but rather it equates to the last sequence in a successful day. The second is acquiring the psychological conditioning that whatever you put off until tomorrow is something desirable that you will enjoy performing. If you can practice these with religious precision, then you will begin to recognize that success means the last step is released and the next is anticipated. For me, maintaining this for three days a week (Sunday through Wednesday morning) and then simply relaxing has molded me into an entirely new person.

Awareness Is the First Step

The weekly patterns we focused on, though a good framework for anyone, are patterns that only work for some people. Self-awareness is crucial in this area, as is honestly assessing your needs and biorhythms. Adding the human element into each of our scheduled patterns is what makes them both unique and predictable. We are all different, but frailties and dissimilarities are predictable. Take baby steps and determine which steps work for you. Remember that someone who changes everything will fail at everything. Make small changes one at a time, and keep the successful ones. In this respect, I have drawn heavily from Buddhist teachings about reducing suffering, which have been well documented and practiced over the years. Use these types of ideas, as well as those of other successful religions, to begin your quest.

Remember that what makes us enjoy ourselves is a harmonious relationship with our surroundings. The things that disrupt this harmony will reduce our enjoyment as we become less able to make sense of our surroundings. For example, if you witnessed a bird flying upside down, it would trouble your mind, and you would begin to look for a logical explanation. The longer you are unable to find a logical explanation, the more uncomfortable you will become. Once you find a convincing explanation, such as the existence of a mirror, it resolves your cognitive dissonance. As long as you experience such dissonance, you will be unable to relax and find enjoyment.

356

I believe that we use music to resolve our unresolved feelings. Music that expresses our turmoil makes us feel that we share that turmoil with someone else. This sharing helps resolve the feelings of turmoil. Many of us have learned to find such resolution in music as well as in many other forms of art and entertainment. Knowing how to find comfort in music and other art forms and entertainment helps to make us effective people. As an exercise, review the songs that interest you and compare them against the categories of the enjoyment of processes. Though incomplete, the list at the end of this chapter may help you start your own list.

Being self-aware includes understanding your social interactions so that you can tell when, where, and how they affect your personal stability. We all need to feel accepted and as if we belong, which is what many of our civic encounters, including attending church, fulfill. I have heard religious leaders give good descriptions of two types of relationships. We participate in consumer trade or trade relationships on a day-to-day basis, which involve the exchange of goods or services. These relationships are mutually beneficial, but the benefits are limited to these transactions. Community and church environments provide human interactions that do not involve goods or services but that are important to people. These are voluntary, and all parties meet and interact entirely of their own volition and contribute free of commitment. As long as these relationships do not require any one party to provide or commit to transactions, these relationships can remain interdependent. For the sake of your stability, remember to keep these commitment-free relationships maintainable in your life cycle.

When evaluating your social interactions, understand what they do for your emotional state. Whether they put you at ease or irritate you may depend upon how much they affect your internal thought length. We all need activities that place us in the mindset of brevity and fun thoughts and that shorten our thought lengths, which become relaxing or at least not stressful. We walk away from these environments feeling relaxed and refreshed; our mental focus is entirely relieved. Because some of us have a natural tendency to enjoy a longer thought length, we may take pleasure from a thought-provoking lecture or sermon. Others of us who have a natural tendency to enjoy shorter thought lengths may enjoy sporting events or dance clubs where less thought is required. Either way, we find ourselves with a comfort zone that matches our own needs.

Our social interactions synchronize us with those around us; this is what many of us may only know by feeling. We have heard of the mob mentality in which usually calm, average citizens become a riotous group of lawbreakers. Similarly, we know the feelings we get when we find ourselves in a supportive group at church or civic centers. This energy transfers between us by synchronizing the lengths of thoughts in our minds and then establishes a similar emotional state among us, which we feel as a collective emotion of the group. Whichever civic event or activity you choose, attempt to locate an internal comfort zone that fits your nature. If you reach a point in the week or a time of the day when you need to wind down and initiate a mindset that prepares you for calmer activities, for sleep, or for an unfocused, relaxing period, then it is important to attend the right social event to prepare your mindset.

Remember that our mindset indispensably enables us first to enjoy the processes of our lives. As we learned from Forrest Gump, enjoying the things we do on a recurring basis allows us to meticulously complete repetitive tasks with a high standard of quality and efficiency. When we repeat tasks often, the practice makes us become very effective, and this gives us a high standard of quality, which makes our work desirable. Repeated actions also make us become more efficient. Efficiency makes our work more cost-effective since we require fewer resources— including time—to accomplish the same results as others. When we enjoy the process, each of the other aspects required for success falls into alignment.

Mapping Songs to Enjoy the Process

I Enjoy This *(I am singing about something I enjoy)*

- "Crash Into Me," Dave Matthews Band

- "All of Me," John Legend

- "Home," Jasmine Thompson

- "Sweet Home Alabama," Lynyrd Skynyrd

- "All the Small Things," Blink 182

- "Never Let You Go," Third Eye Blind

- "Thanks for the Memories," Fall Out Boy

- "You're Gonna Go Far Kid," The Offspring

- "Hey There Delilah," Plain White T's

- "Hey Stephen," Taylor Swift

- "I'm Yours," Jason Mraz

- "Bubbly," Colbie Caillat

- "Love Story," Taylor Swift

- "Nothing Else Matters," Metallica

- "Comatose," Skillet

- "So Far Away," Staind

Why Can't I Enjoy? *(I am singing about my inability to enjoy something)*

- "One," U2

- "One Headlight," The Wallflowers

- "In Your Eyes," Peter Gabriel

- "Disarm," Smashing Pumpkins

- "Hearts Without Chains," Ellie Goulding

- "Heart Shaped Box," Nirvana

- "How to Save a Life," The Fray

- "A Thousand Years," Christina Perri

- "Let It Die," Three Days Grace

- "Ends," Everlast

- "Don't Tread on Me," Metallica

I Want to Enjoy *(I am singing about my desire to enjoy something, someone, or some situation)*

- "Bitter Sweet Symphony," The Verve

- "Lights," Ellie Goulding

- "Are You Gonna Be My Girl," Jet

- "Want You Bad," Offspring

- "Snow (Hey Oh)," Red Hot Chili Peppers

- "Wake Me Up When September Ends," Green Day

- "Falling for You," Colbie Caillat

- "Leave Out All the Rest," Linkin Park

- "Boulevard of Broken Dreams," Green Day

- "Serenity," Godsmack

- "When I'm Gone," 3 Doors Down

I Changed for Enjoyment (I am singing about changes I made for someone else's or for my own enjoyment)

- "The One I Love," R.E.M.

- "Too Close," Alex Clare

- "Freebird," Lynyrd Skynyrd

- "All Star," Smash Mouth

- "Simple Man," Shinedown

- "Sound of Madness," Shinedown

- "Lose Yourself," Eminem

- "Numb," Linkin Park

- "It's Been Awhile," Staind

- "Second Chance," Shinedown

I Am Searching for Enjoyment (I am singing about the process of searching for enjoyment)

- "Don't Stop Believing," Journey

- "Habits (Stay High)," Tove Lo

- "Spectrum," Zedd

- "Let Her Go," Jasmine Thompson

- "Move Along," The All-American Rejects

- "When I Come Around," Green Day

- "Welcome to My Life," Simple Plan "Semi-Charmed Life," Third Eye Blind

- "21 Guns," Green Day

- "Everything Changes," Staind

- "Voodoo," Godsmack

- "Unforgiven," Metallica

- "Gotta Be Somebody," Nickelback

I Am Not Enjoying (*I am singing about something, someone, or some situation that I do not enjoy*)

- "I'm On Fire," Bruce Springsteen

- "The Grouch," Green Day

- "High School Never Ends," Bowling for Soup

- "Deify," Disturbed

- "It's Not Me It's You," Skillet

- "Epiphany," Staind

I Am Reducing the Pain of My Lack of Enjoyment (*I don't enjoy something or some situation, and I want to reduce the pain it causes me*)

- "Say Something," A Great Big World
- "Almost Lover," Jasmine Thompson
- "Viva La Vida," Coldplay
- "I Don't Care," Fall Out Boys
- "Should Have Said No," Taylor Swift
- "Need You Now," Lady Antebellum
- "Wrecking Ball," Miley Cyrus
- "One More Night," Maroon 5
- "Stan," Eminem
- "What It's Like," Everlast
- "Master of Puppets," Metallica

I Am Preventing My Enjoyment (*I am singing about choices I made that interfered with my enjoyment*)

- "Good Girl," Carrie Underwood
- "My Own Worst Enemy," Lit
- "Who Knew," Eminem
- "Headstrong," Trapt

References

Brown, B. (2010), The Gifts of Imperfection: Let Go of Who You Think You're Supposed to Be and Embrace Who You Are, Hazelden Publishing.

Haanel, C. F., (1916), The Master Key System, Psychology Publishing, St. Louis and The Master Key Institute, New York

Chapter XIII

Reevaluating Your Path

People think they need to pursue success and capture it as if it is an item to be had. I have heard so many people say that success was handed to someone or inherited from family members. In truth, no one can give you or hand you success. They can give you money or a successfully run business, and they can give you the skills to understand how to either build success or maintain a successfully run organization that can be passed along to you. We've all heard examples of how successful companies have failed when new management or next-generation leadership has taken over. This is because the new leadership inherited the ongoing operation of someone else's success, which they could not maintain. They could not keep up the same growth 1) because they lost the requisite conduit for working past where they are, 2) because they did not have the same path and the same unobstructed direction, or 3) because they may not have enjoyed the process enough to keep the same quality or the same standards of operation.

The Influence of Inner Change on the Process Variables

The failure or success of someone who builds or even assumes control of a successfully run organization inherently exists within the individual. Many people go through most of their lives without wanting to plan any of their own direction. They live day to day as though they are in survival mode, simply ensuring that what enters their scope of awareness today is sufficient to last until the end of that day or week. Often this is due to the perspective lifetime in which they find themselves. Each of these lifetimes will have a different set of footings on which an individual bases his or her decisions. Two people, each with an entirely different set of underlying decision-making structures, may come to the same decision but for different reasons. However, when these two people reach opposite decisions, each person's decision may negatively affect each basis of the other person's decision. Let's look at an example:

The Bases of Republican Decisions		The Bases of Democratic Decisions	
1	Stability and maintainability	1	Greater good of most people
2	Organizational control	2	Environmental protection
3	Minimize disruption of status quo	3	Protection of minorities from unfair treatment
4	Belief enforcement	4	Health care for those who cannot afford it
5	Industrial strength	5	Advocate for separation of church and state
6	Protection of the hard working	6	Reduce unfair treatment of disadvantaged
7	Punishment of wrongdoing	7	Protection of individual rights
8	Military strength	8	Support local small business
9	International reputation	9	Enable community program
10	Enable free-market competition	10	Protection of individuals from large interests

If these were the top ten bases for the decisions of a Republican and a Democrat, not one of the things on which these two people use to base their decisions would be the same. The Democrat might make a decision that would benefit small businesses by taking money from international relief and the military to provide grants for any woman or minority who starts a business that supports Eco-star energy usage or that reduces the power of large health care companies. This legislation would meet many of the Democrat's top ten underlying decision-making structures. However, it not only does not include any of the Republican's principles, but it also runs counter to several of them. Such a decision by one person would become an insult or appear evil to the other.

These foundations for decisions change as we turn the corners from one perspective lifetime to another. At one point in my life, I was in a relationship with someone whom I would consider very special—a relationship characterized by a mutually experienced, very intimate connection. Our ages were different enough and my perspective lifetime had shifted recently enough that, while I had turned the corner to my eleventh perspective lifetime, the person with whom I was in a relationship was, in my opinion, still solidly in her ninth perspective lifetime.

The Bases of Decisions in the Ninth Perspective Lifetime		The Bases of Decisions in the Eleventh Perspective Lifetime	
1	Experiment with responsibility	1	Health is a gift
2	Pets are part of family	2	Avoidance of past discomfort
3	Reproductive desire strong	3	People are important, pets are passing
4	Unexplored biologically driven influences	4	Items and possessions do not matter
5	Status is part of confidence	5	Status comes and goes
6	Acceptable to trade health for desire	6	Confidence is accomplishment
7	Possession drives perfection in mate pairing	7	Giving is primary need
8	Receiving is primary need	8	Acceptance and belonging
9	Security and comfort	9	Exceptionally connected relationships are rare
10	Relational opportunities are endless	10	Tradeoff to life continuity not an option

Though I am sure that this list does not accurately capture all of the drivers in this particular dynamic, the point is that the most important decision-making bases for each of us largely did not occur on the other's list. At various times in people's lives, they may have more or less desire to actually take control of the different aspects of themselves if those aspects do not fall within their primary decision-making principles. As life continues, reevaluating the process has to include this aspect of human progression. When you allow yourself to approach and enter these new stages—even to expect them—it will help you transition more gradually. The collapses that I have experienced were in part due to delaying such changes to the point that a logical conflict within me caused instability.

External Influences to the Process Variables

The people and situations that affect our lives also have an impact on our ability to live the process. We have some ability to pick and set these variables, but once they are involved in our lives, they can change without our knowledge and independently of our influences. External influences will mostly emerge in the people and situation portions of our life cycle. Many people will claim that one of these external influences is responsible for their failure or their inability to advance. Although these influences do affect us—and our life cycle—we still control how their input affects us and which of these influences we allow ourselves to have contact with. Knowing our own tolerance for the way that external influences affect us is the most important consideration for these interactions. Some of us may need to remove ourselves from situations, while others can be in the middle of a situation and remain unaffected.

Situational Influences

Earlier in the book, I used the example of visiting someone who lived in an inner-city slum. This resident had directed me to leave a bag of garbage on the curb between their front yard and the adjacent building. They claimed that they would pick it up later and said that, since I was only visiting, I should not bother with it. Upon visiting one year later, the exact same garbage was in the same location. The garbage was mostly flattened into place by foot traffic and was surrounded by a few additions, which made it extremely undesirable even to consider touching. This situational aspect of the lives of the people in that neighborhood was entirely acceptable to all who walked down that street daily.

My reaction to this was utter disgust, but the entire neighborhood accepted it and tolerated it without even seeming to notice. I do not understand how people who have gained a tolerance for this sort of environment could not feel its effects on their lives. At the same time, I cannot imagine how I could keep balance in the maintenance portion of my life cycle while remaining in this situation. Personally, I would have to remove myself from such a situation.

People Influences

The people around us can also have a large impact on us, one that we may not even notice if everyone has adopted the same behavior. In describing my childhood, I characterized many aspects of it that resulted from a strong community influence on each person's life. After moving away from the area where I was raised, I spent several years traveling to different locations and had the chance to sample many local cultures. I was surprised by how the influences within communities that affected each individual varied in different regions of the country. In my extensive travels in the South, I observed that a mindset of independent isolation seems to dominate, whereas in the community in which I grew up, this mindset would not even be an option. Where I grew up, individual decisions were heavily influenced by the community.

Over the years, when I've visited where I grew up, I have noticed that the community influence on decision-making has remained pervasive. Because I only visited, it did not affect me personally, but I noticed how much it seemed to restrain people. The smallest decisions made by certain individuals influenced much of the community. At the same time, people who did not subject themselves to this community influence were scorned. I felt the effect of this influence even though I lived far away when I went through a very difficult time in my life that ended with a marital separation. Although I was not directly aware of the expectations of the community, I found myself with around fifteen fewer Facebook friends after I made the decision to separate from my wife. This public response to my decision came from people who lived halfway across the country from me.

I began to understand this influence much more while living in Colorado after I met a friend who was a former member of a Quaker community in eastern Ohio. He had moved to Colorado with his family in the 1960s after faulty wiring in his home caused a fire that burned it to the ground.

He explained to me that the Quaker community's beliefs were such that, if individuals experienced misfortune, it was believed to be God's wrath for some aspect of their lives that they had lived in defiance of his will. Because of my friend's misfortune, his community required him to enter a penitent stage voluntarily and to check himself into an institution similar to an insane asylum. His penitence was to last for two years, and no one in the community was allowed to associate or do business with him should he not perform that penitence.

I was surprised to learn from further research that this penitentiary system of Pennsylvania, one of the leading correctional institutions in the nation, was most likely the foundation of the entire prison system of the United States. But what most interested me was that the impact of the Quaker community mindset, which is prevalent among people from this region, had made many people reluctant to make decisions without the community having reached a prior consensus. By ensuring community input on decisions, individuals were less culpable if the decision drew the wrath of God. Human nature has extended this community influence into many aspects of culture without people even being aware of it. I have observed this influence in religious and civic circles throughout Pennsylvania, as it has become a social norm due to the Quaker influence introduced by the state's founders.

Such influences from both people and situations can be entirely outside of your control, and at times, you may not even be aware of their existence. Although these are only examples, external influences can be numerous and can have extreme effects on you. When all you know is being in the same situations or being surrounded by the same people, the only way to get a new perspective is to explore new situations or new influential groups.

Interactive and Social Influences to the Process Variables

People brought together in a situation produce another form of influence, which I will classify as social influences. In the chapter "Thought-Length Hierarchy," we discussed how the average length of time spent on thoughts determines people's emotional states. This is apparent when people cohabitate and when they are continuously exposed to shared thoughts and conversation. When multiple mechanical or computer components are operating on a single communication cable or a single power supply, they synchronize and can even appear to operate with simultaneous precision. This harmonic operation is due to moving or processing sequences while taking exactly the same amount of time to complete each portion of movement—but on different pieces of equipment.

When people harmonically synchronize with each other, we see things like women having the same menstruation cycles as their roommates. In groups, we can witness the mob mentality in which people are incited to act inappropriately or to become emotional, excited, or aroused, as if they are all connected. This unseen force can move people in a positive or negative direction, occur for short periods, or persist over an extended, possibly unnoticed period. In my own experiences working with other people, such as couples who go through a divorce or toxic group environment, the couple often finds themselves in a harmonic pattern in which they constantly divide each other's thoughts through learned coping behaviors. In these cases, often both parties in the couple will reach a diminished thought-length capability and a reduced emotional maturity at the same time.

This destructive thought-length dynamic often results in one or both people feeling as if they were incapable of having any control in the situation. When it persists for years, sometimes people simply give up and begin to believe that they have a biological limitation or that they are defective or mentally ill, when it may really be an issue related to the harmonic synchronization of their social interactions. Cults have used this manner of control effectively to gain extreme control over their followers. Through a convincing message and belief-reference programming, cults have persuaded followers to go as far as mass suicide and human sacrifice.

More positively, in areas such as Silicon Valley, ingenious innovation is the norm more than the exception. Residents are influenced by the social milieu. Competition and lavish personal spending are part of the culture. Visible wealth indicates an individual's status and, by inference, how ingenious the individual is. In Silicon Valley, everyday people in a Starbucks, for example, are millionaires. Ambient conversations and connections with people in such a place become vehicles for spreading ordinary private thoughts. The extent to which people are actively building their futures can bring the acceleration that we discussed in the chapter, "Working Past Where You Are." Ideas for innovation accompany the knowledge of the innovative ideas of others.

These social influences are found in many places. Some of us are more skilled while others are less skilled at dealing with social influences. Your awareness of your strengths and weaknesses is the key to understanding how to reduce the social influences to the process variables in your life. I have found that the ability to be aware of social influences is more of a learned skill. People from highly motivated, bustling, or political environs have often gained these skills early in life. Such skills, which may fall in the social engineering arena for many people, will be considered acceptable or wrong depending on our beliefs or background.

Learn how to succeed by repeating successful patterns and by optimizing less successful patterns. Fundamentally, your life path will continually refresh and renew. You will always be required to adjust your direction and branch out from your path. Augment and refine your path so that you can provide yourself constant motivational feedback. Let's look at a process for continuously reevaluating our paths to adjust for the changes that we may not even see in ourselves if we do not take this time to reflect.

Exploration Cycle

Self-exploration is something we have talked about throughout this book, in many areas relating it to the process of designing your future. I have repeatedly explained that influencing your future behavior requires an understanding of the present—specifically, your traits and your current behavior. When I began my self-exploration some years back, the hardest part was discovering where to start. This book was designed to shed some light on that. I don't believe I have all the ideas, but exploration cycles have to start somewhere. In the age of the Internet, many resources now exist that did not a few years ago. You can do a quick search and find out more things to begin to explore than you could possibly finish in your lifetime.

How to explore is a process in itself. Many of us are aware of the first portion or the first step of gathering details. We can spend our lifetimes collecting data and learning details. What can we do with it all? We can apply to be on a quiz show to flaunt the wealth of facts and details we have amassed. That may provide a means to showcase our talent, but the real reason you should acquire knowledge is to be able to use it to affect your life, refine your behavior, optimize your effectiveness, and become the best version of yourself.

Good self-exploration starts when we document our actions, as discussed at the end of the chapter, "Working Past Where You Are." Each of us will have moments when we come across tasks or situations that we decide we are incapable of handling. The words "I can't" usually trigger this decision within us. I challenge myself to write down each of these things that I decide I can't do. As you are reading, I recommend you do the same. Write down the tasks or projects that you think are beyond your capabilities.

Why might the items I list be beyond my capabilities? First, they may be things I don't want to pursue, so the phrase "I can't" can be more of an escape clause. Excluding the tasks and projects on the list that I don't want to pursue, I like to take a few minutes to perform a brief exercise for each thing on my list that "I can't do." Here is the exercise: First, determine if any other person can actually do this. If so, then think of someone whom you believe is capable of performing or accomplishing the task. What attributes do they possess that makes them capable? Start by creating a list of all the qualities you can think of. Gradually, you will begin to see that this list covers simple attributes that took time to develop and that then influenced that person's list of achievable tasks.

Hypothetically, if you have decided that you could not run for the office of state senator, then you should examine what is necessary to achieve that position. The current state senator—let's say it's a woman—did not begin one day by simply saying she wanted to run for office. She may have taken the path of becoming involved with a local charity, during which she enjoyed the process of meeting and helping new people every day. She may have spent time each day after her previous job, meeting and proving her worthiness to person after person, only to become acquainted with at least 50 percent of the people in her small neighborhood. Next, she may have run for an unpaid position on the school board because she had looked at future trends and compiled a list of ideas for the future direction of the community. The people who knew her from helping out at the charity then propelled her into her first position as an elected official on the school board, which gave her access to more groups of people, both on the school board and in other communities. One at a time, the steps that brought her to a given level of fame were

374

merely steps on the path that led her to look at the future and "work past where she was." Then she repeated those steps because it was rewarding to enjoy the process that had led her on her chosen path.

The exploration cycle loops to your life path as you compare yourself against the people whom you believe can achieve the task, determine what qualities they possess, and design your path to develop those qualities in yourself. Each level on which you currently find yourself includes tasks specific to that level and tasks that apply to the next few levels. Recognizing what qualities to develop, understanding how to acquire them, and knowing how to expand with each level is a practice of documenting the present and evaluating the future.

Mindset

When we are children, we do not think about our emotional state. We flow with human desire and with what we feel that we want at each moment. We start to self-explore when we begin to identify our emotional states. Whether because of continuous input from our parental figures or because we gain a certain level of consciousness and want to begin the process on our own, we realize that we react to situations involuntarily and that we have some ability to overpower our unconscious reactions. Let's look at this a little deeper and try to map all the emotional states, noting how often we experience them and identifying those in which we spend the majority of our time. We may be unaware that we spend much of our time agitated because we do not desire to do so, but the exercise of thinking about it and documenting it may show otherwise. Below are some categories of emotion that you may want to use for your process of documentation.

Human Emotions:

Acceptance	Doubt	Hatred	Paranoia
Affection	Ecstasy	Hope	Pity
Aggression	Empathy	Horror	Pleasure
Ambivalence	Envy	Hostility	Pride
Apathy	Embarrassment	Homesickness	Rage
Anxiety	Euphoria	Hunger	Regret
Boredom	Forgiveness	Hysteria	Remorse
Compassion	Frustration	Interest	Shame
Confusion	Gratitude	Loneliness	Suffering
Contempt	Grief	Love	Sympathy
Depression	Guilt		

After exploring emotional states, let's look a little deeper into the mindsets in which we find ourselves. These are often a bit more involved and more difficult to categorize, but at the same time, it is easier to determine which one we feel at any given time. Our mindset is the largest contributor to our driving force. Similar to exploring emotional states, determining the mindset in which we spend the majority of our time is the first step toward positively affecting it. Within the exploration cycle, you should also keep track of the mindset in which you find yourself the most often as well as the one that is the most effective for making progress along your particular life path. Remember that this is not the same for everyone, as a UFC fighter will require a different mindset than an accountant or a politician.

Human Mindsets:

Exuberant - outgoing, explorative
Driven - focused, productive
Positive - controlled, logical
Bubbly - anticipatory, optimistic
Determined - hopeful, structured
Indifferent - resolved, passive
Anxious - nervous, cautious
Concern - pessimistic, worried
Despair - hopeless, uncertain
Undirected - confused, doubtful
Agitated - uneasy
Worthless - shameful, unproductive
Hopeless - ineffective, incapable

We will work with this mapping exercise later when we start to examine the usefulness of and

the adoption of a particular mindset to increase our effectiveness. Moving from one mindset to

another will require you to control your thought lengths, to place yourself in beneficial situations,

and to address the biological triggers that shift you from one focus to another. We will continue

to talk about this more in the last chapter, "Living the Process." Remember that the table of

mindsets is not intended to be all-inclusive. Use it as a guide, but do not expect your list to be an

exact match.

People

The next area to address within the exploration cycle involves the people who have influence

over your life cycle. Understanding the relationship between these influences, their ability to

influence, and the magnitude of their effect is vital to this exercise. As you start to document each of these influences in your life, take some time to place them in the order of the table below. Notice that "Least Changeable - Most Influential" is at the top. These people will have the largest impact, and you will probably want to identify them by name. As you reach the lower levels of the chart, names will be less important than classifications or groups.

As you identify these people and groups, note the dynamic of the interactions between them and you. Are they positive interactions on average? Are they negative? Does the person or group introduce poison into your life? Think about the impact these people have on you in terms of the negative or positive events that occur. Later we will explore the following questions: If I no longer connect with this person, do the interactions or events stay the same? Do they get better, worse, or go away?

Least Changeable - Most Influential

Family
Friends
Neighbors
Co-workers
Authorities
Acquaintances
Organizational peers
Member peers
Conformity leaders (church)
Demographic peers
Inspirational peers
Motivational influences
Passersby
Virtual social network

Most Changeable - Least Influential

Lastly, in our interactions with the people aspect of our life cycle, think about what we prefer. What effect do we have on the situation? Do we enjoy being around people who are better, more skilled, more mature, and more experienced than we are? Do we enjoy being around peers more often? Would we prefer to be around people who are less capable, less intelligent, or needier than we are? The answers to these questions will give us some insight into our personal needs, and these will often change along with mindset. Noting how we relate in these three areas for each mindset will also be beneficial. Later, we will look at how we can affect our mindset to create a more desirable or more productive condition by addressing the feeling we get from the people who surround us.

Situations

The final area in which we should evaluate ourselves is the situation in which we choose to place ourselves. Do we choose our situations based on how we arrange and determine our schedule for an effective week? Do we select our situations based on our emotional state? Do we select our situations based on input from other people? Knowing how we function requires an understanding of what compels us to choose situations. Many people will choose what they consider a good situation—something they are supposed to do, such as attend church. However, they do it because of the expectations of others, and they become so miserable from their participation in this seemingly beneficial situation that they create negative energy within it. The reason we choose situations is as important as the choice itself, for that establishes our ability to enjoy the process. Explore the situations you choose and the reasons for your choice, and document them.

The second exercise related to situations involves documenting what you introduce that affects each situation. While taking notes on each situation, examine what your involvement does. Do I add value to the situation? Do I add positive energy to the people involved? Do I remove positive energy from—or add negative energy to—the situation? Do I alter the situation or interact with it at all? This exercise also will change along with your mindset, so noting how this interacts with each of your mindsets will add to your exploration. Later, we will discuss the influences we add to situations and delve into how to adjust them. The reason for selecting a situation becomes important at this stage because it will affect our enjoyment when it modifies our mindset and will affect our relationship to the situation.

Refinement Cycle

As our lives are never static, throughout this book we have been looking at each portion as a process. Defining the direction and the components that affect each portion as they constantly flow requires a refinement cycle, which is a process of reevaluating each area of our life cycle and path. A refinement cycle should examine which stimuli affect us in each mindset that we identified. Interestingly, the same stimulus can affect me differently in each mindset. Of course, it is not practical to address every mindset, but you probably noted problem areas as you went through the exercise of mapping mindsets. I have found that I only need to address 3-5 problem areas, while the rest of them seem to take care of themselves. As I mentioned in other parts of this book, my problem areas involve my self-defined flaws and my biological responses to anxiety and stress.

Collecting the Details

Addressing the problem areas is the first step, which will be more of a reactive practice directed at avoiding discomfort. The proactive part of the refinement cycle involves a process used in engineering and scientific organizations. The details we collected regarding ourselves in the exploring and path-creating sections will become the first step in this process. Many things will stand out, and solutions will pop into mind immediately. I call these "Oh, wow" moments. Others may take some time looking at the information and actually adding up how often triggers occur or what percentage of the time we spend in certain mindsets and emotional states.

Scrutinize the differences when the same stimulus occurs at different times, when the only thing that has changed is you or some portion of your life cycle. Also, view this through the lens of the different stages of your life. Did you react differently? What changed? Were the changes because of you, or were they because of influences, triggers, skills, situations, etc.? The collections of your actions are usually revelatory because you can view yourself from a vantage that is often different from the way others describe you from their outside viewpoint. Examine each set of information while considering whether the influence that changed was internal, external, or social. Have changes occurred over such an extended period of time that the change is only noticeable when you compare yourself to different times in your life? The collection and comparison of details will lead to the next step, which is when you begin to engineer yourself into the best possible version of you.

Create a Hypothesis

We can often find multiple hypotheses—possible solutions—when it comes to ideas for how to adjust our lives. Multiple things may need to be adjusted at the same time, and often combinations of these will be the best solutions. Adjusting one or two of the life cycle elements, while holding the remaining one or two constant, is the best way to think about creating hypotheses. In exceptionally turbulent times, adjusting all three may even be required to avoid a disaster. I will give you a few ways to think about adjustments, and asking yourself these questions may help when creating a hypothesis.

Can I Change My Reason?

Often, we do things without knowing why, and it causes us problems on many levels. We lose our motivation to do things that do not benefit us. Finding the benefit of our actions, in terms of which actions make us feel like ourselves again, is important when making adjustments of this nature. Changing the reason you do something can make all the difference in the world. When we set up a path, we benefit from the work because it moves us in a direction that invites the most satisfying treatment.

Earlier in the book, I presented an example of two ways to play a game of chess—one in which we were looking ahead to the next move to determine if the opponent had gone in the expected direction or not and the other in which we moved based on what we saw after each move by the opponent. The anticipation of the opponent's moves gave us a feeling of excitement; while aa reduction of pain approach gave us the feelings of avoiding the results of each move, which then caused us anxiety. Changing the reason we do things can keep constant the situations and people aspects of our life cycle, but it can change the way we look at and interact with those aspects when adjusting our enjoyment. We can focus on an adjustment that makes us feel fulfilled about our personal progress, or we can make an adjustment that makes us feel better about the processes we performed. Either or both can often be done with the same adjustment.

Can I Change My Location?

The next hypothesis poses the question: can I think the same, keep the same actions, but change my location? This question is also valid when we think through our actions in response to stimuli and when we find that we either do not want to or do not need to change how we think or act. In my personal life, I write and spend a lot of time thinking, so I determined to change my location to one where I felt the most inspired to do those things. People who have a desire to become a musician or an actor often change locations to be among like-minded people who will most likely improve their chances of success in that industry. An adjustment as simple as changing to a new fitness center or community center right down the road may make all the difference in the world.

Can I Change My Mindset?

Taking a vacation, listening to a motivational seminar, or even scheduling some personal time are all adjustments that change mindset, an objective for which we previously discussed how to plan. These changes are the easiest, and they often become the only hypotheses on many people's lists. However, I have found that they usually only work in combination with another adjustment. Many of us spend a lifetime thinking that this is the only portion we have control over, only to make several temporary adjustments to a larger problem that we feel powerless to control.

Can I Change My Choices of Situations?

Asking this question will result in thinking about how you can adjust your choices of situations. Can you decide when and why to choose one situation over another based on what we learned in our exploration cycle? When you feel sad, does your choice of situation cause you to slip further into a state of depression? If so, consider the choice of activities available to you when you feel sad and attempt to avoid the particular situations that may exacerbate your sadness. In my own life, I have often reserved some time to study in the evening, while saving for the morning those things that require some activity. I used to go to the school library after class where my interaction with many other people and my fatigue limited my productivity. When I changed my situation to do some busy work at home, relax, and be social in the evening then go to the library in the early morning, my productivity increased significantly.

I addressed both my biological and my social needs with the same adjustment. Even though I was able to study in the evening, I found as I aged that my mental ability fell off later in the day, while my ability to do busy things did not. Although intrinsically difficult because I felt I would have less time in the morning, making this change allowed me to get more work done in a shorter time. A change of situation will often have to be gradual and coincide with a change to either your mindset or the reason for your actions.

Bridge the Gap

My last example shows how I used the information I collected about myself to make a hypothesis, which I then tested with good success. This third stage of bridging the gaps between details, ideas, and actions is, for some reason, the hardest part for many people, including me. We are usually good at talking about what we see, and we often have inferences about how those collections of information could be used in some way. On the other hand, making the step to take action is the point at which we often fall short. In the chapter "Working Past Where You Are," we discussed the process of using the present, in which one task at a time links to a future task that has not yet occurred. Using the habits gained from that process and applied to this one, we have a practice for documenting our refinement cycle as we proceed and for determining the patterns that give us the best results.

Doing this has changed me more than anything else has. Most significantly, my performance improved in general as I added more regularly occurring downtime and vacation time. By almost forcing the weekly cycle, which includes very active and fun events for each cycle of productivity to sociability to activity, I am able to rest more fully and thus to work harder and more productively. The addition of a monthly or quarterly long weekend of rest and an annual month-long period of rest increases my productivity. I worked for years taking hardly any of my available vacation days off, and all it yielded was unhealthy living, which resulted in having to take the same number of sick days off.

Bridging the gaps consists of adjusting an action or activity and looking for the hypothesized or expected result. If you need to be more social when moving into a situation, then adjusting to a shorter thought length will get you to an appropriate mindset. Likewise, if you need to focus on topics that are more complex, you can perform exercises to extend thought length. If you have identified the adverse, biological triggers that cause discomfort, which leads to dislike and causes an undirected mindset, then address the triggers by either changing your input to them or avoiding the other influences that contribute to them. Gradually, the discomfort will subside, and you can address the dislike, add rewards, and move to a mindset of indifference. When determination crosses these adjustments, positive results bring recurring affirmation when others notice the change. You might even end up actually enjoying the exact same activities.

Other adjustments that I have made include noting when I feel a certain way and deciding to do an activity or go to a location as a result. Like alcoholics who drink when they feel bad in order to forget their problems, this creates a biological reward system for your emotional state. However, your intended response should have a positive result. Other things that I do for myself include calling and talking to a particular person when I am in a certain mindset. I think all of us, as we become more emotionally mature, have identified quite a list of items of the form "avoid this when…," and I do this for myself because it benefits my mood.

Helpful Supportive Items

This process will benefit from a few tools that I have found to support the refinement cycle. Knowing how you think best and identifying your personality type are the first two things I recommend that you determine about yourself. The determination of what style of thinking best suits you will help you locate your most productive environment. When I discovered my thinking style, it was like an awakening. I learned that many of the situations I had encountered—a good portion of which were beyond my control, sometimes because of teachers—were so contrary to what I needed in order to think well that they became poisonous to me. I recommend taking the Kolb Experiential Learning Theory (ELT) test to understand the type of environments that will work best for you personally (Kolb, 1999). The ELT categorizes into four types the ways that different people learn, which we will further discuss later in the chapter.

Knowing how you most effectively think is part of meeting your human needs. If you place yourself in a situation in which the stimulus is contrary to your personal needs for thinking, you will not be productive. No matter what basic need you have—whether it involves the way that you think best, relates to an area defined on Maslow's hierarchy of needs, or even simply is a temporary health or nutritional need—not allowing that need to be fulfilled leaves you in an unbalanced state. Even if you are not consciously aware of such needs, the continuation of the imbalance gradually creates a divide between your logical decisions, which do not satisfy your needs, and your body's biological cravings. This results in the feeling that something is illogical or unresolved.

The personalities of individuals—including your own—can produce harmony or conflict, which may be addressable by knowing a little bit about the different types of personalities that people exhibit. The Myers-Briggs Type Indicator (MBTI) is a good place to start to learn about your personality type (Briggs, 1962). Most readers may be familiar with this as it is widely utilized in school systems across the Unites States, even at the grade school level.

Optimize Your Best Worst

When we reevaluate our paths, our main objective should be to reset the clock on our own motivation. Back when we looked at determining a path, we made a list of "situations that make us feel alive," and I indicated we would further discuss them later. The situations that make us feel alive reset the clock on our motivation. The continued process of reevaluation should incorporate such situations in addition to efforts that later return positive feedback from others. The support for and the positive affirmation of progress are essential to resetting motivation. If we add situations in which we are performing actions that we admire by other people, we will feel like the people that we want to be like. Possibly even more important, these will fit into the ideal image that we started to construct when we defined our paths. Whom do I envy? How do I want people to see or view me? How do I want others to treat me? With whom do I want to surround myself? In what environment do I want to be? This improved version of you will gradually appear as you interact with others and aim to elicit the responses you want to receive.

Another part of reevaluating your path is to set and reset your emotional state to whatever makes you most effective. For example, commonly in the military, solders are drilled and trained to trigger their own aggression. For occasions when they find themselves scared, tired, or in despair, being able to trigger anger or aggression is more effective for the tasks required in their jobs than those vulnerable emotional states. Thus, identifying useless emotions for a given situation and triggering the emotional state that is required to be effective will give you a measure of control. Such self-control is often seen as a part of emotional maturity. Gaining emotional maturity in these situations starts with mapping your own emotional states, making a list of them, recognizing which mindsets are more effective, and knowing how you can trigger each of them in yourself.

The practice of adjusting your mental states may also require adding some influences over time. Often your ability to see yourself as capable of achieving a particular status will depend somewhat on your perceived self-worth and on how others view your reputation. In other words, people relate ability to status. For instance, we would not elect as president of the United States someone who had not been a senator, governor, general, or head of a large organization. Why is this? It is because we perceive that person's ability through the lens of that person's experience. Thus, a part of the reevaluation of your path is to identify and add these types of influences.

Many of us consider condoning vices to be wrong—a belief often instilled at early ages via negative reinforcement. The reason for this is most likely that what has been traditionally considered a vice in the past includes things that were physically enjoyable but that have been found to be unhealthy according to modern science. At various times in the past, drugs—the effects of which were unknown or little known—were the commonly desired vices of choice, but that is not as relevant now. New vices have replaced them, such as physical pampering, palate-pleasing treats, self-time for games, scanning Internet content, or even time away from the stresses around us. In my opinion, having some vices is essential to satisfying your human needs. Explore what sorts of things you enjoy, and if you have come to believe that those things should be stopped whenever they cross your mind, then examine where and how you acquired those beliefs.

Mental and Thought Support

As the focus of this book is on how you should look internally into yourself, optimizing the inner workings of the mind is central to this view of self. We talked about exploring and refining cycles. Now let's look at building on that so you can become the best version of yourself. Both from other resources and from those that we first looked at in the earlier chapters of this book, we now have many tools to work with. Let's discuss some of these and explore how we might use them to help ourselves along this journey.

Thinking Styles

The Kolb Experiential Learning Theory (ELT) is a great tool, as mentioned in the last section. The chart below shows the four primary learning styles and some details about the traits a person exhibits in each of these categories (Kolb, 1999). Some people will fall solidly into one of these categories while others may straddle two types. A few will even sit in the middle with some traits from each. Most people, however, will find that one or two fit and that their exact opposite is on the other side of the chart. This is important because being forced to operate in the conditions of your exact opposite learning style will be poisonous for most people.

Accomodating
Concrete Experience + Active Experiment
- Hands-on and concrete
- Wants to do
- Discovery method
- Sets objectives/schedules
- Asks questions fearlessly
- Challenges theories
- Adaptable
- Receives information from others
- Gut feeling rather than logic

Diverging
Concrete Experience + Reflective Observation
- Real-life experience and discussion
- Imaginative
- More than one possible solution
- Brainstorming and group work
- Observe rather than do
- Alternatives
- Background information

Converging
Abstract Conceptualization + Active Experiment
- Hands-on and theoretical
- Analogies
- Specific problems
- Tests hypothesis
- Best answer
- Works alone
- Problem solving
- Technical over interpersonal

Assimilating
Abstract Conceptualization + Reflective Observation
- Theories and facts
- Theoretical models and graphs
- Talk about rationale rather than do
- Lectures
- Numbers
- Defines problems
- Logical Formats

How is this information useful to us when we think about engineering the best version of ourselves? Using the information on our mindsets, situations, and people that we collected in the exploring cycle, we can now identify in which category the stimuli of each of those aspects fall relative to our need for productive thinking. If you identify with the "Converging" category in the lower left of the diagram, then sitting in a think tank with people who discuss virtual, intangible theories may not be the best place for you to be productive. You would be better off situating yourself in a practical learning environment where you can disassemble and reassemble physical equipment. Topics containing theoretical objectiveness with multiple possibilities may be poisonous to you.

The ELT will have its highest value when choosing the situation and people aspects of your life cycle. This is not to say that you can never be around people with opposite thinking styles, but when you need to be productive, choosing to avoid those will help you to dodge the poisons to your thinking style.

Hierarchy of Thoughts

The taxonomy of thoughts that we first discussed in the chapter "Thought-Length Hierarchy" will be of value as you begin to identify which mindsets or emotional states you desire to adjust in a positive direction at a particular time. Progressing from one mindset or emotional state to another is effectively done by shortening or lengthening your present thought length. If you feel somber, worthless, or anxious, then your mind is thinking about long, deep topics that often relate to shame, remorse, guilt, or some other deep, self-contemplative thought. Making a conscious effort at these times to shorten the time you spend thinking a particular thought will start to lower your thought lengths from the "Conceptualizing" and "Exploring/Expanding" categories on the following chart down to the category of the "Brevity and Fun" thought lengths. This serves to arrest the deeper, contemplative thoughts needed for questioning self-worth and establishes a more relaxing mindset and thought length, as in the green region of the chart. Since humans have a comfortable, unstressed level centered on the state of brevity and fun thoughts, the mind starts to relax from its tense state, as if a muscle released from flexing.

Thought-length progression

	%
Ascending	0.01%
Self-Enlightening	0.04%
Revolutionizing	0.10%
Utilitarian	0.30%
Hypothesizing	0.65%
Compiling and correlating	0.80%
Replicative	1.40%
Exploring/Expanding	3.00%
Conceptualizing	4.00%
Organizational	8.00%
Individualizing	17.00%
Distinguishing	20.00%
Brevity and Fun	19.00%
Interactive-reproductive	16.00%
Staying out of trouble	6.00%
Instinctual	2.00%
Survival	1.00%
Physically Sustaining	0.50%
Involuntary	0.20%

In addition, you can adjust your thought lengths in the other direction to begin a focused routine that moves you up the thought-length chart, which I will discuss later in this section. Once they are aware of the direction toward which they seek to proceed from their current mindset, anybody can determine the required thought length for a particular mindset. Moving up and down this chart becomes a characteristic of practicing two processes: one that shortens and one that lengthens thoughts.

This has been an amazing revelation to me, both for my own use and for my work with counselees. People often contact me in a confused or agitated state in which they do not understand—or in which they are unable to see past themselves to realize—that a series of biological triggers has trapped them in an emotional rut. The wonderful and dangerous thing about thought lengths is that you can lead other people up and down this chart simply by making them listen to you and follow along with your tempo and thought patterns.

My son, a deep thinker, has often called me on the phone in a depressed mindset in which all he can think about is why people don't talk to him at school. One time at school, he encountered a new kid whom he noted had made multiple new friends after only being there a week or so. His contemplation of this made him analyze all that he thought was wrong with the situation, reflecting on it at length to try to determine where he had gone wrong. He was so depressed on the phone that I first led him to a distraction, so we talked about a new movie he had seen. I began to compare that movie to others we had seen and quoted random funny lines from movies that I knew he would relate to and would laugh about with me. After about five minutes of lighthearted, casual conversation, which only requires shorter thoughts, I asked him how he felt, and he was amazed to say that he felt great.

Next, I went back to a longer thought and explained how children learn at an early age by watching the faces of the people open to interaction. Those who make no facial movements and stare off into the distance with unchanged facial expressions are deep in thought, and if interrupted, they are not emotionally available for interaction, so even at young ages people instinctively know this. In contrast, when children see people whose eyes bounce around from place to place, augmented by rapidly changing emotional cues, they know that those people are in a mindset of brevity and fun thoughts and that those people have time to attend to children. I told him that he could watch this dynamic play out when a child will not even give the people who are deep in thought a second look when they are in the same room. Often you can note the fear on a child's face when they see this, which is most likely because they live with someone who will snap at them when disturbed from this mindset.

393

I continued to say that as adults we have all gained this understanding and that we subconsciously know who to address and who not to. His contemplation of why people would not talk to him actually put him in a long thought length and caused him to exhibit the kind of facial expressions that those people instinctively interpreted as cues not to address him. This made it possible to then tell him that there was nothing at all wrong with him. I explained that human nature is such that people would address him if he changed his behavior to display the nonverbal cues that send the biological signal to others that he is approachable.

In another example, I have spoken with people late at night who had worked themselves into a frenzy of short thoughts and who were nearly hyperventilating with anxiety. Having been in this situation many times, I have learned to start slowing down as I talk, actually stretching some words out to intentionally make them longer than the other person would anticipate in normal speech. I would transition from the shorter topics by stretching them into longer ones and then by repeatedly linking other related attributes until we were contemplating some deep topic for five minutes or so. Then in the same manner as with my son, I would ask those people how they felt after resetting their thought length, and then would explain how they could continue to do this themselves by practicing each time they received the same or similar biological trigger that started the experience.

By using thought length as a tool to adjust emotion and thus mindset, we can help others as well as ourselves when needed. We are all familiar with this kind of stretching and shrinking of topics because comedians, politicians, ministers, and other skilled orators all use this as a tool to captivate their audiences. As a word of caution, be sure you are using this to benefit the human race, not to maliciously control or manipulate people.

In my last two examples of how I support others with thought-length therapy, I explained both shortening and increasing thought length. To move up the thought taxonomy requires a forced lengthening of thoughts. To move down requires shorter, more rapid thoughts. To lengthen my own thoughts, I use this process.

- Let the details slip out of focus
- Group previous thoughts
- Find contrast and similarities
- For each contrast, make a list of possible bridges
- Document what you discovered
- Move up or down detail level, repeat

The first thing is to let your current surroundings slip out of focus. This skill often generates the most questions, so I have determined the things that enable its use. Most people contribute a few things, some of which are complete opposites, to enabling the loss of focus. The list of what makes us focus may also help, as minimizing these from your environment when you need to focus is just as important as setting up the proper variables. What makes you lose focus also often puts you to sleep, so finding the balance between the targeted thought length and sleep is a challenge. Let your mind lose focus while your body is physically stimulated. To remain on the conscious side of this balance, you can use stimulants such as coffee, social interaction, movement, or physical discomfort, such as a hard chair. Try some of these in different patterns and combinations to determine which work best for you.

What makes us lose focus	What makes us focus
- Safe environment	- Unsafe
- Something you are familiar with	- Unfamiliar environment
- Things are taken care of for you	- Unique stimuli
- Repetitive stimuli	- Uncomfortable physical conditions
- Biorhythms (low energy)	- Biorhythms (energy exertion)
- Boring (surroundings)	

Remember that, as your biorhythms change at different times of the day, week, or month, some of these may require augmentation. Our natural biorhythms may alter how effective our desired change may be or even how able we are to recognize our own state. If you are at a low energy point of the day, it may not be as easy to notice that your mindset has turned foul. In addition, if you have entered a more social time of the week, then adjusting to a longer thought length for one task or situation may not be optimal. It may be better to reschedule the activity that requires deeper thought for earlier in the following week when you plan to focus and when you will have some time for deeper thinking.

Step-by-Step Process to Think Deeply

I. Remove stimuli that distract you by overwhelming your input. What does this mean? For example, if you sit in the middle of a flock of birds, you do not see any single bird because the flock becomes a blur. Your visual sense diminishes, and your focus on the individual stimulus fades.

II. Add the types of things that make you lose your focus on the things outside of your mind. For example, put on some headphones and play the same song (or a short list of songs) repeatedly until you are so familiar with them that you don't think about them anymore. This is really the same as number one, except removing the auditory stimuli.

III. Give yourself time to think. If you don't know what you're about to write when you sit down, you will sit and look at the screen as your work blurs in front of you—just like the exercise in step one, except in an unproductive way. I go biking or do some quiet, independent activity, and then I plan to think only during that activity each day. Don't sit down until you have about ten thoughts to write about. Then when you run out of those thoughts, go back to the activity that helps you think.

IV. Have a process for thinking, and practice lengthening your thought process. Here is an example of a process for thinking deeply about a topic. This process can be applied to any topic you like, and you should practice doing it for topics other than those you need to write about. Merely repeating this on a regular basis builds your cognitive ability.

1. Think of the topic (any topic you like).

2. Make a list of all of its attributes in your mind.

3. Group similar attributes into categories in your mind.

4. Make several hypotheses related to the groupings.

5. Connect and contrast the groupings to each hypothesis, and see which of the hypotheses are more accurate or which hold up best.

6. Connect each attribute to the hypothesis, and see if the same accuracy still holds up.

7. Make conclusions and define each path between the groupings, categories, and attributes.

8. Now it's time to write three lists.

   - On one side of your list, write down the thought process you went through on your topic from steps 1-6.

   - On the opposite side, write the list of conclusions from step 7.

   - Your unique work, the most valuable piece, is now the bridge between these two lists, which is your third list. The content that fills in the gaps between these two lists will be the value you add to the world.

9. After making these lists, write the summary of the process, including how you went about each step and the results of your lists in step 8.

V. Practice this process using small topics over longer periods each day. Eventually, you will do this process without thinking, will have stretched your ability to think in longer thought lengths, and will have strengthened your overall cognitive ability, much a like an athlete builds a muscle—repeating the same exercise and building up resistance and difficulty in achievable increments over a long period of time. Thinking it will come fast or overdoing it will only frustrate you or overwhelm you, which will cause you to give up.

Interpersonal Needs

Optimizing our interpersonal interactions can have a substantial positive impact when we take the time to set up interactions that fulfill our personal needs. Self-denial is often so ingrained into many of our belief structures that we apply it across our entire lives, intentionally increasing the number of areas where we do the opposite of what we desire. We use clichés like "no pain, no gain" because we have learned that growth is achieved through resistance. However, we often fail to balance this growth with some time for rest and healing, which includes breaks from social interactions.

Our bodies have involuntary reactions that prepare us for when things are wrong, that help us stay out of trouble, or that prevent difficult situations. Internally, we simply know when something appears to be wrong or is not progressing in a beneficial direction. We feel uneasy as our body prepares to initiate an anticipated corrective action. The average number of stimuli in the world around us has increased by many orders of magnitude in only a few generations of human development. Our bodies' natural reactions, which served to protect us from physical danger, are less relevant in this age, while the stimuli that cause involuntary reactions are more prevalent than ever. We need to plan to rest and relax from the physical and social stimuli that trigger those biological reactions.

I have often been accused of not being spiritual because of my logical approach to everything. The premise of such an opinion seems to be that logic and spirituality are polar opposites. According to my assessment, spirituality is the extent to which we are attuned to the involuntary cues within ourselves and to those we receive from others. The extremely spiritual people I have known appeared to exhibit the belief that their spirituality related to how much they accepted the same involuntary, uncontrollable, and unknown behaviors that I attempted to understand with logic. Recall both the Kolb learning styles and the Myers-Briggs personality tests, both of which recognize the opposing forces of sensing versus intuition or of thinking versus feeling.

A counseling group inquired about how I would approach helping individuals address the emotional aspects of traumatic situations. My immediate thought in response was that I did not have a way to deal with emotional trauma, but upon further reflection, I realized that emotional trauma is a series of situations with stimuli and responses. I recalled my years of visiting counselors, during which sessions we dug up and discussed—one instance at a time—the discomfort I felt in various situations of my life. Each situation in which discomfort had plagued me for years involved an unresolved emotional response or feeling. Each was only resolved within me when I understood what I had felt, why I had acted, or what stimuli I was responding to. Thus, in my case, the acceptance of and the comfort with the situation meant logically understanding it.

In my opinion, we each need to resolve one of these two things. Do we try to understand a situation? Alternatively, do we accept that we should not try to understand it and thus become comfortable with the situation's lack of resolvability? Since I am quite predisposed to being a sensing-thinking person, I cannot speak for people who possess an opposite disposition. However, when people attempt to become at ease with situations and when they accept them as irresolvable, they will have to do so repeatedly throughout their existence. The logical understanding of the same situation constructs a mental compartmentalization that allows you to move past unresolved feelings, which cause biological discomfort by repeatedly revisiting the illogical progression in your mind.

Needs for Fulfillment

Each human has a need for interpersonal involvement with others. Whether we admit it or not, as we talked about in the chapter "Thought-Length Hierarchy," an interactive nature that stabilizes humans begins in infancy. The infant and its primary caretaker actually form a dialogic

400

relationship in which the infant's right brain develops by following the caretaker's cues for emotional responses in situations that affect the developing human. This continues into adulthood, and we need to interact with others to observe their reactions to stimuli. Even if only subconscious, we need this validation of how others react to the same situations in order to stabilize ourselves. This is why people who are isolated from others become increasingly eccentric or disillusioned.

While we need interaction, we may often experience nonstop interaction in our modern age, so we need time away from the stimuli of others as well. In any instance of exposure, moderation is the key to stability. This includes social interactions, intellectual stimuli, self-indulgences, praise, acceptance, supportive guidance, or motivation. Each of these human needs should be included and optimized to determine the best level of exposure.

Personalities You Need to Have Surrounding You

Understanding which people or personality types are best for us at a particular time or in a particular mindset can most effectively address what we need for our interpersonal fulfillment. When we looked at defining our paths, we made a list of personalities that we would like around us. Refer to that list while you optimize your best and worst. Certain personalities will be calming, while others will be challenging, and at different times, both will be beneficial. Depending on what we are attempting to accomplish or what mindset we desire for ourselves, choosing the people to interact with can aid or obstruct the desired outcome.

When we need to focus on creating a product that requires deep thought, we might want to surround ourselves with people who have intellectual, pondering personality types, but when we want to sell the product, we should want to be around people who have extremely confident, conversational, interactive personality types. After work, we may want to take a class and surround ourselves with the personality types of teachers or mentors. In any instance, the major contributing factor is your own personality type. You will notice that you feel supported by some personality types, while others will feel disruptive. When a particular type of personality or style of thinking is completely contrary to your own, it will usually feel disruptive. Sometimes opposition is necessary for a task to be effective, but the discomfort you feel also needs to be addressed and limited.

Use the information from your exploration cycle to optimize the personalities with which you surround yourself. Determine which personalities you work best with in situations required for your success. If a particular personality type makes you extremely productive or unproductive, position yourself accordingly. Though it is not all-inclusive, the list below is a good place to start. Map how you work with these types, and identify which make you more or less productive. Start with your problem mindsets and remove what influences them. Then begin to augment the times when you need to be productive with the people who possess the most supportive personality types.

Argumentative, challenging
Intellectual, pondering
Passive, peaceful
Conversational, interactive
Supporting, coaching
Communal living
Spiritual, religious
Social, group activities
Self-improvement, fitness
Individual or team sports
Enlightened social events or parties
Independent, isolated
Teacher, mentor
Student or understudy
Less fortunate
More fortunate
Extremely confident
Eclectic, diverse
Material collector

Physical Needs

Optimizing your physical needs is also important to your stability and productivity. Many people

are familiar with needing enough nutrition and sleep. We can also find many resources regarding

what caloric intake or what regularity of excretion we should have. However, most of the

directions you can find on human needs address the building or maintenance of the physical

body. Few focus on mental needs or on improving productivity. As we have discussed earlier in

the book, productivity requires incorporating the aspect of time into your physical needs. We

need to be able to be productive for a desired period and to align that time in a way that makes

us most productive. Doing so requires us to sustain the same human needs and variations

thereof.

Address when and how you have energy, when you are able to produce and maintain body heat, and when you are most focused. Utilize the times when you are most interactive, and respond to your biological and sexual triggers. Adjust each of these to cyclic or seasonal patterns. The optimization of physical needs should follow a trial-and-error process that attempts to meet the bounds of the alignment of successful demographics, which we discussed in the chapter "Enjoying the Process." Combine this optimization with the reduction of biological triggers, also discussed in that chapter, and determine the best and worst for your own success.

Environment

We can change only the things we have control over. We may have control over which environment we choose, but we cannot control the components that comprise it. We can often address our internal selves or the way in which we interact with our environment. Matching our biorhythms to the needs of our environment is the best way to start optimizing ourselves for that environment.

If you have difficulty waking up in the morning or if your biorhythms are sluggish throughout your early waking hours, you very likely experience low body heat production, clouded thinking, and low energy production. This was the case with me. For years, I struggled to figure out a way to overcome the morning rut. I was typically able to get started in the late morning, usually about 2-3 hours after I had awakened. I noticed that I became hungry when I was no longer chilly, and my thinking cleared up when the desire for food became the focus. I made adjustments to wake up earlier at first, which aligned my natural biorhythms with the time I needed to start working. Later, I optimized again by adding a routine to raise my body temperature as soon as I awoke.

This engaged my mental focus and sparked my desire for food earlier so that I was able to shorten the time required for my entire biorhythmic routine.

Most of us struggle with biorhythms at times during the day, often in the mid-afternoon around 2:00–3:00 p.m. Some people may also experience a low period from the late afternoon until after dinner and then may come alive in the late evening when sleep becomes necessary to prepare for the next day. Either of these can often cause low productivity or disrupt daily or weekly cycles. Once again, some preparation and planning will align your biorhythms, which you can do by shifting your schedule or by arranging a stimulating event or activity. Some people will have luck with shifting the time when they eat, altering the types of food that they eat, or adjusting their body temperatures, which may be the opposite at other times of the day. Other options include doing an exercise, scheduling a social event, attending an entertainment event, or just taking a break from the subject of their focus. Certainly, when all else fails, add a stimulant such as coffee. Shifting, changing, or adding influences or mitigating the negative impact of our own biorhythms are all ways of changing ourselves, for they are the parts of our environment over which we have control.

Multiple Life Cycle Component Changes

At times in our lives, we will need to change multiple areas of our life cycle at the same time. These junctures are often planned in people's lives and even expected at various times. For instance, a young person may be expected to leave home, go off to the military, or attend a college after high school. This expectation is planned for and anticipated as a milestone for most. In these cases, many people are making this change together, at the same time, which lessens the adverse effects since everyone is open to forming new sets of friends and to looking for new situations together. In the case of a teenager leaving for college, all three portions of the life cycle will most likely be changing at the same time.

When we evaluate our life cycle at various times in our lives and then determine that all three aspects are progressing in negative directions, sometimes the only approach is to decide to change all three. During the writing of this book, I have changed all three. I realized that I had changed and that I did not desire to maintain the effort required to barely prevent all three of my life cycle components from sliding in a negative direction. Many of us will hold on for years in the spin cycle of a minimal capacity to maintain stability. After I realized the three areas of the life cycle, I decided that I would make a change to all three and reset. This decision came as much from my desire to design my life while I was writing about that process as it did from my need to make a change in all areas.

Like a person who takes a year or so from their normal grind to hike in the Andes of South America or to follow in the path of Christ or the Buddha, I decided to practice my own processes. I wanted to start from ground zero, set a path, initiate a process of working past where I was, and find my enjoyment in a new area to pursue. The enlightenment I have found in doing so has not only changed me but also has enabled me to document these processes, which I used to embark upon an endless path with great potential for achievement. I have changed and adjusted each area of my life cycle in every way in order to design a successful life and to build a valuable, successful business.

References

Kolb, D. A., Boyatzis, R. E., Mainemelis, C., (1999), Experiential Learning Theory: Previous Research and New Direction. Department of Organizational Behavior, Weatherhead School of Management

Briggs, K. C., Myers, I. B. (1962) Myers–Briggs Type Indicator

Chapter XIV

Rebuilding After Life's Low Points

The times in my life when I was the most dangerous were when everyone had given up on me and I was nothing. These times actually present a significant advantage that you will not have at any other times in your life, which is that no one expects anything from you. Here's how you can capitalize on these times.

As you learned in the chapter "Thriving at the Low Points of Our Lives," I have experienced several of these times, as most of us do. We like to keep them very private. We don't talk about them. In fact, most of us will not even remember them because we block out the memory. Yes, we activate logical thought stoppers for that memory, block it, and divert our attention away from it as if it does not exist. If we don't remember it, does it really exist? Unfortunately, if we have a hyperarousal response to the situation, we may unknowingly default to being irritated whenever similar situations arise or are discussed or depicted. This is why the people who are guilty of something will sometimes be the first to condemn it in others.

I have seen people who have endured situations like divorce be the hardest on others who are enduring similar situations. People who have had an extramarital affair wrongfully accuse their partners of the same betrayal. However, even the greatest figures in history are responsible for the most monumental failures—as well as, of course, the greatest successes. This truth of human nature is that we have short memories when it comes to the emotional associations we make with both others and ourselves. The memory of a great blunder followed by a great success becomes the emotional memory of two large successes. We made a strong emotional connection in the past, and now we switch to the present situation and emotional state.

So let's engineer our lives so that others remember us as having succeeded when we go through these situations. Let's use what we have seen repeatedly throughout history to make ourselves great. A saying I used when I confronted my last few low points is, "I will be silent and out of sight until one day when you notice the castle, which I have erected in the shadows of your party." By making this my motto and entering a building phase, the significance of each low point has been dwarfed by a subsequent accomplishment.

You will find that the times when everyone seems to disengage from you and disregard their interactions with you are a gift. You will be like a fly on the wall; your observations and interactions will often lead you to the third part of secondhand realizations. Use these moments of realization to your advantage. These euphoric moments will give you some insight into people and into how members of society interact. Focusing on this gap and on how things come together for the best will be the next phase of your life. Use this enlightenment to bridge your momentum into the next phase.

I have euphoric moments in the recovery from each collapse. Only those who have experienced this can really understand. During the breakdown preceding a collapse, parts of my personality entirely disappeared. In the unbalanced disarray, this loss was not entirely noticeable. During recovery, however, the part of me that died—or that I killed—came back to life at some point. This enlightenment was unlike any other in my life. You strive to understand how this could have slipped away without your even noticing, and then you discover what else you have lost.

One time I experienced the overall loss of my sexuality when my partner informed me that she was repulsed by me. It did not return for years, and when it did, I was shocked that I hadn't even noticed its absence. The day it came back, it was as if I were a child again, unable to control it.

I have talked to people who were victims of rape or violent crime who expressed that a feeling of validity returned one day, which they did not know they had lost until the moment of its return. They had shut out the entire event, never admitting to their conscious self that it was gone.

In my case, I did not feel I had value to any other person after my total collapse. Why would I bother entertaining the notion that a woman should want to date me? My sense of value returned one day after I observed that a co-worker, whom I perceived as having much less value in the work environment than I had, showed me pictures of his new girlfriend. His wife had left him only a few weeks earlier, and he had met someone new already, while I had not entertained the thought for three years. I had gone out on dates, but at the time, I felt that I was deceiving those women because I did not believe that anyone could value me.

One of my collapses came full circle when I was laid off from my job. I felt that my work ethic, organizational skills, and validity in the work environment had been lost in the layoff. For some time, I felt that I was trying to trick each company at each job interview into hiring me. This surfaced during the interview process, and I was turned away, interview after interview. When you do not believe that hiring you is a good decision, you cannot sell yourself. I did not regain my sense of validity and get positive outcomes from job interviews until I quit trying to find a job and began building my own business. This occurred one day after a client told me that the reason for my rejection was that they could not afford someone of my level, so they wanted to pay me for a lesser consulting role to help them identify a more appropriately skilled—and more junior— person in my stead.

410

Who and What Is Normal?

I hope that, from reading this book, you are getting the picture that what is normal for people in collapse is abnormal for them in every other period of their lives. As the human mind has the ability to improve throughout life, it can also regress when the influences of the life cycle align negatively. In my opinion, if you find yourself in a collapse, you have just received your gift, and the sooner you can accept that what you are going through is perfectly normal, the better off you will be. All of the people and influences telling you that you are not normal will eventually fade away. Some will never come back, and others will become enlightened when they realize otherwise.

The progressions of more capable and less capable times in your life are perfectly normal, so stop beating yourself up. It gives you the amazing opportunity to restart from scratch and to follow the processes I have laid out for engineering your life to make it the best it can be. Nearly everyone I talk to thinks that someone or something else is normal, even as they think that their own lives and minds are not. We all live in the same prisons of uniqueness: our minds. Our common trait is that we are all unique.

Each collapse I have endured was a different, yet similar experience. I am one of few people who have had the gift of evaluating multiple collapses in a single lifetime. I refer to it as a gift because I have been able to compare and contrast these times with the relatively calm periods of my life, but since I have experienced more than one of these times, I have been able to appreciate the similarities and differences as well. This is what I consider the primary strength in my unique life experience. Given the fact that normal, everyday people as well as very exceptional people experience these periods of collapse, we can recognize that these periods are entirely normal

and potentially repeatable, and wonderfully, possibly avoidable—or at least quickly remediable.

As a child thrown into a situation of extreme prejudice that was contrary to the modern age, I

had the first of these experiences. Like a victim of mind control, I was repeatedly pressured with

irrational thoughts and attitudes that contradicted the logical progression of my thoughts. These

extreme contradictions affected me more than it did others who might not have had the same

logical and intuitive conflict that I had, but in any case, I broke. I had to abandon one of the

directions to avoid developing a split personality. I had to shut off the process that would have

made me inflict on myself the control of accepting without logically understanding. Although at

odds with everything around me, this control falls perfectly within normal human patterns, as

anyone struggling with contradictions can be affected in the same way.

My extreme resistance to contradictory thoughts and attitudes drove me again while I was in the

Navy. As I explained earlier, my fellow sailors accepted that they should continually profess to

understand what was expected of us, even as they acted in opposition to what was expected. I

resisted this paradox precisely as I had earlier in my life. However, the same human inclination to

contradict logic also affected me over time and triggered a collapse that I resisted longer than I

believe most people could. Although my resistance to something that I believed was beneath my

personal integrity created this conflict, and although I refused to bend in my principles, conflict

such as this, maintained over time, will have the same effect on any human.

My ultimate collapse, the rock bottom of my life, was also simply a case of someone placed into a

situation in which thoughts and attitudes contradicted facts of the environment. As is the case in

many interpersonal relationships in which one person is mentally unstable, the person

attempting to maintain stability will be the most at odds with what is irrational. Thus, symptoms

412

of instability will often occur first in the person closest to the unstable individual. Because of my personality flaw, which leads me to accept all the blame, it took years of counseling to resolve this flaw and realize that the situation in which I was placed would have led anyone to the same conflict. Though I knew and accepted that it was out of my control, I was able to accept this knowledge more and more as I watched the same thing happen to other people in the same situation.

The subsequent collapses that I personally experienced followed a somewhat different progression from that point forward, but they were also entirely normal in light of the limitations and rationalizations of people in general. These can be classified as an internal conflict either due to fading humanity and loss of health or due to the achievement of milestones common to everyone's life. When we encounter the limitations of our frail human existence, the loss of health and the degradation of mental stability affect everyone. We can all expect the day when we meet the end or learn of its proximity, whether it happens in our fading seconds or originates from the knowledge of impending, unmaintainable bodily functions. People's reactions to this realization and to their reduced capabilities are entirely normal. Whether you are losing your health or reaching a milestone, such as your children leaving home, you should not be fooled. Every one of us will have these entirely life-changing experiences, which we think we have handled worse than anyone before us did. These situations are all a normal progression of life.

Questioning Your Competence

Throughout people's lives, they will have periods of increased cognitive ability and periods of decreased cognitive ability. We will all experience these repeated cycles, from collapsing to excelling and back, though some of us will have more than others will. The most exceptional people in history have had both the highest peaks and the lowest valleys. Like tracking a stock market chart, however, you can observe each of our patterns gradually decline to ever lower points and then briefly ascend to modest peaks, but as we learn this process and accept our own limitations, the pattern reverses. Higher peaks follow the low points, and each valley is shallower than the previous one. Rock bottom does not mean that it's over—just that you have learned how to address it and how to convert that process into a positive result. What demonstrates success is the ability to design each collapse so that it has its own integrated reset that compels your return to loftier levels.

In my own collapse, I began the process that became the foundation of this book. I turned to something that I had already begun for my life path. I was chipping away at a college degree and finding relief in going to class, where I found a way to enjoy the process of learning. It freed my mind from the whirlwind that had become my life. My college education became a path to work along, during which I had the passion to look beyond my college days and to devote my energy to projects that would fit into the direction of my work, which I imagined at the time would involve merging the hardware and software aspects of the computing world. Parallel to my academic studies, I worked to understand myself and to understand why I had been able to become a great achiever and underachiever. This questioning of my competence is what led to this book, while my work in computing led to my success in the world of cyber security.

By maintaining this path and enjoying the way that learning liberated my mind from the problems on which I would otherwise focus, I pushed forward year after year. When I neared the end of my bachelor's degree in computer engineering, I had already transitioned to a master's degree program. I decided to delay my graduation until I had completed my master's degree in order to combine the ceremonies. By the time that I had completed my first master's degree, I

414

had overlapped into the beginning of a second one, and my focus once again was on the path and not on the goal of completing the degree. When I stopped to think about what had happened, I realized that education had only recently become a part of my life, and I enjoyed the process so much that I decided to attend industry events and lectures as if they were social outings. At some point, I transitioned from the underachieving kid, who had learned to thumb his nose at the people who had put him down, to the college graduate, who had earned several master's degrees. But I was the still same kid from the country, one who had simply trained himself to engineer his life actively by advancing in the direction he had determined. Because I still feel like the same person, these educational accomplishments are more the product of my persistence than they are any gift or ability I possess. I believe that anyone can achieve this status and accomplish what I have.

Health and Perception of Self

In many cases, people find themselves in these situations of collapse because of a change in their health. In fact, everyone will go through this at some point in life. I will tell you about the road I know from my own life.

I had always been healthy, so a significant portion of my self-image revolved around my health. The thought of being physically incapable of performing necessary actions broke me in a way that I did not think possible. When becoming an underachiever has previously helped you progress through a situation in your life, it can become a coping mechanism much like withdrawing. Nevertheless, can you wait—and how long do you have to wait—to get past a change in health? The answer is that you don't ever get past it because you can't simply wait it out. Becoming at peace with aspects of your health will be among the most difficult challenges you will face. The healthier you are and the longer your health persists, the more it will take to get over the first time you confront a health crisis from which you cannot recover.

Though I am sure that you can find many books on how to move forward and on how best to regain your health, I will not focus on the physical. What I will talk about is how it affected me in my collapse situation and how I refocused and regained my values by channeling the same types of physical effort into other aspects of my life. By following these very processes of life engineering, I found other activities that I could pursue and that I could focus on. I believe this is vital to recovery because you must return to the same confidence in some aspect of your life, or else your body will not be able to recover to its best possible condition.

When I was training for strongman competitions, my ultimate collapse occurred, and I was unable to continue training. I could, however, change my focus and devote the same level of commitment to something I could still work on. I found ways to translate every aspect of working out to my mental and intellectual development. I poured myself into education, building my mind as I had built my muscles as a bodybuilder. Each aspect had a parallel. As a bodybuilder for years, I not only saw my muscles expand, but my bones and interconnecting systems also changed. I was no longer merely a boy with a great build—my bone structure had strengthened as well. As for my cognitive activities, things that were difficult at first became second nature later. During my freshman year of college, writing a four-page paper and sustaining a cohesive theme throughout would have been a huge task, but after a few years in graduate school, my eventual work produced a ten-page paper that left researchers questioning whether their direction was the norm.

I noticed that my health did not start to improve until my attitude and swagger—both robust when I had been a bodybuilder—returned in another aspect of my life. When people started to look at me with reverence and respect, which my physique used to elicit, in response to my accomplishments in this new area of my life, all of a sudden my health began quickly improving. The process of life engineering and of refocusing allowed me to overcome this major hurdle, which we all will experience. The process of positively engineering our lives and redirecting our paths will reduce the control that life's setbacks have over us.

Framework for Rebuilding

When you find yourself in a collapse, you have to have somewhere to start—a basic one-two-three process that explains what to do first. Let's examine such a framework for rebuilding. We need to begin developing a new self. First, we need to balance ourselves and then set up maintenance, projects, and direction. We will naturally want to distract ourselves at these times, and we will not want to think about whatever we are thinking about. We will want to stop our discomfort because not feeling is better than pain. Having a situational masker and a counselor to start balancing the mindset portion of your life cycle will be essential, so I recommend starting there.

Shrink to Maintain

Next, we start the process of setting up the framework. Recall the Life Balance Diagram in which people, situation, and mindset are all contained within the maintenance section of the diagram. We need to shrink this entire aspect of our lives until it is positively maintainable. People who do not do this will eventually have it done for them. Friends will leave, or jobs will get lost.

Prolonging this step could result in a degradation of sanity or even institutionalization. If you

become confused or unable to distinguish reality from unreality, rationality from irrationality, or

logic from illogic, then you may not be able to see your own situation. There is no shame in this,

but unfortunately, the most confused people turn to the wrong influences. When others try to

help, it only adds shame and makes it worse—to the point that the individual may not feel

capable of improving.

This shrinking process needs to include the new understanding that you're not going to have the

same capability for maintenance that you did before. These areas do not simply require

reduction—they require more reduction than you think is necessary. Continue working on

shrinking the cycles with a wait-and-see approach for a while, but ultimately, the faster you can

grasp your new reduced capabilities, the better off you will be. I have watched people in this

situation sort through their physical qualities, and they were repeatedly unable to relinquish the

one area that has become larger than their entire maintenance circle.

When you start to look at your new life path and new direction, remember that these are choices

and that other people or surroundings are not pushing them on you. If you choose not to

determine a path, one will still appear, but it will not be your choice. Your first decision should be

to break the chain of events that previously affected you negatively. If you were the bad guy

before, choose not to be on that path. Most of us are familiar with the novella, *A Christmas*

Carol, by Charles Dickens, which depicts this manner of change. If you were stressed out before,

do not return to the same path, which produces stressful conditions.

When it comes to the people in your life, you should sever ties with the influences that lead to

disastrous results. Break any of your codependent patterns, such as by avoiding an ex-wife who is

418

still causing problems in your life after ten years. Often, this will resolve itself when the people who were causing the most problems no longer benefit from their continued involvement in your life. Since these people often view you as a "has a" type of person, using you for something that you wanted to maintain, the involvement fades away when you are no longer the source of whatever they seek. The choice here becomes about whether you should bring them back into your life later—and if so, on what terms. Make sure you set the terms of such involvement if you determine they must be or should be back in your life.

Finding a Path

How do we start to find our path? I will not even accept as valid the notion that your path could be the same that it was before. The truth is that most of us will not have thought about what our paths were before this event. It may not even exist, or it may have simply happened incidentally. We probably chose a career because we went to college and then went to work for each employer who needed our skills and hired us based on our resume. I recommend starting this process by making three lists. First, list the things you do well. Second, list the things you enjoy doing. And third, list the things that can earn you a good living. When you have more ability, you should set a path and use all the selected categories that I outlined in the chapter "Determining a Path." For now, in your reduced capacity, you will want to start with something simple. Most likely, by this time in your life, you have already built a valuable skill set and assembled a good list of things you enjoy.

Since you are likely to consider a significant career change, you will need skills that previously you may have avoided acquiring or considered beyond your reach. That was the case with me. The new path that I considered required skills that I had previously tried and failed miserably to develop. I thought I might try to develop these skills if only I had some ability that I thought I lacked. In my experience, a person is never inherently "not good" at something. What I have found is that when I tried and failed to develop certain skills, I lacked the interest to become good at these skills. Since realizing this, I have come to recognize that people are never inherently "not good" at something. They lack interest, so they don't spend enough time or effort. Thus, they are simply not as practiced as others are. In short, you can do anything that interests you.

Don't be constrained by the fact that a skill is unfamiliar or that it is something with which you have little practice. If you have read to this point, you probably would not have guessed that the skill I lacked until my most profound life-rebuilding phase was writing. In fact, I was so miserable at writing that I vowed never to do any written work in my life. Nevertheless, I identified skills that I had that related to and were transferable to my next path, which also required writing. The key is to find as many relatable and transferable skills as you can carry forward to the new path and then start to fill in the gaps around them.

Get up and Show up

The next thing to start doing is to get out there. Remember that you have a get-out-of-jail-free card. No one is watching you or expecting anything from you, so there is no pressure. Start quietly chipping away at the achievable portions of your next path. Don't shut yourself away, but don't surround yourself with all the same influences from before either. Even with related tasks and situations, choose new environments. If you go to a particular social group, such as a church or a VFW post, change to another one. Give yourself a break in order to build this initial stage in peace.

420

Take a personality test to help choose the new social situations that will be important on your new path. You will need to socialize with people who are supportive and not competitive or confrontational. At these times, I have been comfortable around people with a calm resolve and people who are experiencing a similar traumatic life event, as in a support group. The Internet is great for this. Find a support group. Bounce your ideas off others as you develop your new path.

Byproduct of Recreating Myself

In the most severe collapse of my life, I noted an interesting byproduct that I have seen repeatedly in others and myself. It encompasses how humans handle situations and how our minds develop. Recall the chapters in which we discussed the way that strong emotions and traumatic events establish human reactive programming. We also touched on the way that the effective doubling of the ability to process several of the last levels (or lengths) of thoughts can develop a person's cognitive abilities over the course of a lifetime. Then I explained that, at these low points in our lives, we actually reduce our cognitive ability as if we were at an earlier stage in our lives. Now I will explain, based on my experience, how these processes combine to produce an exceptional result.

When I was at the lowest point of my life, there was nothing left of the previous person that I was. In the aftermath, I had to recreate and rebuild the person that I was going to be from then on. Since then, I have also spent some time watching and helping others through life collapses. With great interest, I have repeatedly observed the childlike regression and reduced emotional maturity that we all exhibit, but an exceptional growth in some area always follows thereafter. The most effective religious leaders in my memory had turned to religion in the course of one of these life events and had been exceptionally effective at communicating how this event had brought them to their religious convictions.

At the lowest point of my life, I continued my college career and later became remarkably effective in areas related to my studies. From speaking with other individuals with different talents, I heard similar stories of rags to riches after major collapses. The similarities among the ways that people had gained exceptional, specialized skills during these times led me to look at myself and at what skills I had gained during such times in my life. When I was at my lowest point, I was stuck between the labels of mental illness and government fraud. At the same time, I was reduced to a collapsed internal mindset that made me wonder which of these labels applied. I studied how I functioned internally because I wanted to understand how I had reached that state.

During my rebuilding phase, I pursued computer science and business education, but I also continued to visit my VA counselor more regularly, adding the third tier of self-awareness to my rebuilding skills. Because at that time an individual had poisoned the people aspect of my life cycle by proclaiming that their path called for them to persecute me based on their religious views. That person's religious views implied that I could be dehumanized to the point that my removal from my own child's life was justified. As the object of persecution, I felt that I had no recourse within the bounds of that person's religious structure. Once again, this created such confusion in me about the purpose of religion that I altogether avoided seeking solutions that involved religion.

I have spent some time since then comparing my description of myself to those that others have arrived at from similar collapse situations. While others often base their definition of self on religious convictions, I base mine on the logical influences to which I was exposed during this rebuilding phase. Other people I used for test cases turned to social media for comfort, and they ended up becoming masters at understanding and influencing people in cyberspace. Those who had turned to work or to sports lost themselves in those worlds and found great success in their

422

chosen fields. In each instance, the person's expertise correlated with the subject in which they immersed themselves at times of duress. While studying this behavior and the results of these times, I realized that the nature of the person's condition and the psychological effect of the events that had created that condition could explain this correlation.

Based on my conversations with a few divorced couples in which each spouse appeared to have suffered a complete collapse at nearly the same time, either near the end of the marriage or after the divorce, it seemed that the combinations of their life cycles had made them both poisonous to the people aspect of each other's life cycles. I noticed that they both seemed to have simultaneously suffered from extremely reduced thought-length capabilities, and thus both possessed very little emotional maturity. The disharmony between their biorhythms naturally turned them in a negative direction. From my perspective, my divorce and subsequent collapse seemed to have followed essentially this same pattern. The ability of people in close proximity to affect the thought lengths of one another seems to be the basis for these parallel changes in emotional maturity. Their disharmonious thought lengths divided, causing both people to progressively shorten each other's thoughts, which is a phenomenon we discussed in the chapter "Thought-Length Hierarchy."

The collapsed state seems to reduce people to the emotional maturity of someone much younger. In fact, their emotional maturity resembles that of people in the latter stages of their eighth perspective lifetime. They begin to redevelop many of those traits and are similarly susceptible to influences. In my case, I estimate that my thought-length capability, though recoverable, diminished to a level comparable to my eight-year-old's first life decision. Of course, the strongest influences in my life, established during the ages of 8-12, were entirely replaced by new influences created during the roughly three years following this collapse. Once again, there is much more research to be done on this subject, but I assess that the reduction of my thought-length capability to the level of the lower age made the content I learned during that time as deep-seated as childhood memories and influences.

Fragile Mental State

When in this state, you actually have a great gift that most people will never have. Not only does no one expect anything from you, but you also have the ability to rewire who you are. This offers an amazing opportunity for a new start. But if you hide out and ignore your feelings until you pull through it, you can squander that opportunity. It is a travesty that the institutions that adjudicate divorces and settle child custody disputes support relentless litigation. They thereby condition people at their most susceptible times to occupy the rest of their lives with dispute and conflict. Nevertheless, let's focus on how to make this benefit you, and let's accept this gift to reprogram our lives to become our best selves.

First, avoid resorting to and thus immersing yourself in the stereotypical growth-stunting areas that people have traditionally taken up during those times. Decide what you want to pursue according to what matches your accomplishments and aligns with the rest of your life's direction. If you have been an accountant for fifteen years, then choosing a seamstress as your situational masker, whom you will shadow for two years while you build your thought-length capability, may make you the best seamstress in four counties, but it may not help you become your best possible self. If you have a medical condition and decide to dwell on it during that time, then you can easily become a hypochondriac. You can decide at that time if you will spend the rest of your life as a monk or a priest and can reprogram yourself to feel entirely content as one. Definitely be aware that your condition while rewiring will make you exceptionally committed and quite susceptible to indoctrination and will expose you to severe misguidance should your comfortable choice or situational masker happen to exhibit cult-like tendencies.

424

When I was recreating myself, many things would have been valuable for me to know. The process of life engineering, which is the foundation of this book, is based on precisely this premise. These include concepts such as the influences of previous perspective lifetimes, thought lengths, emotional maturity, and many others that I had never experienced before but that are normal in these situations. To explain these better, I will describe something I call "the dark road analogy."

Imagine that you are driving at night down a dark, winding coastal or mountain road on which you have never driven before. Your senses are heightened. With every turn around which you cannot see, you imagine a cliff slightly off the edge of the road. You slow down; your visible distance is only as far as your headlights can reach. Your actions must be executed within distance you can see. What will you do if your headlights gradually dim? As the distance you can see shortens, you slow down to make sure that you can adapt and react. You may have steered clear of hazards and may be driving down a road through a field, but your reduced field of vision makes you assume that danger lurks just outside of your view.

This is how we fall into these periods of reduced thought length. Consider the difference if the same conditions arise on a road you have driven every day of your life. You could probably turn off the headlights completely and still drive the road with moderate skill. Your confidence in your ability to drive stems from knowing what to expect. You know that the road becomes curvy a mile ahead and that you need to start slowing, but you also know that when you exit the serpentine section, you can speed back up. Life is always a dark road and is always unknown. What would happen if we added to the first situation a passenger who knows the road well and who can tell you what to expect? You can now approach the same situation, which you navigated uncertainly before, with a bit more confidence. The passenger can point out the curves, know when to expect a bump, and inform you when you can relax. Let's look at a few of the road hazards you may encounter while recreating yourself so that you will know what to expect from this process.

Putting the Process Into Action

Here are some closing recommendations for starting out after one of life's low points, assuming that you have decided to read this book after such an event. Before you move on to the next chapter, "Living the Process," I recommend putting some basics in place.

First, find some kind of mind-mapping software and learn how to use it. If you are already familiar with such a tool, simply start a new map to begin creating the new you. Don't copy anything from the past or reuse someone else's map. You will want to think about every aspect of your life as you decide whether it belongs in your life from this point on. Start working past where you are by documenting the present, and for each thing you add in the present, note two future possibilities in your map. After a while, start to add two possibilities to each of these possibilities, and update another one with each current task.

Set up a way to capture ideas on the fly, such as when you are walking or doing any other activity. Use a smart phone app to capture your ideas, or carry around a journal and pen. Begin your schedule with the things you enjoy, and only do something that you don't like as a self-directed immediate prerequisite for a task you enjoy.

Chapter XV

Living the Process

When we first decide to take control over a previously uncontrolled area of our lives, it will seem like an awakening. At the same time, it will also be difficult to maintain that control. This is normal and expected. Recall that the process of working past where you are begins with the knowledge of what lies in your future path. By gaining awareness, you gain knowledge of your future path. The practice of thinking about future necessities will cause you to inadvertently make small additions at first, followed regularly by more and more. Consistency will lead to habits that will lead to competence. Mere awareness puts you on the right path and advances you beyond those who have not yet gained awareness.

Setting up Success

Often, one's perception of an incident is more important than what actually happened. Examples of this are apparent with many famous people. For instance, do you know what Albert Einstein is famous for? Some of you may know that he developed several scientific theories; others may even know that he developed the theory of relativity. Beyond that, very few people have actually read any of his published work. How can people become so famous if we know so little about them? The secret to success is to know what influences people, to assess the status of others, and to be able to implement those influences. The processes I have laid out in this book not only help individuals become successful—they also help individuals carry out a progression of steps that make others view them as successful.

Remember that talent and skills are not biological. They emerge after years of incremental development. Mr. Universe didn't become Mr. Universe in the seventh grade by picking up 250-pound dumbbells. We gain skills and become talented because we are interested in a particular subject and because we enjoy the processes that increase our competence in that particular set of skills. The arrangement of processes that lead to that point is the only real secret that successful people keep from the less successful. When initially setting it up, however, this will seem foreign if you have not engaged in such arrangement before. Next, I will share how to take the first step toward being successful.

Fake It Until You Make It

Start simply by taking the first step. Decide on a good influence to incorporate into your life, and perform the first task toward that ultimate result. It is entirely normal to feel like a complete failure. People never feel competent when they first begin on a new path, so you should expect to feel inadequate and incompetent. Work past that by doing the task a few times. You will gradually reduce your feelings of inadequacy once you become skilled at performing the task for long enough periods that your emotional memory of self transforms. Remember that you do not need to have it all right away. Establish a routine to continue what you have started, and the confidence will follow.

You may not feel like the sort of person who is competent or successful at the things you set out to achieve, but observers cannot ascertain that you feel that way. Many of you may have heard the expressions, "Fake it until you make it" or "Project it until you perfect it," which mean the same thing. People see you based on what you appear to be, not how you feel inside. I have often told people who are entering a new situation to picture someone who acted successful in the same or similar situation and to emulate that person. On the inside, you may feel as if you are entirely inadequate or even as if you severely mishandled a situation. However, others see the same thing in you that you saw in the person whom you emulated. They only see a successful, confident person. They do not see the nearly vomiting, scared child that you feel like inside.

People who have succeeded often do not know it. As I have been saying throughout this book, in order to be successful, you need to set up the progression that makes you successful. Doing this requires that you forget about pursuing success. You must purely enjoy the process that gets you there. When the routines you have established and have come to enjoy become rewarding enough, you will forget about being successful. Then one day, suddenly something will happen that you never believed possible.

Don't overdo it. Choose the right tool for the right job. I was once advised that a carpenter does not use a golden hammer. Practicality and discretion will be a great recurring self-check. Success is not perfection—it is the culmination of many small, achievable, successfully executed tasks. At the same time, this does not mean that it's okay to be sloppy or complete things halfway, because such poor work practices would be noticed. Know your audience and perform at, or slightly above, the level required for what you seek to accomplish.

The involuntary absorption of your surroundings will also be a significant factor at the beginning of your path. Since your environment will always seep into your mindset, you should choose a desirable environment along with your effort to "fake it until you make it." That way, instead of trying to shut out your environment, you can allow it to guide you. If your path is as a musician, then Nashville is the place you want to be. If you plan to be a movie actor, then move to

Hollywood. If you want to be a successful engineer, then pack your bags for Silicon Valley. If you want to be successful in the financial industry, then head to New York City. If you want to be a successful politician, then convince the voters to send you to Washington, D.C. In short, if you want to be wealthy, then go where the money is.

As you begin to live the process, many things will discourage you. I have found truth in the saying, "A prophet is never accepted in his own town." The people in situations with you are comfortable with the "you" that they know. The oddest interactions I have encountered involved either people whom I expected would not at all be affected by me or people who would benefit from my success. Some people may resist your improvement as if some portion of them had run amok. Be prepared for this.

Finally, act like success is already yours. In the chapter "Reevaluating Your Path," we introduced a sequence of steps for reevaluating and determining your path to coincide with the process area of working past where you are. Once you have completed the refinement cycle and have identified a method for bridging the gap, you should act as if the bridge is complete. Think beyond the progress. Imagine that you have already accomplished the set of tasks. Many people do not recognize their own achievement until all aspects of it are complete, but in life, nothing is ever finished. I often advise clients during interviews that experience is like an oak tree: whether a two-hundred-year-old oak tree or a sapling, it is still an oak tree; the same is true of experience. Don't sell yourself short. Own your future, and believe in your abilities.

Address Fear

It is normal to feel uncertain and even fearful about your capabilities or about what the future may hold. A Congressional Medal of Honor recipient once confirmed to me that "Courage is not the absence of fear, but having fear and moving forward anyway." In the chapters "Working Past Where You Are" and "Enjoying the Process," we talked about many ways to address fear with processes that gradually remove the unknown, processes that address personal anxiety, and processes that yield recurring affirmations, which reduce your fear of rejection. Many people have expressed to me a great fear of failure, and I point out to them that when they begin to work on a list of achievable tasks, each task advances them another step toward successful completion. The only way to fail is to stop working on the task. Success is not something you have; it is the culmination of the time spent enjoying the processes that lead to something greater.

Participating in support groups will help you along your path; many of us know this instinctively. Ensure that you are not using a support group to validate your decisions, but instead to share your results. Seek out supportive people who are further along on their path than you are, and help others to begin their journeys. The former will give you something to strive for, while the latter will provide a sense of validation. Create a relationship with an exceptionally experienced person who can serve as a mentor. If you are enduring a low point in your life, find someone to act as a situational masker to help get you back into the world.

Positive Control of Life Cycle

The only thing we have control over is the way the world affects us. If you associate with people who are aware of this and who attempt to adjust only to what the world throws at them, then you will be able to develop with those individuals. With a group of such people, you can make a mountain. When you associate with people who believe that the world needs to be adjusted to suit them, you will notice that their influence brings negative energy. My recommendation is to disconnect from those influences gradually. Seek out and align with influences that create positive energy and flow. Adjust your perception of what is possible.

Mindset

The most important thing for creating a mindset of positive energy is to be aware of yourself, know which mindsets you frequently adopt, and understand how to identify them. Create a method for yourself for triggering a shift from one mindset to another. In order to produce outgoing positive energy, you should align the components that enable you to enjoy the processes in your life, whether those include the situation, the avoidance of biological triggers, or an internal adjustment. Remember that you contribute to each situation when your mindset influences the life cycles of those around you. Adjust your mindset to the desired situation. For each negative mindset you have identified in yourself, know how to change it to one better suited to the situation.

Think of each person around you as the "is a" type of person. Determine their value to you based on who they are, not on what they possess. When we view people as the "has a" type of people, we begin to devalue them as individuals and see them more as objects for use. Seeing others as less valuable leads to treating them with less respect, and this adds negative energy to

432

situations. View people either as if you can learn something from them or as if you can gain comfort from the things they say that you already know. Avoid the mindset of using people in order to feel superior to them. Above all, try not to be a poison to people whose personality type or thinking style differs from yours.

People

Choose the length of your exposure to people based on the positive or negative energy they bring. Even in the same, daily situation, each person brings a different mindset. Individuals will be in different emotional states and will have either longer or shorter average thought lengths depending on what they have been exposed to in previous situations. Discovering people's current thought length, adjusting who you are, or pursuing brief, synchronizing exercises will aid in establishing positive energy during the interaction of the people involved. At the onset of the interaction, project facial cues to signal the desired emotional state required for the encounter.

Remember that synchronizing thought lengths among people equates to making a connection. Shorter thought lengths typify fun, nonthreatening, and safe interactions. Longer thought lengths can be ascribed to bad news or the invocation of authority, but they will always reduce the capacity for nonverbal synchronization and will make nearby people feel more uncertain. It is important to reduce the biological triggers that affect both others and you. The uncertainty of longer thought lengths at the convening of an interaction is a biological trigger that produces uncertainty. Avoid other biological triggers that create discomfort, such as challenging widely held belief structures, summoning the fear of retribution of trouble, or arousing sexual provocations.

Situations

People's reasons for selecting a situation are driven by mindset. Knowing how to positively affect the situation you have selected is the first step toward emotional maturity. For each situation, ensure that you add value to those around you. To contribute positive energy, resolve to provide more value than a random passerby would. Then grow that energy until the situation would suffer in your absence. Even if you are merely a small part of a large situation, your positive energy can derive from the fact that you are an identifiable individual, as opposed to an anonymous participant. Selecting a situation that adds positive energy to your life and being able to return positive energy to the situation should be your goal for each situation in your life.

Be sure that your life includes situations that meet your human and personal needs for fulfillment. Know which thought lengths benefit you most of the time, and choose the situations that support that thought length in order to create a progressively peaceful mindset. Find harmonic thought-length activities that naturally match your abilities and require little effort, and identify some that expand your abilities. Understand the foundation of your decision-making for your perspective lifetime. You should arrange situations that address your needs for fulfillment according to Maslow's hierarchy of needs. Organize your time so that you feel a sense of progression and do not flounder on plateaus.

Surround yourself with influences that provide recurring affirmation of your contributions and value. Like-minded people will benefit your path's direction, so remember that no matter what situation you choose, the influences will seep into you whether you want them to or not. Plan for this and surround yourself with the influences that will guide you along your path. Reduce the influences of unwanted thought-length categories by curbing your suggestibility or by choosing different situations. Remember that prolonged situations of disruptive thought lengths equate to insanity. Above all, choose some activities that will help you reset and relax.

Closing

Begin to construct a life path that best suits your personality. Be honest with yourself. The key to success is enjoyment, and the key to enjoyment is accurate self-identification. Form your lifestyle around the way you work best, instead of letting your work form your lifestyle. Find soothing things that clear your mind and that allow you to progress. Often, a logical understanding of where you are, how you feel, or how you arrived at a situation will provide this clarity. If we cannot determine why we feel, act, or progress in a given direction through life, it makes us uneasy. If we do not understand what brought us to our current situation, we feel unsettled or even helpless. Then we have moments when everything about a particular topic becomes clear, and we are able to relax with the knowledge that we understand ourselves. Logic and understanding put us at peace with ourselves—hence, the logic of life.